The Jacobite Army
in England
1745

For Pauline and Lucy

The Jacobite Army in England
1745

THE FINAL CAMPAIGN

Frank McLynn

JOHN DONALD PUBLISHERS LTD
EDINBURGH

ISBN 0 85976 488 5

First Paperback Edition 1998

Printed in Great Britain by Bell & Bain Ltd., Glasgow.

Introduction to the Paperback Edition

A handful of military campaigns, and sometimes a single decisive battle, have changed world history. Salamis, Actium, Hastings, Yorktown and, in our own era, Stalingrad, are examples of the battles; Caesar's war against Pompey after he had crossed the Rubicon, Cortes's conquest of Mexico, Elizabeth I's defeat of the Spanish Armada, are good examples of the campaigns. The Jacobite Rising of 1745 carried within itself the potential to be such an earth-shaking event: for a start, if the attempt to restore the Stuart dynasty had been successful, the first global conflict, the Seven Years War of 1756-63, could not have occurred. And the key moment of the '45 was not, as is commonly supposed, the battle of Culloden in April 1746, but the invasion of England by the Jacobite army in November-December 1745.

In his brilliant essay on historical counterfactuals, the great German sociologist, Max Weber, ingeniously demonstrated how historical causality is predicated on 'alternative' history. What would have happened, he asks, if the Persians, not the Greeks, had won the battle of Salamis in 480 BC? To deny that this is a meaningful question is, in effect, to insinuate an extreme form of historical inevitability. If we accept the arguments of the cynical historical positivists, the way historical events turned out was the only way they could have turned out. It follows that historians should abandon their otiose quest for causality, and simply concentrate on dates, facts and figures of a past, dead in more senses than one. Fortunately, Weber's arguments have won this particular battle in historiography, so that sophisticated people no longer think it pointless to ask: what would have happened, if?

The invasion of England by Prince Charles Edward Stuart ('bonnie Prince Charlie') in November-December 1745, is one of the most famous counterfactuals. What would have happened if the Welsh Jacobites, under Sir Watkin Williams Wynn, had made good their boast and hastened to enlist under the Jacobite banner? What would have been the consequences if Louis XV, having heard of the Prince's landing in Scotland, had at once committed the might of France to his aid, instead of stalling and sending pointless missions to Scotland? Instead of realising, too late, that he had been presented by the Prince with a golden opportunity of taking England out of the War of Austrian Succession, might he not have solved problems that were still plaguing France in the era of Napoleon? What would have happened if

v

the Prince had got his way and marched on to London instead of being forced by his regimental commanders to retreat to Scotland? The last is the most intriguing scenario of all, for it is my conviction that the Prince would then have regained the throne of his ancestors, even without French aid, and in the teeth of Hanoverian sea power.

Since I wrote the book you hold in your hands, even more evidence has been unearthed, by myself and other scholars, such as Professor Jeremy Black and Professor Murray Pittock, which points in the same direction. In the text I discuss the military options which reinforce the correctness of the Prince's desire to press on from Derby. But one might also add to this the tottering nature of the Whig/Hanoverian elite in December 1745 as it reeled under a series of financial hammer blows — all caused by a general crisis of confidence. The index of Bank of England stock fell from 141 in October 1745 to 127 in December; because of continuing uncertainty engendered by the rising (which was still a serious threat in Scotland until the end of March 1746) bank stock did not rise above 125 in these months.

At the Council at Derby on 5 December 1745, when Lord George Murray defeated the Prince in the debate on whether to advance, he used to telling effect the idea of a monolithic London. He argued that if the Jacobites raced the Duke of Cumberland to London, the duke would pick up numbers all the time while the prince's strength remained unchanged or diminished as a result of skirmishes. The Whigs, on the other hand, knowing the uncertain temper of the London mob, were not at all certain that the increased numbers might not accrue to the Jacobite side instead. Aeneas MacDonald, one of the 'seven men of Moidart' who landed with the Prince in Scotland in late July 1745, was later imprisoned in the Tower of London, where he held conversations with the Lord Mayor. The Mayor, who had no reason to concoct fictions now that the Jacobite threat was past, confided to MacDonald that if the Prince had advanced from Derby, no more than five hundred men in the militia would have volunteered for the Hanoverian militia.

Here, then, is a great story crying out to be retold in the light of all the most recent scholarship. But it was not just the historical significance of the drama that attracted me. I was deeply impressed by all the visual and circumstantial details in the primary sources: the Nifflheim-like fog and mist at the siege of Carlisle; the snow and ice on Shap Fell; the moonlit armed clash at Clifton; the Prince beside himself with frustration and rage at the Derby Council; General Oglethorpe oversleeping at Orton; Marshal Wade pennypinching while his soldiers froze to death; the barefaced cunning of Dudley Bradstreet, the duke of Newcastle's secret agent.

I wrote this volume as the second of my quartet of books on the Jacobites, and, nearly twenty years later, I still remember the excitement of building up a chronicle painstakingly from disparate unpublished sources. It is sometimes embarrassing to revisit the results of one's early labours, but I feel that in this instance I have nothing to apologise for. Without wishing to sound arrogant, I hope I can take pride in an account that has stood the test of time and that subsequent scholarship has not been able to impugn or dislodge.

Twickenham, 1998   FRANK McLYNN

Introduction

THERE have been many accounts of the English campaign of November-December 1745 before, either as part of a general survey of the '45 or in a few cases with the specific object of illuminating the campaign itself. There seems, then, a *prima facie* need to justify adding to the number. My reasons are twofold. In the first place all of the traditional accounts make use of a limited and somewhat narrow range of sources; moreover there is often little attempt to discriminate between the reliability of one version and another, so that in some popular works (Winifred Duke's *The Rash Adventurer*, for example) the narrative consists of a stitching together without comment of some of the more obviously available eyewitness accounts (such as those of Elcho, O'Sullivan, Murray of Broughton etc.). The Thucydidean task of comparing the stories of Whig and Jacobite (and also contrasting Whig with Whig and Jacobite with Jacobite) and so on has not been performed for the entire range of the 1745 campaign. Secondly, much work has been done in recent years on detailed aspects of the '45 in England (particularly in the work of Rupert Jarvis and Eveline Cruickshanks). This modern research has not as yet been incorporated in a comprehensive narrative account. As Jarvis says of his *Collected Papers on the Jacobite Risings*: 'The present papers therefore seek mainly to examine certain aspects of the Jacobite movement, divorced from any narrative as such — the web rather than the thread.' The day by day chronicle offered here incorporates this modern research and directs attention to those aspects of the campaign that have been traditionally neglected, such as the French factor and the movements of Marshal Wade.

The campaign of the Jacobite army in England in 1745 can be considered final in two important senses. It was the last time the dynastic issue was contested by force of arms (and was thus the last internal rebellion in Great Britain), and it was the final occasion when a military campaign was fought on *English soil*. The skirmish at Clifton on 18 December 1745 produced the last casualties in battle in England itself. The beginning of this quasi-legendary story dates from the arrival of Prince Charles Edward Stuart in Loch-nan-Uamh with the 'Seven Men of Moidart' at the end of July 1745. Until the invasion of England, Charles Edward's progress was a series of spectacular triumphs: the raising of the Stuart standard at Glenfinnan, the tactical outwitting of Sir John Cope in the Highlands, the capture of Edinburgh and finally the rout of Sir John Cope at Prestonpans on 21 September. By the beginning of October the Jacobites controlled the whole of Scotland except the castles of

Edinburgh and Stirling and a few Whig outposts. It is from this juncture that an invasion of England became a serious possibility and it is at this point that the story of the English campaign properly begins.

My thanks are due to Dr. Eveline Cruickshanks who read the manuscript and made a number of helpful suggestions. Needless to say, she cannot be held responsible for any errors that have crept into the text.

Contents

Abbreviations used in Notes

Add MSS   Additional MSS, British Library
AEMD   Archives Etrangères, Mémoires et Documents, Angleterre
HMC   Historical Manuscripts Commission Reports
LCAS   Lancashire and Cheshire Antiquarian Society (Transactions of)
LCHS   Lancashire and Cheshire Historical Society (Transactions of)
LM   The Lyon in Mourning
LP   Lockhart Papers
SP Dom   State Papers, Domestic, George II. Series 36 (bundle/number)
SP Ireland   State Papers, Ireland. Series 63
Staffs CRO   Staffordshire County Record Office
VCH   Victoria County History
VP   Vernon Papers
WO   War Office Papers

The Jacobite army in England

1

Preparations and Counter-Preparations

PREPARATIONS in England to receive the threatened invasion from the Highland army — expected even before Prestonpans — fell into five main categories: disposition of regular army units; the raising of new regiments through the associations and subscriptions for the defence of England; raising the militia; anti-Catholic and anti-Jacobite security measures; and the gathering of intelligence concerning the likely movements and strategy of the Highland army.

Immediately the news of Charles Edward's advance through Scotland was received, orders went out from London for the recall of troops from Flanders and for reinforcements from Ireland.[1] Seven regiments of infantry and three of guards were sent back from the Continent and two regiments plus 1,000 men drawn from miscellaneous regiments were transported from Dublin to Chester. The arrival of these battalions in England helped to calm the panic caused initially by news of the 'Young Pretender's' landing in Scotland. A military committee was formed, consisting of Field Marshal George Wade, General Ligonier, Lord Stair, and the Dutch commander, to draw up a plan of military operations.[2] On 4 October 1745 they produced a report, showing that twenty-nine battalions of infantry and sixteen squadrons of cavalry were currently available for action. It was decided to divide these into two armies, one commanded by Wade, the other by Ligonier. Wade was to march north immediately with thirteen battalions of foot, including 6,000 Dutch auxiliaries, and six squadrons of horse (the cavalry to be under the command of General Wentworth).[3] He was to make his way to Newcastle which in the days after Prestonpans was thought the most likely Highland target in England. Major-General Huske would go on ahead to Newcastle to superintend its defence, while General Cope, Commander-in-Chief in Scotland, would be ordered down from Berwick to join him. Two thousand Swiss mercenaries were also ordered north.

Wade made his way north through Nottingham and arrived in Newcastle at the end of October, delivering arms to the various county Lords Lieutenant en route. His original rendezvous point was Doncaster, chosen so that he could proceed thence either to Tyneside or Lancashire, depending on the Highland army's movements.[4] With no signs of activity from the Jacobites in Edinburgh, he moved up to Newcastle on 29 October.[5]

Ligonier meanwhile was to command fourteen regiments of cavalry and infantry and to place himself on a line running from Nottingham to Chester, in case the Highlanders bypassed Wade.[6] He was to oppose and attack any movement south of

1

this line or into Wales. In the event that his forces and Wade's made a junction, Ligonier was to come under the orders of Wade. Ligonier was granted the normal powers of a commander-in-chief in matters of finance, discipline and quartering and given £20,000 in cash for contingencies. He was to keep the principal Secretary of State (the Duke of Newcastle) informed of all developments and to suppress any risings or disaffection among the population.[7]

Ligonier was unhappy about his orders for two reasons. He considered them to be vague, and he doubted that he was the right man for the job. In an audience with George II at Kingston, Ligonier expressed the hope that the king's favourite son, the Duke of Cumberland, would be sent for; in the panicky state of English public opinion, he felt that he himself, as a Frenchman, might not receive the necessary support either from the people or the administration, whereas Cumberland was sure to. George II, however, expressed full confidence in Ligonier and clarified his orders, while acceding to his requirements in other areas. Ligonier now received a set of contingency instructions. He was to march to Chester and defend a line along the river there. If the Highlanders got to Chester before him, he was to cover the terrain between the Severn and the Trent. If, on the other hand, the Highlanders had made no move by the time he reached Chester, he was to move across to Nottingham prior to joining Wade. Ligonier's humane concern for his troops — a rare quality in the eighteenth century — was also to be indulged. There was to be proper care for the sick and a blanket and pair of shoes per man. Ligonier himself was to receive a military staff, an artillery train with engineers and eight tin boats. As it transpired, he was delayed in London for nearly two months, so that these orders turned out to be largely irrelevant.[8]

Under Ligonier's command were the regular regiments of Montagu's, Kingston's, Turle's, Skelton's, Howard's, Bligh's, Sempill's, Johnson's, Douglas's and the King's Own Dragoons. In addition he was to take over the newly raised regiments of Lords Gower, Montagu, Halifax and Granby. It was the issue of these new corps formed specifically to combat the threat from Scotland in 1745 which was to be so contentious. In addition to the four mentioned above, other regiments were to be raised by the following aristocrats: Rutland, Kingston, Herbert, Falmouth, Derby, Cholmondeley, Berkeley, Bedford and Lord Kildare in Ireland. The question to be decided by Parliament after its opening on 17 October concerned the composition of these regiments and the status of their officers. The original offer of these lords had been to raise and pay the new troops themselves, but they soon tried to foist the expense onto the county while retaining control over their organisation and all benefits accruing in their own hands.[9] Only Lord Kildare proved willing to honour his original offer, but such was the political weight of the Whig aristocrats that the costs of the new regiments were assumed by public money.

As for their officers, the big question was whether these newly appointed worthies would retain their rank once the regiments were disbanded. Henry Pelham and the Duke of Bedford favoured the retention of rank but the king, initially at least, opposed it. Henry Fox, later Lord Holland, argued George II's case in an angry debate in Parliament on 31 October. He pointed out that to grant permanent rank to these new officers would be a terrible blow to the regular army officers, especially as most of the new commissions were granted out of barefaced nepotism.[10] A major clash within the ruling elite was averted when George II changed his mind, thus causing the motion opposing the permanency of the new commissions to be lost in the House of Commons.[11] Like many of the wrangles within the inner circles of government during the '45, this issue too turned out to be largely irrelevant for, as Horace Walpole pointed out in his memoirs: 'It is certain that not six of the thirteen regiments was ever raised nor four employed.'[12] Indeed one Jacobite observer went so far as to claim that the raising of the new regiments was good for the Stuart cause, since it impaired recruitment to the more reliable regular regiments, and because the decision that the officers of the new regiments should have equal ranking with regular officers could only cause resentment.[13]

Apart from the proposed new regiments, warrants were sent to the Lords Lieutenant in the counties, empowering them to form their own companies and battalions. In addition, warrants for this purpose were issued to the mayors and magistrates in Hull, Bristol, Liverpool, Exeter, Newcastle, Carlisle and Berwick. This action greatly irritated the Lords Lieutenant in the counties, who regarded it as an infringement of their authority, and poor relations between town and country deriving from ancient rivalries were further exacerbated. As it happened, the corporations and cities turned out to be a reluctant military force. The magistrates balked at having to support the troops they raised out of voluntary contributions and pressed for them to be sustained at public expense.[14]

On 14 October 1745 the Duke of Newcastle, in a letter to the Mayor of Nottingham, effectively quashed any hopes that this would be done. He drew a distinction between the regulations governing those regiments specifically authorised by George II as additions to the regular army and the volunteer regiments raised by town magistrates and Lords Lieutenant in the counties. Whereas the new regiments of the former type were put on the military establishment and paid at public expense, those raised by voluntary subscription were not (and as a corollary were not bound by military regulations). It was for the corporation or county at whose expense these kinds of companies were 'raised and subsisted' to determine their duties. The authorities in charge of raising the voluntary companies usually responded by stating that, since the new regiments paid at public expense seemed reluctant to serve outside the locality in which they were recruited, they too would only serve outside the town or county if all their expenses were reimbursed.[15]

The disputes about the 'new' and 'voluntary' regiments paled beside the confusion surrounding the militia. In many counties in 1745, because of political factionalism within the Whig party, there were no Lords Lieutenant actually in office. Even where there were, there was considerable uncertainty as to whether the county militia could legally be called out without specific statutory warrant. Technically, as the law stood (especially after the expiration of the 1734 Militia Act), the militia could not be constituted as a legal body until the crown had repaid to the county the previous month's pay and subsistence expended by the county for the upkeep of the militia. This technicality could not be dealt with until Parliament passed the necessary statute, and it could not do this while it stood prorogued. It could not be convened until the king's return from Hanover, since George II had refused to delegate to a council of regency the power to summon Parliament in his absence.[16] Small wonder that one Minister wrote in September: 'Everything is done that can be done by an administration that has no power and whom the king will hardly vouchsafe to say one word about his own business. He grows angrier with those who want to help him out of it. He may run the risk of losing another kingdom by the folly of his advisers, just as he has already lost one by bad advice.'[17]

Even when the legal difficulty about the month's pay was removed, by a bill which received the royal assent in November, poor drafting of the act meant that uncertainty about the legal status of the militia remained. This was to have momentous consequences at the siege of Carlisle in November 1745.[18] Apart from all this, the militia, raw and half-armed, was not considered a potentially significant force anyway. There were even those who doubted whether the militia in certain counties could be trusted to oppose Charles Edward, though in clearly pro-Jacobite counties it was thought best to call out the militia anyway, on the grounds that those thus drafted might otherwise have joined the Highland army.[19]

For all these reasons, the county authorities tended to prefer some force other than the militia for their defence. Technically there were six forms of raising troops in 1745, apart from regular army recruiting or the militia. These were: troops raised in the counties by the Lords Lieutenant; troops raised in the counties by lords other than the Lords Lieutenant; companies formed in the boroughs and cities by mayors and magistrates under royal warrants; the 'subscription soldiers' raised by the associations for the defence of England; men raised under blank commissions; and the thirteen additional regiments on the establishment, originally raised by noblemen. We can, however, more lucidly reduce the strata of defence in England in 1745 to four: the pre-existing regular army units; the new regiments on the military establishment; the militia; and all other troops raised by county, city and borough authorities and the associations, by whatever name they went. For all this, the only credible fighting force consisted of the regular army units. Even there the Whig defences were weaker than they seemed because of the large number of Dutch and Swiss mercenaries, to say nothing of unreliable Highland regiments recalled from Flanders like the Black Watch.

In general the military position in England did not inspire confidence and led to much recrimination. A commentary on the preparations in Yorkshire is typical: 'I am sorry that county is not better prepared but alas, it is not easy to be prepared in a country rendered so artificially unwarlike as England. What signify all the speeches of the Orators, or rather of our ignorant, perhaps knavish babblers in Parliament against the army? What has been the consequence of their insisting so often, contrary to common experience and common sense, that our Navy was a sufficient security? They only misled honest gentlemen. Their frothing words will not restore tranquillity and public credit, nor repel the Highlanders. The Roman orators were also warriors; even Cicero was, I believe, a better general than most of ours, who have not forgot the Art of War . . . they never learnt it.'[20]

The enthusiasm apparently evinced in the associations and subscriptions for the defence of England might have seemed a pleasing development, but here too there were doubters. All over England in 1745 associations had been formed for the defence of king and government, and subscriptions to raise additional forces had been collected. In some counties men associated themselves together to protect the realm and the church; this was the method used in York. In other counties subscriptions were raised, so that out of the funds a more formal force could be equipped and maintained. Some units, such as the Yorkshire Royal Hunters, were raised by royal warrant. Several of these bodies produced impressive results. In Derbyshire subscriptions were raised and commissions granted and the Derbyshire Blues were created.[21] In Yorkshire the aforementioned Hunters were created by General Oglethorpe and have often been considered the first instance of volunteer yeoman cavalry.[22] In Lancashire the county's nobility, clergy and gentry met at Preston and entered into an association to raise five hundred men.[23] In Liverpool a company of 'Blues' was formed. Other localities unable to raise men made financial contributions instead: the town of Ripon sent £400 unrequested; in Wiltshire an association of tradesmen and clothiers from the towns of Trowbridge, Bradford and Melksham pledged themselves to supply arms to George II's forces.[24]

Nevertheless, for various reasons the subscriptions and associations did not achieve the results expected of them. In general England was apathetic if not hostile to the whole idea. Even in London, where the Common Council voted £1000, both Carteret and Granville refused to subscribe.[25] In Oxford the association 'for the preservation of Church and State' was vehemently opposed by the Tories, on the grounds that it was a party political measure by the Whigs, reeking of partisanship, and was reminiscent both of the unsavoury Whig manoeuvrings of the 1690s and of the era of Cromwell.[26] The Oxford association was signed by none of the Tories, not even Lord Cornbury, now widely regarded as a political 'trimmer'. And even when likely enemies of the regime, such as Tories and Catholics, did subscribe, this was regarded with suspicion. Archbishop Herring, in his correspondence with Lord Chancellor Hardwicke, quoted *timeo Danaos et dona ferentes* in this regard, and Hardwicke replied in the same vein *aliquis latet error; equo ne credite, Teucri.*[27] Moreover, it was feared that in many counties the commission granted to the gentry to raise volunteers might later be used on behalf of Charles Edward rather than against him. Apart from this, the forces actually raised by the associations were of dubious value and when actually put to the test, as with the Derbyshire Blues, proved a humiliating failure.

Attitudes in the northern counties most likely to be in the line of the Highlanders' march varied considerably, depending on a number of factors: the strength of commitment to the Whig regime; the likelihood that the particular locality really would be occupied by a Jacobite army; the state of local defences; and the proximity of regular government forces. These differences can perhaps best be illustrated by the example of four major towns, two in the north-west and two in the north-east. In Newcastle considerable panic was in evidence even before the battle of Prestonpans.[28] Although General Huske was sent to command the forces there, many of the contingents were short in numbers, many of the troops were sick, and the Scottish and Irish soldiers were considered unreliable against a Stuart prince. For all that, spirited attempts were made to equip the town to withstand a siege.

Morale gradually rose as Charles Edward made no attempt in October to march south from Edinburgh, and the town was greatly relieved when Marshal Wade arrived with an army of some 8,000 men at the end of October.

In the staunchly Whig town of Liverpool, where a Jacobite march through Catholic Lancashire was considered a distinct possibility, a good, loyal, pro-Hanoverian spirit was evinced.[29] The Duke of Newcastle's licensing of the Mayor of Liverpool to raise troops and form companies did not lead to any jealousy or friction between the town authorities and the Lord Lieutenant of Lancashire. The voluntary force formed on Merseyside, the 'Liverpool Blues', though it never saw action, was one of the success stories of the Whig side in the '45. Colonel William Graham was sent from London to take command of it, and much effective reconnaissance work was performed during the Highlanders' advance through Lancashire.

In Hull, where there was a total absence of Jacobite feeling, there was nonetheless a reluctance to be committed wholeheartedly to the Hanoverian cause.[30] In addition, violent rivalries arose between the town magistrates, granted the power to raise companies by the Duke of Newcastle, and the Lord Lieutenant of the East Riding, who had similar but distinct powers. So although the walls of Hull were fortified and General Pulteney was sent as Newcastle's liaison officer, the town disappointed the authorities in London by its attitude.

Perhaps the most interesting case of all, in view of its central role in the Jacobite invasion of England in November 1745, was that of Carlisle.[31] There were three major problems here. One was an intense rivalry between county and corporation, thrown into focus by Newcastle's granting the power to raise troops both to the Lord Lieutenant and the magistrates in Carlisle. The second was a continuing question mark, after 24 October, about the legal status of the militia, with no right clearly established for the authorities to levy its pay at the very moment an invasion from Scotland was expected. The third was personal dislike, bitterness and hostility existing between the four principal personalities in Carlisle: Thomas Pattinson, the Deputy Mayor and Postmaster; Richard Gilpin, the Recorder, Justice of the Peace and Deputy Lieutenant of Carlisle; John Waugh, the Chancellor; and Lieutenant-Colonel Durand, the governor of Carlisle Castle. The problems encountered in Carlisle, which proved fatal to the defence of the town when the Highlanders invested it in November 1745, were merely more dramatic in form than elsewhere, though completely typical of the chaos and disharmony prevailing in most towns in the north of England. Newcastle, Liverpool and Nottingham were the sole exceptions to this general tendency, the first because of the presence of Wade's army, the second through a rare commitment to the Hanoverian regime, and the third because Newcastle himself was the Lord Lieutenant and in issuing powers to the town authorities was obviously exempt from the risk of giving offence to the Lord Lieutenant on the spot.[32]

The presence of large numbers of Catholics in England might have seemed to pose the threat of a Jacobite fifth column, and there were some Whigs, like Sir Henry Hoghton of Lancashire, who advocated using the full resources of the existing anti-Catholic laws to deal with them.[33] Against this, Newcastle and the members of the inner circle of government believed in *quieta non movere*. There is evidence of bitter dissension among the Whigs about how to implement the anti-Catholic laws and how to proceed against English Catholics.[34] By his insistence on strong measures against Catholic recusants, Hoghton gave offence to influential members of the Privy Council. The government opinion, as expressed forcibly to Hoghton, was that matters should not be pressed further than the tendering of the statutory oath and declaration, with the corollary that those who refused should have their arms and horses and confiscated. Anything else was considered counter-productive, as being likely to convert tacit support for the 'Pretender' into actual taking up arms for the rebels. Hoghton consequently found it hard to make his writ run even in Lancashire; some of his subalterns were reluctant to implement the search warrants which empowered militia officers to search the houses of suspected persons.[35] The Catholic factor was particularly important in both Lancashire and Yorkshire and combined with the excessive party factionalism already existing to produce an even more complex political configuration in these counties, which in turn further impaired the defence preparations for a Highland incursion.[36]

The final principal aspect of the preparations in England for an invasion from Scotland concerned the government's reading of Charles Edward's intentions. A good barometer of rising and falling Whig expectations is to be found in Horace Walpole's correspondence for late 1745. In September, even before the battle of Prestonpans, the Highlanders' purpose was widely reported to be the invasion of England.[37] Curiously, *after* the defeat of Cope on 21 September Walpole recorded the general opinion that it was unlikely that the 'Young Pretender' would attempt anything so rash and precarious as a march on England.[38] The long sojourn of the Jacobite army in Edinburgh during October led to growing confidence that the Stuart position in Scotland would be consolidated in preference to an irruption across the English border.[39] Newcastle told Lord Chesterfield, Lieutenant-General in Dublin: 'The stay of the rebels in Scotland may probably be with a view to give time to France or Spain, or both, to make a descent in some part of the kingdom.'[40] On the other hand, there were those who felt that if Wade's army was sent north to Newcastle, to block the obvious entry point of an army marching to London, this would tempt the Highlanders to make a forced march to Carlisle and thence to Lancashire and Wales.[41] As Lord Chancellor Hardwicke expressed it: 'They have the best intelligence, they will certainly not disperse for reasons of fear . . . they will not come into England unless it appears an eligible scheme . . . if they do slip Wade, they will march like a torrent.'[42]

When the movement south from Edinburgh did commence at the end of October, there was considerable divergence of view concerning both the strategy and the tactics of the Highlanders. One view was that the incursion into England was simply to pre-empt an English invasion of Scotland; another that the march was clearly designed to link with a French landing from Dunkirk.[43] These opinions presupposed that the invasion was a reality. Others still assumed that the southward movement must be a feint. Wade considered that the Jacobites wanted him to think that their objective was Carlisle so as to draw him out of Newcastle, their true goal. Others worked out from the disposition of the various contingents at Kelso, Wooler and Moffat that Carlisle must be the objective but doubted that the thrust in that direction was wholehearted.[44] After causing a stir in the north-west, this version ran, the Highlanders would return to Central Scotland via Dunbartonshire. Even those who thought that the Highlanders were making for Carlisle and were in earnest could not imagine that they would actually attempt to invest the town. Newcastle stated: 'If the rebels are heading for Kelso it is a fair bet they are heading for Lancashire as in 1715 possibly to join with the French. They will probably get to Preston before Wade.'[45] Walpole's analysis of the situation, once it was known that the Highlanders were outside Carlisle, is particularly interesting. After pouring scorn on the government for sending Ligonier to block the road from the north-west only when the clansmen were already on it, he conceded that the long-term prospects for a Jacobite army were negligible. As he saw it, the Highlanders did not have the numbers to besiege Carlisle. They would, therefore, bypass it and march into Lancashire. Once they were in Lancashire, Wade would move out from Newcastle and get behind them. The Jacobites would then have three choices: to proceed to London or Bristol or North Wales. The last course was not feasible since they could not live off the land in Wales unless there was a rebellion in Ireland so that they could be supplied from there. The choice of London or Bristol entailed fighting two armies and facing certain annihilation; according to Walpole, Wade's army alone was an object of dread to Charles Edward, which was why he had avoided it at Newcastle.[46]

It is worth noting that almost none of these projections materialised. The Highlanders *did* besiege Carlisle with less than half the men Walpole had credited them with when he declared such an investment impracticable. Wade did *not* cut off the Jacobites either on the march south or the retreat north; neither Wade's nor Ligonier's army was able to offer any effective barrier to the intended passage of the Highland army to London.

If the Whig elite was experiencing great difficulties in the defence of England in the autumn of 1745, its leaders at once overrated and underrated the followers of Charles Edward. On the one hand, they credited them with a fixed and certain strategy but could not decide what it was; on the other they considered that the actual military threat, wherever it materialised, would be negligible. They were wrong on both counts, and how far the Jacobite leaders were from unanimity can be seen from events in Edinburgh in late October.

On the evening of 30 October 1745 a Council was held at Prince Charles Edward's headquarters which made the fateful decision to proceed with the invasion of England, but not before something much less than total commitment had been displayed by the clan leaders. In an ancillary decision, Carlisle was chosen as the primary objective of the army once in England. This was the culmination of six weeks of uncertainty, from the time the Highlanders first entered Edinburgh. So at last there came to pass what some Whig leaders had expected ever since the raising of the Stuart standard at Glenfinnan and even before Prestonpans seemed to make it inevitable.[47]

By the end of October Charles Edward could procrastinate no longer: either his army would have to retreat to the Highlands or it would have to press on into England. The logic of the momentum of events was better grasped by the Prince than by some of his advisers. There were three main factors, in ascending order of importance, which disposed the Council in favour of an advance across the border. First, there was the risk of desertion in the Highland army because of its inactivity in Edinburgh; even Lord George Murray had to admit that the six-week sojourn in Scotland's capital had made the clansmen frustrated and impatient.[48] Secondly, the longer the invasion of England was delayed, the greater the number of troops the Hanoverian dynasty could assemble to oppose them south of the border. Already there were Dutch and Swiss mercenaries in England as well as the regiments recalled from Flanders, and new regiments were being raised weekly through the subscriptions and associations.[49] In the opinion of many, Charles Edward had missed his chance through not proceeding into England immediately after Prestonpans, although at that time his exiguous numbers made such an operation impracticable. This showed the crucial significance of the decision taken by Macleod and Sir Alexander MacDonald of Sleat not to 'come out'. If they had declared for the Prince, Charles Edward would have had sufficient men to commence the invasion of England in September. It also demonstrated how fateful was the vacillation of the French. If Earl Marischal Keith, the doyen of exiled Scottish Jacobites, had been able to land in Scotland early in September with 3,000 men from France, insurrection in Scotland would have been near-universal and the Highland army might have reached London even before George II's troops had been recalled from Flanders.[50] Alternatively, if Lord Elcho's suggestion had been implemented and the entire Irish Brigade had been landed in fishing vessels on the English coast before the British regiments returned from the Low Countries, the reluctant Skye chiefs Macleod and MacDonald of Sleat would have joined the Prince. Above all, the English Jacobites would have risen. As Jacobite agent George Kelly had made clear as early as 1740: 'The English Jacobites will not fail to join *such troops as the king of France shall send.*'[51] (My italics) This point was re-emphasised by MacGregor of Balhaldy (another Jacobite agent) to Charles Edward on 11 November 1745 when he made it clear that Lords Barrymore, Beaufort, Sir John Hynde Cotton and Watkin Williams Wynn would not rise until the French landed — lack of arms and officers made it impossible for them to do so earlier.[52]

Thirdly, there was the overriding factor of money. The long stay in Edinburgh had exhausted the public monies. On the other hand, Charles Edward neither dared nor had any desire to collect the hated malt tax.[53] The choice, then, was between retreating to the Highlands, to live off the land there, or advancing through the Lowlands to England, where fresh collections of excise and cess could be made.

The faction which supported Lord George Murray in opposing an incursion onto English soil made a number of different points in answer to Charles Edward. They argued that an invasion would have made sense immediately after Prestonpans but not now. In September Lord George Murray had seemed particularly keen to be at the Dutch and then favoured a strike into England. But the available forces for such an operation, after depletions because of the departure of many Highlanders at harvest-time and the detachment of others to escort prisoners, numbered only about

1500. It was obvious madness to cross into England with such a small force, and recruits could not be had in large enough quantities.[54] Not enough volunteers had come forward even to make up John Roy Stewart's Edinburgh regiment, and Lord George had had to transfer fifty of the Strathallan men from the Atholl Brigade to bring it up to strength. By the end of October it was felt that the opportunity to catch the Whigs off guard, while the bulk of their forces was in Flanders, had gone; the armies ranged against them in England were now too strong. Nor was Lord George Murray sanguine about the likelihood of desertions from the British army. He did not share the Duke of Perth's ingenuous view that regular soldiers would not fight against their 'lawful' king, even though John Murray of Broughton, the Prince's secretary, claimed to have positive assurances from one colonel, whose regiment then lay in Kent, that he would commit his entire corps in the Prince's favour when the time was ripe.[55]

Other arguments advanced by the 'no invasion' faction were: the failure of the French to declare their open support for Charles Edward; the non-appearance hitherto of any sympathetic showing from the English Jacobites; and the fact that the Prince had made no plans whatsoever to co-ordinate with his English sympathisers. Accordingly the coterie opposed to an English adventure summed up their case under three main headings: Charles Edward should proceed into England only when his 'friends' there expressly invited him; he should refrain from entering England in any case, since the advice from the French seemed to be that they would not continue to aid him if he were defeated; and, at the simplest level of all, 5,000 men could not defeat 30,000.[56]

The Prince countered with a number of arguments. He declared with great conviction that a large body of English Jacobites would rise once the clan army was across the border. And he used the envoy from France, the Marquis d'Eguilles (whom Louis XV had sent to Scotland early in October) to insinuate cleverly the argument that the French would not venture a landing in England without positive proof of support there, and this support could only manifest itself by a rising of English Jacobites to join the clan army.[57]

Most of the clan leaders were opposed to an advance into England. Lord George Murray supported them, but with mixed feelings. He scouted the Prince's arguments concerning the French, since in his view an English adventure was irrelevant to the issue of their support anyway; he considered a French landing on the south coast of England highly unlikely and imagined they would favour 'pump-priming' activity by sending discrete picquets of reinforcements to Scotland. On the other hand, he feared a repeat performance of the risings in 1715 and 1719 (in both of which he had participated), when a retreat to the Highlands had led to a melting away of the Jacobite army.[58]

In the end, the decision to attempt an invasion of England was carried by just one vote, thanks to the support given the Prince by Lord Elcho and the Duke of Perth. Had John Roy Stewart been on the Council, the vote would have gone against Charles Edward.[59] In late October Stewart was the only colonel not on the Council, and he was a staunch exponent of the 'Scotland-first' policy. Stewart's view typified that of the half of the councillors who had been narrowly overruled. Their strategy was based on the conviction that no invasion should be attempted while the castles of Edinburgh and Stirling still held out against them. To reduce these fortresses, heavy artillery was needed, and it was proposed to send to France for proper cannon, against which the castles could not stand for more than three days. Meanwhile the Highlands should be systematically raised, one section by Lochiel, Keppoch and Stewart of Ardshiel, another by the MacDonalds, another by the Atholl Brigade, and so on.[60] If the entire fighting force of the pro-Jacobite Highlands, some 30,000 men, could be raised, and a token force of 3,000 Frenchmen landed as an earnest of Louis XV's intentions, the march to London could then commence with a formidable host. Such an army would be bound to draw out the English Jacobites and even if it failed to do so, it would be more than capable of defeating the combined Hanoverian forces. If the worst happened and no help came from France, the Prince's army should bide its time in Scotland, making periodic forays into England to collect the public money. This Scottish faction remained confident that there was enough food, money and resources in Scotland to enable such a holding action to be implemented successfully. Their reluctant acquiescence in the majority decision at the Edinburgh Council meeting was later to produce a backlash effect at the Council in Derby on 5 December, with all the momentous consequences that flowed from the decision taken there.[61]

The next issue to resolve was the best itinerary for the army in its movement into England. Charles Edward confidently proposed an advance via Berwick to meet Wade at Newcastle, rather than an approach by way of Carlisle and the north-west.[62] The prince made a number of seemingly cogent points: Wade would not long have arrived in Newcastle and his troops would be weary after the long march north, following hard on their campaign in Flanders; Cope's defeat meant that morale was now low on Tyneside but would pick up again if Wade's troops were allowed to rest; Wade had no great superiority in numbers; the reduction of Newcastle would make the Jacobites masters of Northumberland and Durham, provide their friends in Yorkshire and Lancashire with compelling incentives to join them and would cause panic in London; moreover, to march to Carlisle would be bad for the morale of the Jacobite army, as it would look as though the prince was shunning Wade.[63]

This was a formidable array of arguments. Undoubtedly a second victory, and especially one on English soil, would have shattered Whig confidence and might well have cleared Northumberland of government troops and caused the north-country Jacobites to show themselves. Had Charles Edward's intelligence been better, he would have known just how parlous was the state of Wade's army and been even more encouraged in his resolve to offer battle.[64]

But this time it was the turn of Lord George Murray to carry the Council with him. He dealt with the argument that a battle with Wade would encourage the English Jacobites to join in by saying that, if this were the reason for fighting it, it should only be joined on the most favourable terms. On the other hand, should the unexpected happen and the Jacobites be defeated, retreat across the Tweed would be very difficult.[65] Moreover, the proposed road to Newcastle via Wooler and Whittingham had been badly affected by the recent rains and might well be impassable to artillery. And even if it were not, Berwick, which lay on the route to

Newcastle, was a walled town, garrisoned by three hundred regulars and a large party of militiamen. The artillery the Highlanders possessed was not powerful enough to breach the walls of Berwick, and, in any case, sieges were not the clansmen's strong point. Carlisle was a much more desirable objective: though it was walled, it did not expect an assault from the Highlanders, and there were no regular troops there; in addition, a march to Carlisle kept all options open, since the Jacobite army could still cross to Newcastle and fight Wade later. Above all, the proposed march on Carlisle would still keep the authorities in London guessing as to the Highlanders' ultimate objective, which on this itinerary could be either London or Wales, whereas a movement towards Newcastle only made sense as the prelude to an advance on London.[66]

Lord George Murray then summed up his case in a masterly exposition of strategic thinking which, though by no means watertight in its reasoning, greatly impressed his audience.[67] Let us suppose the best possible outcome for ourselves on a march to Newcastle, he said. Even if we bypass Berwick by taking the road from Kelso to Newcastle, Wade would probably retire behind the walls of the latter town, from which he could not be dislodged. If we ourselves then withdraw, Wade can follow us and possibly even trap us between his own army and the other force commanded by Ligonier coming up from the south. Moreover, the march into Northumberland presupposes a far greater accession of Tyneside Jacobites to the army than in 1715 — a most unlikely contingency with the county swarming with Hanoverian troops. Murray then neatly outlined the advantages of a march on Carlisle. This would immediately force Wade to undertake a long march in midwinter through very difficult country; the Highlanders could engage him on much more favourable terms once he was away from his base at Newcastle, and a single defeat for Wade near Carlisle would be fatal. Moreover, on the west coast the clansmen could await a landing from France, reinforcements from Scotland or a rising of the Lancashire Jacobites.

The Council adjourned until the next day when most of the chiefs revealed themselves in favour of going to Carlisle. Charles Edward was obliged to acquiesce. Lord George Murray expressed himself well pleased with this decision: he pointed out that the Whigs would neither intercept the Highland army on a western march nor slip into Scotland in their rear, where they could be trapped between the Prince's army and that assembling under Strathallan at Perth.[68]

The details of the march to Carlisle now had to be worked out. In order to prevent Wade from sending aid to Carlisle, once he realised that this was the Jacobite objective, a feinting movement should be made by one column, travelling to Kelso as if to proceed via Wooler to Newcastle. There it should halt before veering right on the road to Jedburgh and thence to Carlisle. The other column should advance to Carlisle via Moffat, taking with it the cannon and baggage for which the Kelso-Carlisle road was unsuitable and inadequate.[69]

The main body under Lord George Murray (the Atholl Brigade, Perth's, Ogilvy's, Glenbucket's and Roy Stewart's) and most of the horse left Dalkeith on 2 November with the baggage and artillery and proceeded via Peebles and Moffat to Annandale prior to entering England at Longtown. The second division under

Charles Edward (Elcho's Lifeguards and the clan regiments) marched from Dalkeith by the eastern route via Lauder, Kelso and Jedburgh. The prince spent the night of 7 November at Haggiehaugh on Liddelwater. A third section was detached from his division by Charles Edward to pursue a middle course to England by way of Selkirk and Hawick.[70]

Although the rate of desertion on this march to the English border was high, this was matched by Wade's troubles at Newcastle with the Dutch, who would not budge from the town until their conditions on pay and horses were met.[71] The advance through the Lowlands also enabled the Highlanders to collect further public money and horses — up to 3,000 in all.[72] But Lord George's misgivings about the entire venture — he had already expressed great pessimism in a letter to his wife — seemed justified on the evidence of the march from Edinburgh. Only one border laird in the Lowlands had attempted to join, and owing to Charles Edward's failure to forewarn his supporters in the regions through which the army was to march, this man arrived on the road after the Highlanders had marched by. Realising this, he returned home. Many of the Prince's officers, notably Lochiel and Lord Ogilvy, were very much cast down by the failure of the Lowlanders to rise in large numbers.[73]

How sensible was the decision to invade England in November 1745? If we assume that it was based on the probability that the English Jacobites would rise, it can only be concluded that the enterprise was ill-advised. There were three main obstacles to a large-scale rising in England in support of the Stuarts.[74] One was the use of general warrants, whereby Jacobite ringleaders could be arrested promptly and a rebellion nipped in the bud. The English Jacobite leaders feared to sign correspondence with James Stuart, the 'Old Pretender', or in any way to compromise themselves until a French army landed in England. Secondly, there was since the decline of feudalism no tradition of the use of arms; all recruits in England would therefore need careful officering, and Charles Edward was already short of good officers. Few Englishmen at this time had served in foreign armies, and the English gentry later alleged that the principal reason for their failure to 'come out' was a lack of officers to lead their men. Thirdly, there was indifference to the Stuart cause in England. Few cared who won the dynastic struggle between the Houses of Hanover and Stuart, and this apathy worked in favour of the status quo. In contrast to Scotland, there was little emotional attachment to the Stuarts in England. If the Hanoverians were a foreign ruling dynasty, so, it could be claimed, were the Stuarts. If George II was German-born, Charles Edward was of mixed Scottish, Polish and French stock, so incitement to xenophobia was a two-edged weapon. The historian Edward Gibbon summed it up like this: 'In the year 1745 the throne and the constitution were attacked by a rebellion which does not reflect much honour on the national spirit: since the English friends of the Pretender wanted courage to join his standard, and his enemies (the bulk of the people) allowed him to advance into the heart of the kingdom.'[75] Even more seriously, Charles Edward utterly failed to institute an effective intelligence and espionage system or to make contact with the English Jacobites. This was particularly important as, since the establishment of a standing army, only William of Orange had succeeded in overthrowing a regime, and he had compassed this by stealth and assiduous contacts with likely supporters. Charles Edward had not established contact with his actual or potential English friends (the sum total of his efforts during the actual invasion of England consisted of two abortive letters, to Barrymore and Sir Watkin Williams Wynn). When taxed with this failure by his colonels, he attempted to brazen it out and insisted that he did have letters from the English Jacobites. This bluff was to have disastrous consequences when called at Derby.

Moreover, even when the Prince did bestir himself to put out feelers to his likely supporters in England, he chose the wrong men as emissaries. In general they did not make a good impression, being either political unknowns or proving inadequate on grounds of birth, intelligence or *gravitas*. Besides, the messages carried by these envoys were singularly uninformative: they gave no inkling of the Prince's strategy, said nothing about French participation, nor gave any precise instructions on what action the recipient was to take. The dispatch of a messenger to Northumberland after Prestonpans shows all these weaknesses clearly. The Duke of Newcastle's official references to this incident do not convey the extent of the fiasco: 'The man that was seized at Newcastle was going to give notice to the Pretender's friends in the North and North-West that he would soon be among them, and had an order for that purpose, signed by the Pretender's son himself.'[76] The agent, named Hickson, was sent by the Prince, after close consultation with the Duke of Perth and Murray of Broughton, to Northumberland to see who was with them in that county. The message sent with Hickson merely stated that as many as possible of the Prince's friends should join Charles Edward and that they should provide money and provisions so that the county would suffer as little as possible from the march of the Highland army. In the event, of only seven recruits from Northumberland and Cumberland, one deserted, one was too ill to serve and another turned out to be a government spy.[77]

Since the invasion of England was predicated on the existence of a sizeable Jacobite party there, it is worth asking who its leaders were and what their calibre was for mobilising the support for the Stuarts that undoubtedly existed in parts of England. In 1745 the three leading figures among the English Jacobites were Lord Barrymore, Sir John Hynde Cotton and Sir Watkin Williams Wynn.[78] The 4th Earl of Barrymore had been involved in plans for a French invasion since his visit to Paris in 1740 and pledged himself to be on the coast to greet the French invaders on their arrival. He was to be sent blank commissions by James Stuart and was to distribute them in co-operation with the Jacobite Duke of Ormonde who would come in with the French. As a guarantee of his integrity he promised to contribute £12,000 to the costs of a rising in England and sent his son Richard Barry to France in January 1744 to accompany the projected French expedition that year.[79] All the evidence tends to suggest that Barrymore was the most enthusiastic of the English Jacobite leaders — all the more surprising in view of his advanced age at the time. However, Barrymore had already demonstrated a peculiar talent for failing to receive or transmit vital information or resources (as was to happen again in the '45). A large remittance to Charles Edward allegedly went astray in 1744 when sent via Amsterdam — Murray of Broughton put the blame for this on the Jacobite agents Sempill and Balhaldy.[80]

Sir Watkin Williams Wynn had not had such an active role in 1744 and had shown none of Barrymore's apparent zeal, even declining to contribute anything to the expenses of a Jacobite rising. In the '45 Williams Wynn proved himself clearly the kind of Jacobite who would only commit himself openly when there was no risk. A similar tepidity can be observed in the attitude of Sir John Hynde Cotton, widely regarded in France as the most important Jacobite in England. Cotton had been extremely dubious about meeting Louis XV's agent James Butler in 1743 but in the end agreed to do so and promised the fullest co-operation with France. Even then Cotton allowed the mask to slip and revealed his true mettle when he protested about January as the proposed date for a simultaneous invasion from France and domestic rising on the ground that it would be too cold to turn out for a campaign.[81] The same attitude 'possibly more from timorousness than want of inclination' was evinced in early 1745 when Lord Traquair came to England from Charles Edward to sound the intentions of his English supporters. Traquair reported Cotton at first very shy and unwilling to meet him or talk to him about the Prince's affairs.[82]

Another important figure in the English Jacobite party was Sir Robert Abdy, who was one of the six English Jacobites to whom the final military details of the 1744 invasion project had been divulged. Another member of this inner circle was Thomas Brampston, like Abdy an MP for Essex; the sixth was Sir Henry Slingsby of Knaresborough, Yorkshire.[83] Three other notable English Jacobites who had been informed in 1744 of the impending invasion but not its military details were Sir William Carew, Charles Gray and Sir St. John Aubyn. Other figures of importance (though by 1745 more symbolic than actual) were the Earl of Lichfield and the Duke of Beaufort. Beaufort had been named by Murray of Broughton as a person from whom the Jacobite army could expect much assistance, but no contacts were ever made between him and Charles Edward during the '45.[84] In any case the Welsh Jacobite David Morgan, who had been his secretary, may well have been right in his assessment of Beaufort: 'He looked upon him as a recluse and so cautious a man that he would not in this examinee's opinion' — this was after Morgan's capture and investigation by Newcastle's agents — 'risk the smallest part of his estate.'[85]

With men of this calibre leading the Jacobites in England, it was clear that any excuse offered by Charles Edward for inactivity would be seized with avidity. If the potential of the English Jacobites was a principal factor in Charles's mind when he launched the invasion of England, the enterprise was an even bigger gamble than the sceptics like Lord George Murray already thought it was.[86]

NOTES

1. McLynn, 'Ireland and the '45'.
2. Whitworth pp. 108-10.
3. Add. MSS. 33004 passim.
4. SP Dom 69/54.

5. SP Dom 72/20, 73/124.
6. McLynn, 'Nottingham and the '45'.
7. Whitworth p. 110.
8. Ibid; HMC, Hastings iii. pp. 52-53; *Birmingham Gazette* 11 November 1745.
9. Ilchester, i. pp. 116-17.
10. Walpole to Mann, 4 November 1745, Walpole, ii. p. 146.
11. Ilchester, i. pp.118-19.
12. Walpole, *Memoirs* i. p. 447.
13. Stuart MSS 272/92 A.
14. Jarvis, i. passim.
15. McLynn, 'Hull and the '45'; Climenson, i. pp. 112, 175-76, 194, 209-13, 214, 217.
16. Jarvis, i. pp. 97-171.
17. HMC, I p. 115.
18. Mounsey, passim.
19. McLynn, 'West Midlands and the '45'; cf. J. R. Western, *The English Militia*.
20. Midgley pp. 237-39.
21. Simpson (1826) pp. 216-42.
22. SP Dom 68/31 & 95; 69/68 & 69.
23. Williamson pp. 1-60.
24. SP Dom 74/72; Hardwicke-Herring p. 548.
25. Sharpe, III. p. 532.
26. Ward, pp. 59-60, 81, 153, 162, 166.
27. Hardwicke-Herring pp. 544-49, 721, 724-25.
28. McLynn, 'Newcastle and the '45'.
29. Jarvis, i. pp. 229-49.
30. McLynn, 'Hull and the '45'.
31. Jarvis, i. pp. 15-80; Mounsey, passim.
32. McLynn, 'Nottingham and the '45'.
33. Miller pp. 170-72.
34. HMC, 12 v. p. 196.
35. HMC, 14 iv. p. 473.
36. Collyer, 'Yorkshire in the '45'.
37. Walpole to Mann, 20 September 1745, ii. p. 133.
38. Walpole to Mann, 27 September 1745, ii. p. 137.
39. Walpole-Mann, ii. pp. 143-44.
40. Newcastle to Chesterfield, 9 October 1745, SP Ireland 408/148-49.
41. Add. MSS. 32705 ff. 294-95.
42. Hardwicke-Herring p. 725.
43. SP Dom 74/8; V.P. p. 517; Stuart MSS 272/92 C.
44. Harris, ii. p. 184.
45. Add. MSS. 32705 ff. 294-95.
46. Walpole to Mann, 15 November 1745, Walpole, ii. pp. 149-50.
47. Marchant p. 127.
48. Maxwell of Kirkconnell p. 54; Pichot, ii. p. 100
49. Manners p. 17.
50. Murray of Broughton p. 96.
51. Stuart MSS 221/107.
52. Cruickshanks pp. 79-103.
53. Maxwell of Kirkconnell p. 54.
54. Tomasson p. 52.
55. Ibid. p. 64.
56. Ibid. p. 67.
57. McLynn, *France and the '45* p. 89.
58. Browne, iii. pp. 93, 108 et seq.

59. Tomasson pp. 68-69.
60. Tayler, *Jacobite Epilogue* pp. 157, 252-54.
61. Tomasson pp. 64-67.
62. Maxwell of Kirkconnell pp. 58-59.
63. Murray of Broughton p. 231.
64. Glover p. 39.
65. Murray of Broughton p. 231.
66. Jarvis, i. pp. 77, 235.
67. Tomasson pp. 69-73.
68. Ibid. p. 72.
69. Harris, ii. p. 184.
70. *Chronicles of . . . Atholl*, iii. pp. 81-82.
71. Tomasson pp. 72-73.
72. Harris, ii. p. 181.
73. Tomasson pp. 86-87.
74. Cruickshanks passim.
75. Gibbon p. 26.
76. SP Dom 70/37.
77. Tomasson pp. 91-92.
78. Cruickshanks pp. 18-22.
79. Ibid. pp. 20-22.
80. Murray of Broughton p. 103.
81. Cruickshanks pp. 18-19.
82. Murray of Broughton p. 424.
83. Cruickshanks p. 22 et seq.
84. Murray of Broughton p. 435.
85. SP Dom 80 ff. 166-67.
86. SP Dom 78/83; Murray of Broughton pp. 56, 58, 83, 106, 141-42, 381; Cruickshanks, passim.

2

The Jacobite Army

THERE were three main elements in the Jacobite army which invaded England in November 1745. There were clansmen who 'came out' on the orders of their clan chiefs. There were the feudal levies, properly so-called, or men who were liable to serve their lords under the terms of their land tenure. And there were the voluntary units composed of Jacobites by principle or interest who offered their services to the Prince.[1] Lochiel's Camerons would be an example of the first type of regiment, the Atholl Brigade of the second, and the ill-fated Manchester regiment of the third. The clan regiments were six in number: the Camerons, Appin Stewarts, MacPhersons, the MacDonalds of Clanranald and Keppoch and the men of Glengarry. Although the numbers in these clan regiments were uneven and in some cases the regiments were woefully under strength, clan loyalties for the most part made any other organisation impracticable. So the Glengarry and Cameron regiments, at about five hundred men each during the invasion of England, were far larger than the others. The rest of the thirteen regiments of infantry consisted of the three from the Atholl Brigade under Lord George Murray, Perth's, Lord Ogilvy's and John Roy Stewart's regiments, plus the north-eastern regiment under the command of Glenbucket.[2]

At the head of the Atholl Brigade was the redoubtable Lord George Murray, the military genius of the Jacobite army. Fifty-one years old when the rebellion broke out, Murray was a committed ideological Jacobite, who had joined the Prince with considerable misgivings and scepticism as to the rising's chances of success.[3] Though a veteran of the '15 and the '19, Murray's appearance under the Jacobite standard had amazed Scottish Whigs like Duncan Forbes, Lord President of the Council, who had long considered him reconciled to the Hanoverian regime under the influence of the Whig Duke James of Atholl. Instead, he threw in his lot with his other brother, the Marquis of Tullibardine, 'Duke William' of Atholl to the Jacobites.

Tullibardine and Murray experienced the utmost difficulty in raising the thousand-strong brigade, and considerable pressure was needed to force out the Atholl tenantry. Whereas the two successive hard winters of 1743 and 1744 — the latter reputedly the worst in living memory in Scotland — had made the Highland clansmen more inclined to follow into 'the plain', the relatively milder winters in Perthshire left the Athollmen with less motivation to follow suit.[4] Eventually, however, three battalions were raised, which included not only the Athollmen but the levies of Sir Robert Menzies of Weem under Menzies of Shian, and Duncan Robertson of Struan's men under Donald Robertson of Woodshiel. Battalion commanders were Lord Nairne, who assumed also the title of brigadier of the Atholl Brigade, Archibald Menzies of Shian and Lord Nairne's brother, Robert Mercer of Aldie.

The other lieutenant-general in the army (apart from 'Duke William' and Lord George Murray) was Lord James Drummond, 3rd titular Duke of Perth. In his thirties at the time of the rising, Perth was widely considered by the Whigs not to be truly *sérieux* — 'a foolish horse-racing boy', one of them scathingly commented — but this seems to have been a deliberate camouflage by Perth. He had a long history of Jacobite intrigue, stretching back to the 1739 'Association', and had been active in discussions about a rising in 1744.[5] The uneasy relationship between Perth and Lord George Murray dated from their deliberations in that year. The other point of great significance about Perth was that he was a Roman Catholic; a good deal of his plotting in 1744 had centred around the Catholics of York. Perth was a sincere Jacobite and apparently well-loved by his men, as the memoirs of John Daniel, the Lancashire recruit to his regiment, make clear.[6] Perth's regiment (including the men brought in by James Drummond, master of Strathallan, a company of Robertsons of Struan, and men raised by Charles Moir of Stonywood) was at the apex of its fortunes during the invasion of England. It took no part in the battle of Falkirk in January 1746, and its strength had ebbed to only three hundred by Culloden, but in November 1745 the regiment numbered some 750 men.[7]

The oldest commander in the Jacobite army was John Gordon of Glenbucket, who in his seventies was a veteran of all previous risings for the House of Stuart in his adult life.[8] Despite his age, he had pressed into service men in Banff, Glenlivet, Strathavon and Strathbogie, brooking no resistance. Glenbucket, invariably described as a stooped figure on his horse, was to reveal his intransigence and impatience with niceties once again during the campaign in England.

Another large Lowland regiment was headed by the young Lord Ogilvy, David, son of John, 4th titular earl of Airlie. Lord Ogilvy was not only one of the most handsome of the Jacobite commanders but was accompanied into England by a strikingly beautiful wife. More detailed information is available, through the regimental order book, on this corps than on any other unit that took part in the descent on England.[9]

Of the truly volunteer regiments, only one existed at the start of the invasion (the Manchester regiment was not formed until the Prince's arrival there in late November). This was a truly proletarian body, largely raised in the Edinburgh slums by the very epitome of Jacobite adventurers, John Roy Stewart.[10] Of the family of Kinkardine in Inverness-shire, Stewart had been lieutenant and quarter-master in the Scots Greys but resigned when refused a commission in the Black Watch. Converted to the Jacobite cause, he was imprisoned for espionage on behalf of the Stuarts in Inverness in 1736 but managed to escape with the connivance of Lord Lovat. Making his way to France, he fought with the Royal Scots in the service of France at the battle of Fontenoy. His opposition to the invasion of England has already been recounted. It was a supreme irony (which contributed to the legend of Stuart perfidy) that it was the members of the two truly volunteer regiments, the Edinburgh and the Manchester, who were left behind to their fate when the Prince retreated into Scotland on 20 December 1745.

Of the clan regiments, the largest was led by Donald Cameron of Lochiel, the 'gentle Lochiel' of legend, a contemporary of Lord George Murray. Lochiel ran his estates in Lochaber, to which he had no clear legal title, as an intelligent and enterprising capitalist.[11] In many ways he was a similar personality to Lord George Murray, to whom he was personally close. Both were committed to bettering the conditions of their Highland people, were concerned for the poor, and were convinced, though reluctant and pessimistic, supporters of Charles Edward. Where Murray concerned himself with mining, Lochiel's speciality was the timber business. Both too shared a profound distrust of France. Lochiel's Camerons were the key force in the capture of Edinburgh and played a major role in all three pitched battles of the '45.

The next largest Highland contingent was the MacDonalds of Glengarry. Its strength was owing to the incorporation in its ranks, over and above the Glengarry men proper, of divers elements from clans who had 'come out' without their leaders, viz. the Macleods of Raasay, MacDonells of Barisdale, the Grants and Mackenzies of Glenurquhart and Glenmoriston, and the MacDonalds of Scotus. The clan chieftain John MacDonell of Glengarry was not 'out' himself, so the clan was theoretically commanded by his second son Angus. Just before the invasion of England, Angus MacDonell returned home with his kinsman Coll of Barrisdale to raise more men, and the command was given to another of Lord George's contemporaries, Donald MacDonell of Lochgarry.[12]

Clanranald's MacDonalds had been the first to rally to the Stuart Prince, even before Glenfinnan. As with the Glengarry MacDonalds, the clan chieftain Ranald MacDonald remained aloof from the fray, so his men were commanded by his son, Ranald the younger. Clanranald's men were distinguished by their devout attachment to Catholicism. Father Allen MacDonald, a Catholic priest and clansman later lodged in New Gaol, Southwark on charges of treason, acted as chaplain and accompanied the regiment to Derby and back.[13]

The regiment of Keppoch MacDonalds, by contrast, had been raised in person by the clan chief Alexander MacDonald. Because of the peculiar circumstances of this clan — Keppoch had no hereditary jurisdiction or documentary title to his lands — the desertion rate, except of course on the march into England, was very high.[14] The regiment was stiffened by the influx of about one hundred and twenty men of the MacDonalds of Glencoe, neither the Keppoch nor the Glencoe branches being strong enough in their own right to form a single unit. Though deprived of regimental command, Alexander MacDonald of Glencoe retained his seat on the Prince's Council.

The Appin Stewarts were commanded by Charles Stewart of Ardshiel, a kinsman of the chief, Dugald Stewart. Ardshiel had a reputation as an expert swordsman and suffered less than most Jacobite leaders from the failure of the '45. When in exile in France his tenants, while paying their rents to the new incumbent of the forfeited estates, sent an equivalent sum to Ardshiel.[15] Ewen MacPherson of Cluny presents an interesting example of ambivalence, reminiscent of Lord Lovat (who did not join the Prince until December). After being taken prisoner by Lochiel's men in August, Cluny decided to support the Prince's cause, provided he was given security for his estate. His MacPhersons were to play a crucial part in the coming campaign in England.

The infantry commanders were in general more fortunate than their cavalry counterparts in the fate that befell them after taking part in the rising in 1745. Keppoch was killed at Culloden, and Perth died aboard ship on the way to France. Cluny 'skulked' in his 'cage' on Ben Alder until 1755, ostensibly to prepare for the second coming of the Prince from France. When this failed to materialise, he joined his comrades in France. Lords George Murray, Nairne, Ogilvy and the other clan leaders made good their escape to France.

The most striking aspect of the clan portion of Charles Edward's army was how few leaders were prepared to be unequivocal or to risk everything on the Stuart Prince's side. Clearly nothing could be expected from the Whig clans — the Campbells, Grants, Munros, Mackays and Sutherlands — but much more alarming was the fact that many chiefs and lairds who had risen in the '15 remained aloof this time or actually supported the Hanoverian government — the Gordons, Seaforth, MacDonald of Sleat and MacLeod of Skye.

The failure of the two latter to join the Prince was a grievous blow. Had their levies come in, Charles Edward could have had an army of invasion in November 1745 of the same size as that which defeated Hawley at Falkirk in January 1746 (about 8,000 men) and this could have had incalculable consequences. So keenly was this loss felt that the Prince took two steps to combat it. On 24 September he sent Alexander MacLeod as an emissary to Sir Alexander MacDonald and Norman MacLeod, with a message containing a host of false inducements.[16] He declared that he not only had written promises of military assistance from both France and Spain but that two independent expeditions were on the point of landing, one commanded by the Earl Marischal, which would make landfall in Scotland, the other, consisting of the entire Irish Brigade, under the Duke of Ormonde, which would descend on England. Meanwhile in England Donald MacDonald of Kinlochmoidart was sent ahead to give out in all places on the Highlanders' route that the MacDonalds of Sleat and the Macleods were following the Prince with a second army.[17]

There were five troops of cavalry in the Jacobite army which even more than the infantry suffered from being under strength. Elcho's Lifeguards, which formed the advance scouting party during the early days of the invasion of England, consisted of about seventy men and their servants under five officers, about one hundred and twenty in all. At maximum strength in Edinburgh in October, Elcho's numbered about one hundred and sixty of all ranks. At Culloden there was about half this number, so the strength of the squadron during its time in England represented something of a mid-point in its fortunes. This cavalry detachment was a key corps: riding ahead of the main army the horsemen created a very favourable impression in their special uniform of 'blue turned with red'. Lord Elcho himself, a scion of the Lowland house of Wemyss, was in his early twenties during the '45.[18] His commitment to the Stuart cause was ardent, and the fact that the gentlemen in his Lifeguards provided all their own horses and arms was an invaluable aid to the Prince. Elcho is said to have turned down the offer of a comfortable bed at Lady Lothian's house in Newbattle, declaring that he would sleep in a hayloft until the day of a Stuart restoration.[19] On the other hand, Elcho's relations with the Prince himself were not of the closest, especially as Echo was an unabashed admirer of Lord George Murray and openly took his side in the frequent disputes between the Prince and his lieutenant-general, both in and out of the Council chamber.

A second body of horse under Arthur Elphinstone (or Lord Balmerino as he became during the campaign) was not complete and contained only about forty men. This contingent was originally to have been commanded by Lord Kenmure, but he deserted the Prince's cause almost immediately after joining him. The command was then given to Elphinstone, like Lord Pitsligo an epitome of the ideologically committed Episcopalian north-east. On 5 January 1746 the fifty-seven year old Elphinstone became the sixth Lord Balmerino on his brother's death.[20]

The Earl of Kilmarnock commanded the horse grenadiers, with whom were incorporated some Perthshire cavalrymen in the absence of their commander, Lord Strathallan, who was left behind as governor of Perth during the invasion of England. This corps was known as the 'Perthshire horse' or the 'Horse Grenadiers' and at its maximum strength contained about one hundred and thirty men organised in two troops. William Boyd, Earl of Kilmarnock, aged 37 at the time of the rebellion, was propelled into the Jacobite army by bankruptcy and the urgings of his fervently pro-Stuart wife.[21] He later declared that so acute was his personal financial crisis that if Mahomet himself had raised his standard in the Highlands, he would have followed him.

Another troop of horse from Aberdeenshire and Banffshire was headed by Lord Pitsligo; together with servants, this was about the same size as Elcho's Lifeguards. Mainly composed of Banffshire gentlemen, it was led by the saintly sixty-seven year old Lord Pitsligo, the very quintessence of the *parfait knight sans peur et sans reproche*.[22] A veteran of the '15, Pitsligo's mystical form of Jacobitism was unsullied by the political opportunism of such as Kilmarnock and Elcho. When he set out from Aberdeen to Edinburgh with his troop, Pitsligo demonstrated his utter unconcern with worldly advantage with the words: 'Oh Lord, Thou knowest our cause is just. Gentlemen, march.'[23]

A fifth detachment, of hussars, nominally under the command of the Prince's secretary John Murray of Broughton, comprised about eighty hussars and was actually commanded in the field by the Irish officer Baggot, who had come over from France with the Marquis d'Eguilles.[24] This troop saw more action than the other cavalry, as it was sent north with the Duke of Perth on his abortive mission to Scotland on 13–15 December — which ended with the debacle of the 'Sunday hunting'. John Murray of Broughton had played a key role in the intrigues which led to the '45. He was close to the Prince personally but a bitter enemy of Lord George Murray, who in turn blamed on his bad influence many of the Prince's wilder decisions. Murray's ultimate attachment to the Stuarts, however, ran skin-deep.[25] He was primarily a political adventurer and entered the Jacobite demonology in 1746 when after the failure of the rebellion he turned king's evidence to save his own skin. It was principally his evidence which determined the fate of that arch-machiavellian, Simon Fraser, Lord Lovat.

The ultimate fate of the five cavalry leaders is interesting as illustrating the very different experiences of defeated Jacobite leaders. Kilmarnock and Balmerino suffered the executioner's axe, while Murray was captured but saved himself in the way described. Elcho escaped to France but such was the bitterness which his somewhat bumptious attitude caused in England during his vanguard duties that he acquired a reputation among the Whigs as a bloodthirsty hothead. It was this reputation which led to his being specifically excluded from the general amnesty offered in the 1770s to Jacobites who has been 'out' in the '45. Pitsligo, on the other hand, was admired for his saintliness even by the Whigs, so the pursuit of him ordained in the North-East was carried out half-heartedly.[26] This enabled Pitsligo to die in peace in his own bed. There is therefore little comfort here for those (like Pitsligo) who believe in the benign workings of providence, for while one adventurer suffered (Kilmarnock), another did not (Elcho), and while one ideological Jacobite escaped the scaffold (Pitsligo), another paid for rebellion with his head (Balmerino). The most reprehensible morally of the cavalry leaders (Murray of Broughton) emerged relatively unscathed.[27]

The best of the cavalry were Pitsligo's Aberdeen cavalrymen and Elcho's Lifeguards. These latter unfortunately found their ranks thinned when about thirty of their number were transferred to Balmerino's company to make up his numbers. The hussars were the weakest arm of the cavalry and incurred the censure of Lord George Murray during the campaign for their poor training.[28] Discipline among the infantry regiments was weakest among the Keppoch and Glengarry MacDonalds, who were alleged to be largely out of the control of their regimental colonels. Whig propaganda made much of this. Lord Chancellor Hardwicke reported that Keppoch's men had spent one day shooting all the Marquis of Lothian's fallow deer. When the officers called on them from the windows of Lothian's house to desist, they too were shot at.[29] Highland indiscipline during the sojourn at Edinburgh in October was a frequent motif in reports reaching the north of England. One government agent in Durham reported just before the march through the Lowlands that the clansmen were totally out of hand, with their officers indulging them 'for fear of disobliging them'.[30] To some extent the indiscipline that did exist was natural. The Glengarry men were commanded by Donald of Lochgarry, who was not the clan chief, while Keppoch had no clear title to his lands and depended on personal charisma to enforce his will. To some extent, also, the tales of lack of discipline arose from misunderstanding. Morale was inculcated in the clansmen by sheer force of personal magnetism rather than the lash so beloved of British army officers. Lord George Murray constantly praised the courage and discipline of the clansmen when under immense pressure, as at Clifton on 18 December, but this state of affairs was produced by a sense of personal loyalty to clan chief or regimental commander, rather than main force.[31]

Apart from infantry and cavalry detachments, the Jacobite army contained thirteen pieces of cannon, though the largest of these was only a four-pounder.[32] The numbers in the army cannot be estimated precisely.[33] Early wild overestimates by the Whigs led later to some equally implausible underestimates. Figures varying from 12,000 to an incredible 30,000 had been mentioned in official reports early in the rising.[34] Lord Chancellor Hardwicke accurately assessed Charles Edward's army at 3,000 strong in mid-September when all others in government circles were putting it as high as 7,000, but no one in London knew for certain how much the Jacobite army had increased in strength at the commencement of the invasion of England.[35] Although Newcastle's best intelligence sources assessed the numbers in the 'Pretender's army' on 18 November at not more than 8,000, opinions differed on how many actual combatants there were.[36] This was very worrying for the Whig elite, and severe penalties were prescribed for those spreading panic by exaggerating enemy numbers, as the luckless landlord of the Crown and Thistle in Rotherham discovered, after a casual public remark that he thought the Highlanders were 17,000 strong.[37]

An exact count remains difficult to this day. John Glover in his memoir of the '45 estimated that there were 6,000 invaders but only 3,000 effectives.[38] By contrast, a count taken at Derby on the nights of 4/5 December 1745 revealed 7,008 'guests' on the first night and 7,148 the next.[39] Among Jacobite participants there is a similar discrepancy in the discussion of numbers. Chevalier de Johnstone produced a low of 4,500 while the Jacobite sources consulted by Home for his history put the figure as high as 6,000, a figure corroborated also by counts made by the government at two bridges in England.[40] Clearly the problem arises from differing conjectures on how to disentangle effectives from camp followers. The other problem was that it was a Jacobite tactic — but one quickly uncovered by the Whigs — to demand quarters for more men than were actually in the Jacobite force.[41] Considerable lengths were gone to in order to prevent an accurate census of numbers being taken by the enemy. Apart from entering a town in two detachments, often at night and usually on different days, Jacobite commanders would confuse the issue by having their men enter and re-enter a town by different gates, so that their numbers always appeared greater than they were. The factor of numbers was all-important during the invasion of England since this was the Prince's Achilles heel. Although desertions dwindled almost to nothing once the army was in England, the desertion rate on the march from Edinburgh to Carlisle was very high, especially in the Atholl brigade.[42] Many Scots disagreed with the objectives of the English expedition; for them, Charles Edward should have been well content with his mastery of Scotland. Others simply entertained a superstitious dread of entering England. The case of John Fullerton of Dudwick, a Banff Jacobite, was typical of many. Having joined the Prince at Holyrood palace, Fullerton left the army when it headed south for England and rejoined it when it returned to Scotland.[43]

The best estimate of numbers is probably arrived at by correlating Sir John Patullo's muster just before the march to the English border with the exhaustive count of soldiers taken by Whig spies at Eamont bridge in Cumbria. Patullo's muster figures produce about 5,000 infantry and 500 cavalry (see Fig. 1)

		Numbers
Infantry:	Atholl Brigade	1000
	Perth's	750
	Glenbucket's	300
	John Roy Stewart's	350
	Cluny MacPherson's	300
	Lochiel's	500
	Appin Stewarts	350
	Clanranald's	300
	Keppoch's	300
	Ogilvy's	500
	Glengarry's	450
Cavalry:	Elcho's	120
	Balmerino's	40
	Hussars	80
	Pitsligo's	150
	Kilmarnock's	130

Fig.1. The Jacobite Army in November 1745

Allowing for desertions during the march through the Lowlands, this would come close to agreeing with the count of something over 5,000 in all at Eamont Bridge. Moreover, at a review in Glasgow in late December 1745 of the army lately returned from England, about 5,000 were counted.[44]

The rate of desertion once the army was actually in England was very low, hardly surprisingly given the attendant risks of deserting in the heart of enemy country. Although the rate for quitting the Jacobite army was allegedly high during the campaign in Scotland, an examination of Lord Rosebery's list of persons engaged in the rebellion shows only thirty deserters out of a list of 2,590 during the entire rising.[45] Only a handful of these deserted in England. Jacobite commanders tended to be lenient towards deserters, since clan culture reinforced the tradition of returning home to harvest crops during a campaign. Those who deserted and were retaken were not shot but strictly guarded and persuaded to fight again.[46] This naturally later made the defence of having been 'forced out' difficult to sustain, as it could be countered with the argument that there was no risk attached to desertion from the Jacobite army. This in turn raises the whole issue of being 'forced out' and the exact status of the rank and file soldier in the Jacobite army. The most common plea of Jacobite prisoners after the failure of the '45 was that they had been compelled to follow their clan or feudal leader because of threats of destruction to their persons or property. It is true that duress played a major part in raising the Jacobite army, particularly in the case of the Lowland lairds, but against this should be set the following considerations. First, the regular British army in the eighteenth century was largely composed of men who had been subjected to economic and judicial compulsion, and sometimes actual 'pressing'. Secondly, the members of the 'loyal' Highland companies, such as that of Lord Loudoun, had also been forced. Thirdly, wardholding or the compulsory performance of military duty as a clan or feudal obligation always contained an element of force. In this sense 'forcing out' was an integral part of the entire pre-capitalist system of heritable jurisdictions in Scotland before 1745.

A perennial problem for Charles Edward's army was that of lack of officers. Indeed, the excuse frequently offered later by the English Jacobites who failed to rise was that the ill-trained levies they could raise on their estates were good enough for breaking up rival election meetings or for general intimidation but would be useless as a military force without first-class officers. Surprisingly, this defence for the inactivity of his English supporters was accepted both by James Stuart, the 'Old Pretender', and by the commander of the abortive French invasion force in support of the Prince in 1745, the Duc de Richelieu.[47] Significantly, however, it was never accepted by the Prince himself.

The shortage of good officers was made worse by the Prince's decided preference for the mediocre French and Irish officers who had come over from France with the Marquis d'Eguilles in October. D'Eguilles had been sent by the French Court before Prestonpans to assess the credibility and capability of Charles Edward's Highlanders, with a view to Louis XV's possible dispatch of a French invasion force in support. With d'Eguilles had come a number of political adventurers in the service of France.[48] Lord George Murray contemptuously remarked of them that their military knowledge barely enabled them to mount guard competently.[49] None of them held a rank above that of captain, but to ensure their fortunes on return to France, the Prince immediately promoted them, some to the rank of colonel. The meteoric rise of Richard Augustus Warren is the best-known example of how a profession of Jacobitism could propel one at speed to a position of privilege. A bankrupt merchant from Marseilles, Warren, after a short period of volunteer service in the French army, during which time he never saw action, contrived to come to Scotland with d'Eguilles. After six months in the Prince's army, Warren was sent back to France to report and embellish the 'Rout of Moy' in 1746. Promoted to colonel for this 'exploit', he ended the '45 with a baronetcy as well.[50]

The scope given by the Prince to arrivistes, opportunists and incompetents, especially if they were willing to indulge in flattery, and the notable penchant for the Irish that he displayed, infuriated Lord George Murray and the Scots. It was particularly unacceptable to the Scottish volunteer officers, serving at their own expense. When the Prince even proposed to make the Irish officers Sir Francis Geoghan and Captain Brown colonels of the new regiments he hoped to raise in England, the Scots finally decided that enough was enough. Charles Edward was obliged to give the command of the one regiment formed in England to an English volunteer. The bitterest pill for the Scots to swallow was that this preferment of Irishmen in the service of France was extended to men who risked nothing if captured. They would simply be returned to France under a cartel, whereas the Scots risked everything — life, liberty and property — for a Prince who largely avoided their company.[51]

The estrangement of Charles Edward from the Lowland officers was a grave mistake and cost him dearly at Derby. By choosing to march with the clansmen in a separate column during the advance into England, he widened the gap between himself and the non-clan Scots. On the march to Derby he saw less of his principal officers than he had done in Edinburgh. They for their part were too taken up with regimental cares to remain in tune with his current thinking. No longer did the Council members assemble with the Prince each morning for discussion. Since Lord George Murray marched with the Lowland regiments, the friction between the Prince and lieutenant-general was no more, but each became dangerously estranged. Charles Edward had frequent contact with Perth once the border was crossed, but Perth had little opportunity, particularly after Carlisle, of conferring with the influential non-clan Scottish commanders. He was therefore unable to close the gap between them and the Prince or to warn him of the possible impending refusal to penetrate further into England. Perth's problems were compounded by the frail health that would claim him next year. On return from scouting expeditions, the exhausted Duke would retire to his room to take a frugal meal of bread and milk. Then he was condemned to sit up all the night in a chair as respiratory problems made it impossible for him to lie down in a bed.[52]

The position of the spurned volunteer officers in the Jacobite army was an interesting one. Blank commissions issued by the Prince were distributed by the lieutenant-general to the regimental commanders, on whom the real choice of officers fell. This choice was largely determined retrospectively by an individual's ability to raise men, but even after raising them the candidate for officership had then to purchase the commission. This was of course a perfectly natural way of proceeding in all eighteenth-century armies.[53]

The social composition of the officers in the Lowland regiments shows a fairly clear-cut pattern.[54] Above the rank of captain, most were landed proprietors. Captains were either from the landed gentry or were farmers and merchants. The use of the term 'gentleman' to designate the officers tends to be not so much tautologous as uninformative, since 'gentleman' was an umbrella term. This can be seen from the trials of the captured Jacobites after the '45 at which individuals may be referred to as 'gentleman otherwise farmer otherwise yeoman' or, even more confusingly, 'gentleman otherwise labourer'. At the rank of lieutenant some social leavening is evident, for besides representatives of the landed classes, we find tenant farmers, sailors, vintners, tobacconists and merchants. Of course the situation in the clan regiments was very different, since there the officers would largely be chosen on a kinship basis, family proximity to the clan chief being the principal determinant.

The rank and file of the army was part clansmen, part proletarian. As we have seen, less than half the army was formed from the Highland clans proper. If we except the men of Perthshire in Perth's regiment and the Atholl Brigade, whose status was intermediate between the clan organisation and the truly feudal system of the north-east, it emerges that some 1,700 men in the Jacobite army were drawn from Edinburgh, Dundee, Kircardine, Aberdeen and other parts of the north-east. The large proletarian element in the rank and file of these regiments contained 280 men designated as servants, 116 labourers, 100 workmen, 84 weavers, and 36 ploughmen. Shoemakers and barbers figured prominently in John Roy Stewart's regiment. Altogether in the non-clan section of the army 106 merchants and 117 farmers can be identified.[55]

If we except the small numbers of recruits who joined Charles Edward in England, certain conclusions can be drawn about the overall social composition of the Jacobite army at its greatest strength. Fourteen peers, including two countesses, were in the Prince's train and over three hundred knights, lairds and landowners great and small with members of their families. Over four hundred can be identified as belonging to the 'middle sector' of society and some 1,400 belonged to the lower middle class (semi-skilled or tradesmen) or 'working class' including agricultural workers.[56] The rest of the army was composed of clansmen. These figures, however, relate to the army at its maximum strength about the time of the battle of Falkirk, and included about 800 men of Lord Lewis Gordon's regiment, which was raised in Scotland during the invasion of England. The exact social composition of the army which was in action in England during November-December 1745 would therefore have to be extrapolated from the overall picture and such precision is not possible.

The arms and equipment of the men in the Jacobite army denoted its status as an assemblage of irregulars rather than a regular fighting force. Ordinary clansmen carried a musket, a sword — usually the basket-hilted broadsword — or a dirk or both and a pistol.[57] The traditional clan weapon, the Lochaber axe, was little seen in the '45. The Highland shield, however (the targe or target), was carried not only in the clan regiments but in the Lowland units as well, as was a small quantity of bayonets. Guns were in short supply among the Highlanders and many of them were antiquated, survivors of earlier Jacobite risings. For this reason the imported French and Spanish firearms of modern vintage were much sought after. Shortage of ammunition was another problem. Just before the march on England, each man was issued with 'twelve shot', but strict orders were issued against waste of ammunition as well as against shooting at livestock. A further supply of bullets was ordered and manufactured for the Highlanders during their stay at Manchester. Twelve rounds of ammunition — spherical bullets, powder and brown paper for holding the charge — was a remarkably small amount even for an eighteenth-century fighting force (Cumberland's men had twenty-four rounds) and bred in some Whig minds the notion that the Highlanders would not be able to stand and fight a fixed battle. The government agent Bracken reported from Lancaster in November: 'In general they are well-armed but, I dare say, the most of them cannot charge quick, for their pistols are of the screw sort and, as to the common men, very few of them have any pistols, and the target, it is plain, is more for single combat than field fighting, so that, when their army is fairly faced, it must be borne down entirely, it is so weak and light.'[58]

Of the thirteen pieces of cannon, six were Swedish field guns in the two to four-pound range and six were one-and-a-half pounder 'cohorns' captured from Cope at Prestonpans.[59] So far from being of assistance during the campaign in England, the artillery was a positive embarrassment. It was Charles Edward's insistence that none of it be abandoned on the retreat from Derby which led to the rearguard action at Clifton on 18 December. No regiment wanted the chore of guarding this artillery, in contrast to the enthusiasm shown by Perth's when it came to forming a pioneer corps. An *ad hoc* force of some fifty men was detached from the Duke's regiment, mainly those with a background in carpentry, gardening and other manual crafts.[60]

Their role in making good some of the awful pre-turnpike roads in the English campaign has gone unsung in the contemporary sources.

The diet enjoyed by the Highlanders during the invasion of England was probably superior to their normal one. Lord George Murray had insisted that each soldier be provided with a haversack containing meal or oatcakes and a canteen of water, so that the order of march would not be disrupted as foragers broke away from the main force.[61] In addition, large herds of black cattle accompanied the army on its march to provide fresh meat.[62] And since nearly every night in England was spent in a sizeable town where provisions could be requisitioned, these supplies could be supplemented considerably. To a great extent, then, the Highlanders lived off the land: 'like locusts they take all they can drive or carry', one hostile critic commented.[63] Some of the resting places must have afforded an unusually rich feast, particularly in liquor. In Manchester twenty men of clan Donald consumed sixty bottles of wine and nine large barrels of malt liquor at the house of a leading Whig who had fled the town.[64] In Derby six officers and forty men billeted in a single house from Wednesday night to Friday morning dispatched a side of beef, eight joints of mutton, four cheeses, large quantities of white and brown bread, six fowls and a large, though unspecified, amount of ale, beer, tea and spirits.[65]

Lord George Murray in particular was concerned for the welfare of the men in his army, and thanks to his foresight and the ease of supplementing the basic diet in the large towns, losses through sickness during the campaign were negligible. Marshal Wade lost as many in five days on the march from Newcastle to Hexham and back in November as Murray did in the entire campaign. Lord George was ahead of his time in his solicitude for the welfare of his soldiers; Wade and Cumberland were notoriously contemptuous of 'pampering' their troops and absurdly parsimonious with military funds.[66] Only Ligonier in the British army saw the importance for morale of a well-fed army.

Quite how much the officers and men received in pay is difficult to determine. Elcho tells us that the daily rate for officers was: Captain 2s.6d., Lieutenant 2/-, Ensign 1/6d., Private 6d.[67] Other sources do not quite bear this out. Balmerino mentions that sums of 2/- a day were regularly received by the 'gentlemen', while amounts of 7d. and 8d. a day for privates were frequently cited during the state trials in 1746.[68] It seems probable that cavalrymen were better paid than the infantry: in Kilmarnock's horsemen's case, a list shows that sergeants received eighteen pence and rankers one shilling; according to Balmerino, his servant received 8d. a day in addition to his subsistence plus an annual stipend of £4.[69] All sources are agreed, however, that as the campaign wore on into 1746, the men's pay fell into arrears and was paid in kind, usually in the form of meal. This was a development in the period after the battle of Falkirk and was not the case during November-December 1745.

One of the most oft-remarked aspects of the 1745 campaign in England — noted with reluctant admiration even by Whig apologists — was the almost total absence of looting or rapine on the march to and from Derby. This was very largely owing to the regular system of financing of the army by the collection of the public monies.[70] In Scotland these included the proceeds of forfeited estates, the cess and malt tax.

During the progress through England the principal source of revenue for the Jacobites was the Excise Tax, supplemented by all monies in the hands of postmasters. Excise charges were due in England on malt, ale, candles, leather, soap and on brewers and victuallers. Since to Jacobites the Stuarts were kings *de jure*, it followed that their rights to collect the royal revenue should be implemented. The same procedure had been adopted in the '15, and in 1745 it was simply a matter of finding Jacobites acquainted with the procedure for collecting the Excise. As long as they came into possession of the relevant entry and receipt books and made out a legal receipt, Jacobite quartermasters did not need to extort payments from English citizens. With legal proof of payment a town mayor knew he could not be compelled to pay the Excise again by the government in London, so saw no reason to resist Jacobite demands. The upshot was that in Lancashire and Cheshire alone £1,373 was uplifted.

The successful collection of the Excise by the Jacobites was thus both cause and effect of the general apathy towards the dynastic struggle which was so pronounced in England. Given that Excise duties had to be paid, and given that the principal aim of a non-ideological citizenry was to be left in peace by government — any government — it mattered little to whom they were paid. The payment in turn made extortion and looting unnecessary. The people of England came to realise that the propaganda tales of child-eating, bloodthirsty Highland savages were untrue. This lessened their inclination to play an active role on the government side. There was, however, one less pleasant consequence of this successful appropriation of the public monies. Because the Hanoverian government had to make good the losses sustained through this removal of the Excise revenue — since they could not charge a locality twice — Jacobite paymasters and quartermasters were marked men after the failure of the rising. Sir John Wedderburn, principal paymaster in the Prince's army, was doomed by the Chief Justice's ruling in 1746 that to hold a Commission of Excise from the 'Pretender' was an overt act of treason.

One glaring defect in the otherwise impressive organisation of the Jacobite army was the absence of a system of espionage.[71] Both Lord George Murray and the Prince's Quartermaster (and Irish favourite) John O'Sullivan argued strongly that this was indispensable if only to ascertain the movements and resources of the enemy. But the Prince was so little aware of the importance of espionage that he did not even make use of the network of Jacobite spies already in existence. The absurd consequence was that reports from agents in London still went to James Stuart's representatives in Paris. During the sojourn in Edinburgh, just one emissary had been sent into England to prepare the ground for a rising there. Unfortunately the envoy, John Hickson, was indiscreet and was captured with despatches from the Prince at Newcastle, as already related. To save himself he then turned king's evidence. A second messenger sent south during the advance through the Lowlands to report on the dispositions of Marshal Wade failed to return. In despair Lord George Murray improvised his own informal system of spying while he was in England.[72]

But if the Hanoverians had the edge in intelligence and espionage, they were confounded once the invasion began by the sheer speed of the Highlanders' advance. The descent on Carlisle was a taste of things to come. With admirable precision the Atholl brigade and the Lowland regiments proceeded via Peebles and Moffat to link up with the Prince and the clans who had marched by way of Dalkeith, Lauder, Kelso, Jedburgh and Haggiehaugh. During the campaign in England the Highlanders penetrated into the heart of the country with a speed that astonished their enemies, used to the testudinarian pace of eighteenth-century armies. Some days the Jacobite army marched thirty miles and on one occasion thirty-five.[73] In contrast to the British army battalions, which usually did not get under way until about 9 a.m., the Scots would march at dawn or sooner if the moon shone.[74] Charles Edward himself set the tone: he ate little at supper each night, did not undress but lay on top of his bed, retired at 11 p.m. and was up at 4 a.m. the next day, ready to march on foot at the head of his troops.[75] Apart from their superior mobility, the Highlanders had another advantage over their enemies: they did not have to worry about lines of communication. The Hanoverian army, on the other hand, was constrained by two considerations: it had to reckon with the possibility of an insurrection by English Jacobites; and it went in fear of an invasion from France.

The superior speed and mobility of the Jacobite army was all the more impressive given the state of the roads along which they had to travel. In the first half of the eighteenth century few roads had been turnpiked and the others were so bad that it is no exaggeration to say that communication by road had been easier in earlier centuries.[76] Running through country that was largely enclosed, the pre-turnpike highway consisted largely of lanes or restricted ways bordered by hedges and ditches. At one side, along its entire course, ran a horse causeway, perhaps a yard and a quarter in width, constructed of paving stones and cobbles and sometimes protected from the wheeled traffic of the adjacent castway by stoops or posts. The castway itself was not systematically paved, though in Lancashire, where there was plentiful sandstone, the worst holes and ruts had usually been filled in. Pack horses and riders could manage well enough on these roads but heavy traffic could not. There was a particular need for a causeway wide enough to accommodate carts. With the coming of industrialism and the transport of heavy goods like coal, the turnpikes would become a necessity.

Some idea of the hardihood of the clansmen can be formed when it is realised that most of them travelled these roads barefoot, to the disgust and derision of English observers who took this as just one more sign of Highland savagery. Even where shoes were available, the clansmen seem not to have cared for them — it is reported that they were particularly averse to the 'wooden shoes of Lancashire'.[77]

Despite orders that 'regimental women' were not to accompany the army, many did, some with their children, and many accompanied their men to the colonies later when transportation was their reward for rebellion.[78] So well disciplined was the Jacobite army that Sir John MacDonald claimed that the few depredations which did occur during the progress through England were the work of women and camp followers. Naturally, it was this accretion of non-combatants that so confused the issue of numbers in the army.[79]

One factor that should have made it harder for people on the line of march in

England to send their goods and chattels away (as many did) was the existence of cattle plague or cow fever (murrain) which became rampant in late 1745.[80] This should have made it harder for farmers to send their cattle south out of reach of the Highlanders, but no official order against moving herds south was issued until January 1747. As might have been expected, the coincidence of cattle fever and Jacobite invasion was too good an opportunity for Whig propagandists to miss. Horace Walpole asserted that the disease had been started by 'papists' poisoning the wells along the expected line of march of the 'Pretender's son'.[81] This conveniently ignored two considerations: first, that such an activity would in no way have helped the Prince's cause, rather the reverse; secondly, that the plague spread *from* the Home Counties to the North, i.e. from Whig strongholds to Jacobite ones. But as Fielding's *True Patriot* amply demonstrated, Whig publicists were no respecters of the truth during the '45.

NOTES

1. Seton & Arnott, iii. pp. 300–26; Home pp. 114–115.
2. Maxwell of Kirkconnell pp. 59–61.
3. Tomasson pp. 7–17.
4. Ibid. pp. 31–33.
5. Jones pp. 199–211.
6. 'John Daniel's Progress', in W. B. Blaikie, *Origins of the '45* pp. 167–224.
7. Seton & Arnot, iii. p. 322.
8. A & H Tayler, *Jacobites of Banff* p. 249 et seq.
9. *Order Book of Lord Ogilvy's Regiment* (Spalding Club Miscellany, Vol. 1, 1841).
10. H. Tayler, *Jacobite Epilogue* pp. 252–54.
11. Lenman pp. 245–46.
12. See 'Lochgarry's narrative', in W. B. Blaikie, *Itinerary of Prince Charles Edward*.
13. SP Dom 96 f. 185.
14. Harris, *Hardwicke*, ii. p. 190.
15. Tayler, *Jacobite Epilogue* p. xiv.
16. Home pp. 310–12.
17. *Scots Magazine* 1745 p. 40.
18. See Lord Elcho, *A Short Account of the Affairs of Scotland in 1744, 1745 & 1746*, ed. E. Charteris (1907).
19. Harris, *Hardwicke* ii. p. 190.
20. Henderson p. 171.
21. *British Magazine* 1746 p. 192.
22. For Pitsligo see A. & H. Tayler, *Jacobite Letters to Lord Pitsligo* (Aberdeen 1930); William King, *Political and Literary Anecdotes of his time* (1819) p. 145; A. & H. Tayler, *Jacobites of Aberdeenshire & Banffshire in the Forty-Five* (Aberdeen 1982) p. 379.
23. Lord Pitsligo, *Thoughts Concerning Man's Condition* (Edinburgh 1854) p. xviii.
24. For the Marquis d'Eguilles see F. J. McLynn, *France and the Jacobite Rising of 1745* (Edinburgh 1981).
25. The Woodehouselee MSS, ed. A. F. Steuart (Edinburgh 1907) p. 89.
26. King, *Anecdotes* pp. 144–46.
27. See Blaikie, *Origins* pp. 3–71.
28. Tomasson p. 61.
29. Ibid. p. 33.
30. SP Dom 72/106.

31. Tomasson p. 33.

32. Maxwell of Kirkconnell p. 64.

33. Jarvis, ii. p. 15.

34. Nicholas, *Intercepted Post* p. 136.

35. Hardwicke-Herring Correspondence p. 539.

36. SP Dom 74/8.

37. SP Dom 83 f. 127.

38. Glover, *Memoirs* p. 39.

39. Ray p. 157.

40. Chevalier de Johnstone p. 60; Home pp. 315–17; Glenorchy to Campbell, 3 December 1745, *Transactions of the Gaelic Society of Inverness* XII (1896–97) p. 161.

41. *Manchester Magazine,* 26 November 1745.

42. Seton & Arnot, iii. pp. 305–07.

43. Tayler, *Jacobites of Banff* p. 198.

44. Home pp. 315–17.

45. Rosebery, *List of Persons* passim.

46. *Gentlemen's Magazine* 1746 p. 525.

47. McLynn, *France and the Jacobite Rising* p. 177.

48. Ibid. p. 69.

49. Tomasson pp. 94–95.

50. Ibid.

51. This resentment is documented in both Elcho's and Lord George Murray's accounts.

52. Elcho, p. 329.

53. Seton & Arnot, iii. pp. 269–80.

54. Rosebery, *List of Persons* pp. 360–62.

55. Ibid.

56. Ibid.

57. Gordon & Arnot pp. 288–93.

58. SP Dom 76/46

59. Chevalier de Johnstone p. 57.

60. Allardyce Papers, ii. pp. 439, 444.

61. Chambers, 'Marches' p. 54.

62. SP Dom 73/93 & 99; *Birmingham Gazette* 18 November; HMC, Various Colls, viii. p. 122.

63. Staffs CRO D/798/3/1/1.

64. *Manchester Magazine,* 14 January 1746.

65. *Derby Mercury,* 13 December 1745; Marchant pp. 212–14.

66. Tomasson, passim.

67. Elcho, p. 329.

68. Allardyce Papers, ii. pp. 387, 460, 471.

69. HMC, Various Colls, viii. p. 118.

70. Jarvis, i. pp. 175–97.

71. Jarvis, ii. pp. 70–109.

72. Tomasson p. 63.

73. *Trans. Gael. Soc.* XXI, loc. cit. p. 167.

74. *Gentlemen's Magazine* 1745 p. 611.

75. Elcho, p. 329.

76. W. Harrison, 'Preturnpike highways', *LCAS* ix (1891) p. 101 et seq; F. A. Bailey, 'Preturnpike Roads', *LCHS* 89 (1937).

77. Shercliffe, *Wythenshawe* p. 134.

78. Jarvis, i. pp. 253, 273 et seq.

79. Jarvis, ii. pp. 298–99.

80. *Gentlemen's Magazine* 1745 p. 557.

81. Walpole to Mann, 29 November 1745, Walpole, ii. pp. 154–55.

3

The Siege of Carlisle

Friday 8th November

EVEN before the battle of Prestonpans, the Duke of Newcastle had thought it necessary to alert Carlisle that the town might receive an incursion from the Highlanders. Of the loyalty of Carlisle itself there was no doubt. The pledge of fealty to George II had been transmitted by Deputy Mayor Pattinson on 12 September and Chancellor Waugh had sent a letter full of loyal sentiments signed by every member of the Chapter of the Cathedral Church in Carlisle.[1] Prestonpans increased apprehension in the town, especially when the citizens were treated to stories of Highland ferocity by survivors of Cope's army, some of whom were 'subsisted' in Carlisle after the battle.[2] Lieutenant-Colonel Durand was sent from London as governor of Carlisle castle at the beginning of October to put the town in a sound defensive posture, but, owing to uncertainty about the operation of the militia laws, he was obliged to pay his men out of his own pocket to retain any kind of garrison force.[3] Pattinson meanwhile received 400 arms from the Duke of Newcastle and distributed them to the inhabitants, but in the town of Carlisle itself — as distinct from the castle — only two hundred men with three officers could be raised; as Pattinson expressed it to Newcastle: 'this extreme nakedness makes me greatly fear the consequences'.[4] Lord Lonsdale, the Lord Lieutenant of Cumberland, was also concerned at the poor defences of Carlisle, and it was his urgent plea for assistance with its defence on 30 September that led Newcastle to send Durand.[5]

Newcastle himself continued confident that Carlisle could not be taken. As he wrote on 19 September: 'If they [the Highlanders] should attempt to make themselves masters of Carlisle, I am persuaded they will fail in it.'[6] Newcastle reasoned that he had only to issue warrants empowering the Mayor to form the voluntary companies, and to instruct HM Keeper of the Stores to provide a sufficient quantity of arms, and the fighting spirit of Carlisle would do the rest.[7] Apparently he had formed a gross overestimate of the numbers of people in Carlisle ready and willing to bear arms.

By the beginning of November, the inadequate breastworks erected at Carlisle, the scarcity of fighting men, the confusion over militia duties, the distance from the town of both Wade's army and Ligonier's, and the quadripartite factionalism between Chancellor Waugh, Recorder Gilpin, Deputy Mayor Pattinson and Governor Durand, had combined to make Carlisle peculiarly vulnerable.[8] For the contretemps that followed Durand was made the principal scapegoat, as he was the only one who could be reached by military discipline.

Just before entering England, Lord George Murray imparted Charles Edward's final instructions to the other two Lieutenant-Generals, Perth and Tullibardine.[9] The Prince planned to be at Reddings on the 8th and to march from there so as to be at Rockly by midday; there he wanted Tullibardine to meet him with 1,500 men, the Swedish cannon, and a plentiful supply of ammunition. These orders countermanded those issued by John O'Sullivan at Jedburgh on the 7th, when the Prince's destination for the 9th was stated to be Brampton, where Tullibardine was to meet him at noon with the artillery. The change of plans was made because a junction with the Prince on the 9th with *all* the artillery proved impracticable for Tullibardine.[10]

The first barrier for the Highlanders was the River Esk, marking the boundary between Scotland and England, and its crossing was an occasion of great symbolic importance. In normal times, without flooding, the Esk was only half as wide as the Seine at Paris (as Chevalier de Johnstone pointed out), so it did not present a formidable obstacle (by contrast with the return journey). Even so, one of the large guns was lost in the Esk by the artillery detachment and one of the gunners broke his thigh-bone in attempting to rescue it.[11] The Highlanders crossed the river with ease and, on reaching the other side, drew their swords, wheeled to the left and faced Scotland, which they saluted superstitiously. Unfortunately Lochiel cut his hand as he unsheathed his sword and this was immediately taken as a bad omen.[12] Some of the clansmen had already decided anyway that the entire invasion was inauspicious, since the Highlanders had lost well over 500 men through desertion on the march to the border. The roads to Edinburgh and Glasgow were reported thronged with deserters, many of whom were seized by the Lowland Whigs.[13] From these large-scale desertions arose the canard that the Jacobite army had mutinied and refused to cross into England but had been forced to do so by the clan chiefs.[14]

Meanwhile, hearing that there was an advance party of Highlanders at Gretna, Durand dispatched Colonel Dacre in that direction with Mr. Kilpatrick as his lieutenant. Kilpatrick took a small party of his men beyond Ecclefechan where he came in sight of 'a great body of rebels'.[15] A Highland quartermaster was somehow captured and sent to Wade's headquarters next day. In this way, the first prisoner of the campaign in England was taken while still on Scottish soil.

The growing menace of the Highlanders was highlighted in a letter by Newcastle's brother Henry Pelham (through whom the House of Commons was controlled by the Pelhams in this period), written that day: 'They [the enemy] seem to act with some judgment and great resolution . . . Our enemies are continually pouring in arms, officers, engineers and money and this has a bad effect on our credit, for though the stocks do not fall much, yet what ready money there is in the kingdom is pretty much hoarded up, and of consequence the raising our supplies difficult.'[16]

From the Jacobite point of view, the first day in England had gone according to plan. Charles Edward accomplished a march through the Rule valley and Liddesdale before the passage of the Esk.[17] He was then rejoined by his cavalry, who had gone via Hawick and Langholm, near Longtown and spent his first night in England at a farmhouse called 'Reddings', then tenanted by a Mr. David Murray.[18]

Saturday 9th November

Charles Edward marched with his division down the right bank of the Eden to Rockliff, where he crossed and took up his position at Moorhouse, two miles to the west of Carlisle.[19] Other smaller parties were quartered that night at Kingmoor and Greendale, a couple of miles outside Carlisle.[20] At Rockliff the junction with Tullibardine was effected.[21] The Jacobite 'Duke of Atholl's' column had marched that day from Lockerbie; Lord Ogilvy's regiment too moved up from Lockerbie to Newtown.[22] Carlisle itself got its first sight of the Highlanders at about three that Saturday afternoon when a party of some fifty or sixty appeared at Stanwix Bank, a hill opposite Carlisle.[23] It was Martinmas Saturday in Carlisle — a market day — and the garrison in the castle could not fire on the Highlanders without hitting the country people thronging the road on the way back from the market.[24] Eventually, after the cavalry on the hill had spent an hour in reconnaissance, the garrison did get an opportunity to fire on them, but faced with this barrage the Scots did not tarry long. Not, however, before this party from Stanwix had sent Mr. Atkinson, a farmer's son from Drandikes, into the town to demand quarters for 13,000 foot and 3,000 horse.[25]

Durand, watching from the Cathedral tower, was left to ponder what he could do without a sizeable body of regular troops.[26] He knew he could look for nothing from either Ligonier or Wade. These two indeed were no further forward than the stage of receiving their detailed orders.[27] Wade's instructions contained little more than the advice that he should concert troop movements with the various Lords Lieutenant in the counties.[28] Ligonier's orders were more ample and more precise: he was to concert with Wade but be under his command, and should pay particular attention to blocking the Highlanders' path, putting down local disturbances, and disarming Roman Catholics and Non-Jurors.[29] Wade received a copy of these orders, from which he at least knew definitely that Ligonier was ordered north, but at this stage the French-born general had still not left London.

Sunday 10th November

This was the day when operations against Carlisle commenced in earnest. The remainder of the Peebles division arrived, and the military planning of the Jacobites for an assault on Carlisle was revealed to be of a high order.[30] The junction of the three columns had been effected with such precision that there was not more than an interval of two hours between the arrival of the first and last corps.[31] In addition, Carlisle was now invested on three sides: one body of Highlanders, under the Duke of Perth, approached the town from Stanwix Bank; another under Tullibardine was at Shaddongate; and the third under Charles Edward himself lay at Blackhall fields and St. Nicholas.[32]

During the morning there was a thick fog, so dense that 'a man could hardly see his horse's ears',[33] but when this cleared up at midday, the Jacobite detachments closest to the 'Irish' and 'English' gates were fired at from the town and castle.[34] The four-gun battery opened fire on Tullibardine's force, the ten-gun artillery on Perth's, while the castle battery directed a salvo at Charles Edward's detachment. Little was achieved by this except to waste ammunition, although a false report was bruited that Tullibardine had been killed by a volley from the city walls.[35] As Carlisle's defenders prepared for an assault, the fog came down again and lasted until nightfall.

At about 3 p.m. a messenger arrived in the town with a message from Charles Edward for the Mayor.[36] The gist of it was that if Carlisle surrendered, there would be no retaliation against its inhabitants, but that if they resisted, the Prince could not answer for the consequences. He advised the Mayor to think very carefully of the bloodshed for which he might be responsible in a sack of Carlisle. No answer was made to this message.[37]

In the evening trenches were opened, under Perth's direction. Captain Grant, an Irish officer in Lally's regiment of the Irish Brigade, who had come over with d'Eguilles, had some experience in engineering and siege works, and this was now put to good use.[38] The trenches, about eighty yards from the town walls, were kept up even when the bulk of the army retired to Brampton.

Charles Edward then withdrew to Blackhall (Blackwell Hall, one mile south of Carlisle, was the seat of Sir Richard Musgrave) to consider his next move. There he received word that Wade was preparing to advance from Newcastle to meet him.[39] After a quick conference, the decision was taken to withdraw to Brampton to await Wade and offer battle at that point, amid mountainous country that suited the clansmen.[40] And so at 11 p.m. that night four quartermasters appeared in Brampton with orders for provisions for 8,000 men on Monday.[41] The troops accompanying them then took possession of the chapel in Brampton, where some of them ate and slept; another small party was quartered in the Half Moon Inn at Brampton.[42] The bulk of the soldiers were billeted in the villages around Carlisle, some with the Prince at Blackhall, some at Harraby, others, like Ogilvy's regiment, at Stanwix.[43]

The coming encounter with Wade was generally welcome; indeed hitherto the Highlanders had been mystified by the Marshal's inactivity. There were four main theories current in the Jacobite army about Wade's sluggishness.[44] One was that Wade was simply too terrified to meet the Highlanders in battle; another that his army was stricken with illness and not up to a winter campaign; yet another, that paralysis of the will in London was such that Wade had been sent no orders. The most sophisticated interpretation was that Wade dared not leave Newcastle because the colliers, always sympathetic to Jacobitism,* were ready to rise to the number of 20,000.

In Whig circles two views prevailed about the likely course of the campaign. One was that Wade would advance slowly across the Pennines, waiting for Ligonier's force to come up through Lancashire, so that the two armies could catch Charles Edward in a pincer movement.[45] The other was that the invasion of England would collapse in a matter of days, since the 'rebels' would either have to fight Wade or

*For this, see Hughes, *North Country Life in the Eighteenth Century* (1952)

return immediately to Scotland. The idea of the imminent abandonment of the invasion was also fuelled by false reports that the Carlisle garrison had killed a great many Scots with its accurate gunnery.[46] In this mood of euphoria Lancashire prepared to greet Ligonier. Colonel William Graham arrived in Liverpool to do what he could for the defence and morale of that town.[47] Sir Henry Hoghton promised Lord Derby, his Lord Lieutenant, that his own regiment would soon be mustered at Preston.[48] In Chester, the Lord Lieutenant of the county, Lord Cholmondeley, received instructions on measures to delay the enemy should they reach Cheshire. Finally, all Lords Lieutenant on any conceivable line of march from Carlisle were alerted to the presence of the Jacobite army there.[49]

Monday 11th November

Except for a token force, the Highlanders left the environs of Carlisle and marched with over one hundred carriages over Warwick Bridge.[50] The force at Stanwix retired in the same direction on the north side of the river, but at noon a fresh party of Scots, from Glenbucket's regiment, came to Stanwix.[51] They plundered Chancellor Waugh's home and destroyed the parish books and registers, allegedly in pique at not finding the church plate.[52] Meanwhile, during the crossing of the Eden, one of the waggons, containing seven barrels of gunpowder, was lost.[53]

In Brampton, Charles Edward took up his lodgings in a house in High Cross Street.[54] Elcho's Lifeguards took up advanced positions at Naworth Castle, seat of the Earl of Carlisle, about three miles east of Brampton.[55] The army spent the day collecting all horses, food and forage that it could use, and destroying all surplus corn and hay so that Wade's troops, when they came up, would have nothing to live on.[56]

At first, the Highlanders' withdrawal to Brampton was widely attributed to their having been severely mauled by the Carlisle garrison.[57] Some people in Carlisle, seeing only a small number of troops in the trenches, decided that the Jacobite objective was not to take Carlisle but merely to recover the quartermaster Brand, who was by this time in a Newcastle jail as a result of his capture and dispatch to Wade on the 8th.[58] Wade himself was engaged this Monday in a Council of War at which it was eventually decided to march to the relief of Carlisle.[59]

The 11th November was chiefly significant for the letter which Charles Edward wrote to Lord Barrymore.[60] Barrymore had already let it be known that he was 'languishing' for the landing of French troops, without which he was powerless to make a move, but that he would join the Prince if the latter could force a way through to him.[61] Charles Edward's letter was succinct and to the point: 'My lord, this is to acquaint you with the success we have had since our arrival in Scotland and how far we are advanced without repulse. We are now a numerous army, and are laying siege to Carlisle this day, which we are sure cannot hold out long. After that we intend to take our route straight for London, and if things answer our expectations we design to be in Lancashire before the 24th inst. Then I hope you and all my friends in that county will be ready to join us. For now is the time or never. Adieu'. This letter never reached Barrymore, since it was given to the earl's son, Lord Buttevant, by the Prince's messenger. Buttevant, who did not share his father's Jacobite sympathies, promptly burned it.[62]

Tuesday 12th November

While Charles Edward and Sir Thomas Sheridan were breakfasting that morning on a couple of ducks and a hot breast of mutton, Peter Pattinson, a grocer from Cockermouth, asked for an audience with the Prince.[63] Pattinson ingratiated himself with the breakfasters by joking that he had just come from Carlisle where the guns had been booming for four days and nights without doing any more execution than killing a cow. Sheridan then asked him if he knew any Frenchman who would be prepared to go to France as a courier. On receiving a negative reply, Sheridan hit on the idea of commissioning Pattinson to take the letter dated 11th November to Barrymore in Cheshire. Pattinson it was who delivered the letter into the wrong hands.

The first important military action of the day for the Highlanders was to choose a battlefield to the east of Brampton, just off the road to Newcastle.[64] A party was meanwhile sent to Haltwhistle to get advance information on Wade's movements. News about Wade was confused and confusing: one report put him as near as Hexham, while a more reliable intelligence placed him still in Newcastle.[65] This on the whole seemed the more trustworthy advice, since the heavy snowfalls encountered to the east of Brampton made Wade's advance from Tyneside unlikely.

When this intelligence was brought back, Charles Edward called a Council to decide on the next move. The issue was whether to await Wade at Brampton or to return to the siege of Carlisle.[66] But some Highland leaders, of whom Perth was reported to be one, raised the question of the desirability of further campaigning in England. This faction made two main points: first that the French had failed to make an unequivocal declaration of alliance with James Stuart, to detain British troops in Flanders or to stop the Dutch auxiliaries being sent to England; secondly, that there were no signs of the promised rising of English Jacobites, who, it was said, should have declared for the Prince after Prestonpans, so that the clans would not have had to enter England.[67] These objections seemed particularly weighty now that Carlisle had failed to open its gates to a Stuart prince, as his supporters had promised.

To retreat without having achieved anything would, however, be an unthinkable admission of failure, so the compromise suggested by Lord George Murray was accepted. A party should be sent back to invest and take Carlisle while another detachment awaited Wade at Brampton.[68] When Carlisle had fallen, it would be time to decide whether to withdraw to Scotland or to march into England. Perth agreed to this proposal and offered to undertake the artillery bombardment of Carlisle if Lord George would have overall responsibility for the blockade. Murray replied in an offhand way, saying that he knew nothing of sieges, but pointing out that morale would be seriously impaired unless all regiments took their turn in the trenches. He proposed that lots be drawn to see which regiment should enter the trenches first, but this proposal was overruled.

Since Charles Edward favoured abandoning Carlisle and remaining at Brampton to fight Wade — which came closer to the strategy he had argued for in Edinburgh — it was decided that he should command the section of the army that stayed there.[69] To confuse enemy intelligence and simulate an eastward march to meet Wade, Captain Hamilton was sent to Naworth Castle to demand billets for 6,000 men the next day. His party arrived at Naworth around noon, conferred with Ogilvy's regiment which was now stationed there, and spent the remaining daylight hours shooting geese and sheep for their supper.[70]

Immediately after the Council a message was brought to Charles Edward that he should not count on the northern gentry to rise, and it is said that some of the disappointment at this was observed on his countenance that afternoon.[71] He spent the time reviewing his army on a neighbouring moor. In Brampton itself the people continued sullen: no church sermons were preached between the 10th and the 12th because of the Highlanders' presence.[72]

If the identity of the messenger who brought the bad news to the Prince is not known, that of one of Recorder Gilpin's spies is. Robert Lee of Whitehaven was sent out on the 12th to spy on the Highland army but was almost immediately taken prisoner and brought before the Duke of Perth. On protesting to Perth that he was a volunteer for the Prince's army, he was made to don a white cockade, drink the Prince's health, and later to assist in dragging two pieces of cannon to Stanwix Bank, since horses could not pull them over the uneven ground.[73]

Although some Highlanders were reported as far down as Crosby, six miles east of Carlisle,[74] it was now Yorkshire that principally feared their advent.[75] Newcastle wrote to Cholmondeley that he now considered the Jacobite army was heading for Yorkshire rather than Lancashire.[76] Against this possibility Lord Lieutenant Sir Conyers D'Arcy ordered five of the North Riding Companies to quarter at Richmond until definite information about the Scots was received.[77] And in Newcastle Wade had still not commenced his march to Carlisle, although as a prelude a regiment of dragoons had been ordered to Bishop Auckland.[78]

Wednesday 13th November

That morning Perth and Lord George Murray departed with the North-Eastern and Lowland regiments to invest Carlisle. Perth took with him to the siege, in addition to his own regiment, the Atholl brigade, John Roy Stewart's Edinburgh regiment, Ogilvy's (moving up from Naworth castle to Riccarby) plus the horse, viz. Elcho's, Pitsligo's, Balmerino's and Kilmarnock's squadron.[79] These forces mustered at Warwick bridge at 1 p.m., where they were reviewed by Charles Edward, who then surveyed Carlisle with his lieutenant-generals before turning aside to dine at Squire Warwick's house.[80]

Perth and Lord George Murray proceeded to blockade Carlisle on all sides. The trenches were opened on the east side, between the Scotch and English gates, under constant fire from the town.[81] Murray spent the afternoon establishing his headquarters at Harraby while Perth and Tullibardine worked alongside the men in the trenches in their shirtsleeves to encourage them. The immediate problem in the conduct of the siege was that the great circumference of the town on both sides of the River Eden meant that the numbers at Murray's disposal were too few for an effective blockade. The command posts of the regiments were too far from each other to be easily reinforced, and Murray feared that the militia could easily sortie and defeat a single regiment before assistance could arrive.[82] In addition, he was worried by the question of how he could set up the artillery battery so that it would not be constantly harassed by small arms fire from Carlisle. On the credit side, Murray drew comfort from the morale of Perth's men, who were much encouraged by the Duke's indefatigable labours on the earthworks, and the general esprit de corps. Once the regiments engaged on the siege realised that they would spend their hours of rest under cover in the small villages around Carlisle, they showed themselves quite willing to stand guard day and night.

Meanwhile at Warwick Hall and Corby Castle a detachment busied itself cutting down fir trees to make scaling ladders.[83] This development particularly disturbed Durand in the castle, for whom events were now turning out very badly. It was now obvious that the Highlanders were in earnest about besieging Carlisle and were going about it in a thoroughly professional way. They had even brought four carpenters from Brampton with them to assist in erecting batteries.[84] There was worse to come for Durand. Just before 5 p.m. he received a message from Wade that he would be unable to reach Carlisle quickly. Another letter stressing the urgency of the situation was sent out to Wade, but this time the messenger was unable to get through the Jacobite lines.[85] The same tight investment also prevented most of the reinforcements from neighbouring towns, Wigton, Whitehaven and Cockermouth, from arriving.

Durand's concern was not shared by the Whigs generally, who considered the castle at Carlisle impregnable to all but heavy artillery. Besides, even if the town of Carlisle fell, the Highlanders would soon have to return to Scotland.[86] In Newcastle, their withdrawal from Brampton was attributed to fear. A Scottish scout taken prisoner at Hexham claimed that the field of battle had been chosen — Rimside Moor between Rothby and Alnwick was mentioned — but that the Stuart prince had thought better of an engagement.[87] In such a context, the atmosphere at Newcastle was cheerful, and minor setbacks such as the disbandment of the Durham militia through dissension (and halfheartedness towards the Hanoverian dynasty) seemed unimportant.[88] The Duke of Newcastle thought that the return of the clansmen to besiege Carlisle was a mistake on two counts: it allowed Wade to come up with them at his own pace; and it meant that Ligonier's forces could concentrate in Lancashire and Cheshire to block a southward progress.[89] It was unfortunate for Newcastle that neither Wade nor Ligonier, nor even Carlisle itself, was to fulfil his expectations.

Thursday 14th November

A heavy storm of snow and a severe frost left the Highlanders besieging Carlisle in a low state of morale by morning. With difficulty Perth managed to prevent mass desertion and the abandonment of the trenches, and he only achieved it by staying with his men all the time.[90] The problems of the besieging force were becoming acute, not from enemy action but from the weather. To spend twenty-four hours on guard duty was a frightful ordeal in the arctic temperature of November 1745. Lord George offered to relieve Perth with three hundred volunteers from the Atholl brigade.[91] This was merely a temporary expedient: the Athollmen would stand guard for twenty-four hours out of personal attachment to their leader, but no longer. Now were seen the pernicious consequences of the overruling of Murray's plan at the Brampton Council. Fortunately for the Jacobites, an hour before the Atholl brigade was due to relieve Perth's, the white flag was displayed in Carlisle.[92]

For if spirits were low among the besiegers, by extending the trenches to within three hundred yards of Carlisle castle they had yet dealt the *coup de grace* to the resistance of the besieged.[93] Concern and disquiet among the militiamen in Carlisle now reached a head. The Cumberland militia had from the very beginning of the rising received no unequivocal authority from the government, no pay and no subsistence.[94] The letter from Wade received on the 13th, telling them to look to their own devices since his regulars could not come to their assistance in time, was the penultimate straw, especially as Wade's inability to help was now known to the Jacobites.[95] With the trenches now three hundred yards from the castle and the prospect of bitter hand-to-hand fighting looming, the nerve of the militia cracked. Food was running short: all supplies within an eight-mile radius of Carlisle had been requisitioned by the Jacobites, and the enemy were now so near the castle walls that the garrison had already started to throw grenades at them.[96] The coming assault with siege ladders was particularly feared: to save face the militia later invented the story that the Jacobite officers intended to force the country people around Carlisle to scale the walls on ladders and so be destroyed by their own side.[97]

The militia accordingly approached Col. Durand and indicated their unwillingness to fight on. On the morning of Thursday 14th, a letter was sent to Durand in the castle, urging surrender. After a meeting in the King's Arms Inn, at which Durand was unable to persuade them to change their minds, he told the Mayor that the town, which was under civil jurisdiction, might surrender, but he himself would withdraw to the citadel and fight on. Durand immediately took action to minimise the effect of the fall of the town to the Highlanders. All bread was bought up, all guns were spiked, ovens were set up in the castle and an improvised mill and forge established. Later, when he saw two large bodies of Jacobite troops marching towards Rowcliff, he sent Lieutenant Hutchinson back to the King's Arms to attempt to persuade the militia to a change of heart.[98]

All was in vain on this score, for the militia could see no future in opposing the clansmen, especially as their siege tactics seemed so professional. They had had little enough support from the government in London; and if the Highlanders took Carlisle after a bloody siege, what reprisals might they not take? So it was that the white flag of surrender was hung out at 5 p.m.[99] Perth, however, would not accept the surrender of the town without the castle. Mindful of the fiasco in Edinburgh, where the castle had remained in Hanoverian hands (ironically on this very day government troops were repossessing the city also),[100] Perth wanted both town and castle delivered up or neither. His terms were that the magistrates should attend the

Prince at Brampton in their robes to present the keys of Carlisle and that the militia be dismissed on a pledge not to serve against Charles Edward for a year and a day. The Deputy Mayor requested that the townspeople be given until next day to consider this demand.[101]

The siege of Carlisle, thus effectively brought to an end, had been a triumph for Lord George Murray. The only casualties sustained were one officer and one soldier killed. The officer was an Irishman named Dalton who foolishly jumped out of the trenches to jeer at the defenders and received a cannon ball through his throat.[102] This was shortly before the white flag was shown. Murray was the only commander who could have induced the Scots to participate in and persist with the siege. The clansmen detested such 'banausic' work and were impatient even with sentry duty. Moreover, Murray's positioning of the besieging forces drew nothing but praise from the French officers with him.[103] Yet Murray's triumph was to be soured and overshadowed by a major clash between himself and the Prince.

Lord George had already unwittingly given offence to Charles Edward by declining to take command at the siege; his offhand remark that he knew nothing of sieges was interpreted as lack of commitment to the enterprise. The Prince then sent all his orders to Perth and ignored Murray. Behind all this lay a story of Scottish-Irish rivalry on the one hand and personal dislike between the Prince and Murray on the other. Murray's haughty demeanour and apparent lack of respect for his royal personage had long since alienated Charles Edward.[104] This antipathy was exploited by the Irish officers, who resented the fact that Murray treated them with contempt and would not go through them to the Prince, but always approached Charles Edward directly. Murray's most vehement critics were Sir John MacDonald and Francis Strickland, who intrigued incessantly against Lord George and spread the most scurrilous rumours about his loyalty.[105] These went largely without rebuttal, since Murray did not deign to descend to that level of discourse in his dealings with the Prince. But perhaps Murray's most dangerous enemy was O'Sullivan, who was jealous of his military talent and his standing with the clan leaders. O'Sullivan was all the more dangerous in that he influenced his royal master against Murray in secret, while keeping a low profile in open Council. He was able to convince the Prince that the military disagreements which were invariable between Murray and the Irish faction were purely the consequences of Lord George's haughty and authoritarian personality. Because Murray tended not to see the covert opposition of O'Sullivan and Strickland but only the open disagreements with the Prince's secretary, the ironical result was that Lord George identified the other Murray as his principal foe.[106] In fact Murray of Broughton had a grudging respect for Lord George. Unlike the Irish officers, who were in the service of France and did not stand to suffer the extreme penalty if the rebellion failed, Murray of Broughton was a realist. He desperately needed the rebellion to succeed and was able to appreciate the sober wisdom of Lord George's arguments as against the wilder fantasies of O'Sullivan.

Such, then, was the background to the storm about to erupt openly with the surrender of Carlisle. Superficially, however, the 14th was a day of calm for Charles Edward.[107] Brampton, where the Prince spent most time in one place during the entire English campaign, presented a quiet scene where the most the army had to contend with was inquisitive sightseers. This, however, was a dangerous pastime: one John Sanderson was later indicted for treason simply for having been seen in the company of Scottish hussars at Brampton.[108] There was at one stage during this Thursday a suggestion that Lochiel might return with his regiment to exact punishment on the people of Dumfries. The townspeople had apparently plundered the baggage waggons left on the road for want of horses, and Lochiel was to be sent to reclaim the looted goods or to raise £2000 in compensation.[109] News of the white flag at Carlisle changed all that.

On the Whig side, plans for the defence of the rest of England were not going well. Lord Derby, Lord-Lieutenant of Lancashire, arrived at Manchester in an abortive attempt to get the militia into a fit state to meet the Highlanders.[110] Derby's only success was to discuss with Thomas Walley, the Manchester constable, ways and means of disposing of the large amount of gunpowder in the town. But the only truly tangible results for Manchester were the expenses granted to the Deputy Lieutenant and the troop of militia. Yet even with pay and subsistence the Manchester militia were to prove of no more use than their unpaid counterparts in Carlisle.

Friday 15th November

By the morning of the 15th the trenches had been extended to about eighty yards from the walls of Carlisle and an assault by escalade was clearly intended. The final reply from Carlisle was anxiously awaited on all sides, but there were already many signs that the discussions over the surrender of the castle could have only one end.[111] At 1 a.m. on Friday Captain Gilpin informed Durand that the militia were no longer lining the walls.[112] By 4 a.m. the militiamen were reported increasingly 'restless', and at 8 a.m. four hundred of them who had agreed to go into the citadel with Durand the day before emerged.[113] Messages were sent to Perth to see whether there could be any concessions in the terms of surrender, but the reply was that the castle had to be given up as the absolutely basic condition for a cessation of hostilities.[114]

When the militiamen reported this to Durand in the castle at 10 a.m., he immediately called a Council of War. This Council concluded that resistance was useless but that a full report should be sent to London, explaining the halfhearted response of the citizens of Carlisle, the problems with the militia, and the absolute impossibility of holding out any further without support from the militiamen or relief from Wade.[115] The decision to surrender both town and castle had immediate effects. The leading Whigs, like Dr. Waugh and his entourage, quit Carlisle just before the surrender.[116] The capitulation was announced to the beleaguering Highlanders, and very soon the Deputy Mayor Thomas Pattinson was on his way with attendant Aldermen to Brampton.[117] The formal presentation of the keys to Carlisle, made by the city Magistrates on bended knee, did not take place until the next day.

The dramatic fall of both town and castle was immediately cast into a more depressing perspective when a major row in the Jacobite camp was triggered by Lord George Murray's resignation as Lieutenant-General. Murray gave as his reason, 'my advice as a general officer has so little weight'.[118] The proximate cause of his outburst was the surrender procedure at Carlisle, but ever since the Council at Brampton thoughts of resignation had been simmering in Lord George. The final provocation in his eyes was Charles Edward's decision that the surrender of Carlisle would be negotiated by Perth and Murray of Broughton. This was obnoxious to Lord George for two reasons. In the first place, the Prince had decided to use the one man, Murray of Broughton, who was most distasteful to his Lieutenant-General. The coolness between the two Murrays was demonstrated when Broughton travelled up to Carlisle to escort the magistrates back to Brampton. The Prince's secretary stopped at Lord George's headquarters to pick up a guide, without sending any message or in any way communicating with the commander. Secondly, and more importantly, the Prince had previously promised Lord George that military personnel would not be used to negotiate the capitulation of Carlisle, yet here was Perth, not just a military commander but a Catholic, in charge of it. Lord George Murray and the clan leaders had always argued that since the Test and Corporation Acts still applied in England, they should still be observed, regardless of whether they were reasonable statutes or not, until Charles Edward was seated on the English throne, when he could legally annul them. Otherwise, they argued, the Whigs would be able to make splendid propaganda about 'popery' and the Jacobites' scant regard for traditional liberties. In the opinion of Lord George, the Prince had committed a major blunder when he appointed the Catholic Duke of Perth to make terms with the civic authorities of the first English town he had conquered.[119]

Clearly Murray felt that he had been slighted twice over by the appointment of Murray *and* Perth to carry out duties which should have fallen to him, and resigned to secure a vote of confidence. This he was not long in obtaining. At first, Charles Edward was disposed to accept Murray's resignation as Lieutenant-General and to take his offer to serve as a volunteer at face value. In a cold and unsympathetic letter he told Murray that the best way he could manifest what he called 'my attachment to the Royal Family, especially the king' was to show himself more responsive to his (the Prince's) wishes.[120] The anti-Murray faction weighed in with their intrigues. Sir John MacDonald declared: 'this was a very good opportunity to get rid of a dangerous man, suspected by all the army except Sheridan and three or four others'.[121] But the backlash was soon apparent. Lord Elcho, to whom Murray had handed over his command (to the fury of O'Sullivan who expostulated: 'as if it depended on him'), openly displayed his disgust with O'Sullivan and Murray of Broughton. He pointed out, rightly, that the invasion of England could not proceed without Lord George, since the Scots would trust no other commander.[122]

A serious split in the army now seemed inevitable. Tullibardine refused to endorse Murray's stand, both because he could not condone any opposition to the Prince and because he could find no fault with the Irish officers, with whom he got on well. He did, however, arrange a meeting between Lord George and Charles Edward, which produced no result. The first breakthrough came from Murray of

Broughton. Realising that the clan chieftains' sympathy lay with Lord George, he informed Charles Edward of this unpalatable fact and added that as the Stuart cause was the thing dearest to his heart, he would henceforth absent himself from the Council in order to assuage Lord George's wrath.[123]

Meanwhile, Perth had discovered the extent of the misgivings entertained by the officers about serving under a Catholic commander-in-chief. Feelings were running so high on this issue that it was suggested to the Prince that he ought to discharge *all* Catholics from the Council and guarantee that in any future case of capitulation Protestants and not Catholics should handle negotiations. Perth now magnanimously declared that since he had nothing in mind except the Stuarts' best interests, he would cheerfully sacrifice himself. He then not only resigned forthwith as Commander-in-Chief but offered, as an incentive to Lord George to resume his command, to take over responsibility for the baggage.[124] This proposal averted yet another crisis, since Lord Ogilvy, who had been assigned charge of the baggage train, had asserted that he would not undertake it after Carlisle and rather than take on such 'dirty work' would resign his commission and serve as a volunteer in the ranks. Reluctantly, Charles Edward agreed to a deal: Lord George would be asked to withdraw his resignation on the understanding that Perth would be given command of the baggage and Murray of Broughton would be banished from the Council. These proposals, especially the latter, 'seemed to quieten Lord George a good deal',[125] so he accepted command of the army once more, not without misgivings, for he knew he must bear a heavy responsibility for its fortunes and account for them to Charles Edward, whom he still saw as a reckless adventurer.[126]

While the Aldermen waited on the Prince at Brampton, Perth marched his men into Carlisle. It was reported that John Lake (later made prisoner at Carlisle) marched at their head with a large walking stick in his hand, striking several people in the street and exclaiming 'Damn you, make way, for the Prince is coming.'[127] Durand and the militia officers were ordered out of town and 'driven like sheep' by an escort to Penrith.[128] No horses were allowed them so that they were fortunate the weather had taken a turn for the better. Durand and his men took with them to Penrith a farrago of rumours, such as the deaths of Lord George Murray, Tullibardine and Glenbucket, and tales of Highland casualties between five and six hundred.

Twenty-five miles further south, in Kendal, Lord Lonsdale's agent was writing to complain that he had had to journey in person from Newcastle to Kendal, since Wade's commandeering of all available horses to draw his baggage meant that there was none to spare for a messenger.[129] For all that, Wade had still not moved from Newcastle, and his continued presence there was causing consternation among the Whigs. Lord Derby informed Newcastle that his ordering the militia out for fourteen days was based on being able to join Wade, so all his efforts, such as bringing two more companies of militiamen into Manchester, would be fruitless unless the Marshal bestirred himself.[130]

Only two factors seemed to excuse Wade's inactivity. One was that the Newcastle-Hexham road might be impassable to his artillery and that therefore his troops would have to prepare to march by way of Barnard Castle.[131] The other was the

possibility — already raised by the Jacobites at Carlisle — that he feared to leave
Newcastle (in the words of one contemporary chronicler 'a place of vast trade and of
great importance to the city of London') for fear of a rising by the Tyneside
colliers.[132] The Duke of Newcastle, whose partiality to Wade during the entire rising
was striking, uttered not a word of criticism of the Field-Marshal. He was now
obsessed with the idea that the itinerary of the Highlanders would lie through the
East Riding of Yorkshire, and his instructions to the Lord-Lieutenants and Justices
of the Peace were that they should above all strive to diminish the food supply
available to the invaders.[133] Meanwhile he wrote to Wade, recommending an
espionage system and ending, 'and if it should seem to be practicable to settle a
correspondence with any of the principal people among the rebels, you are at liberty
to offer anything you may think proper for that purpose'.[134]

Saturday 16th November

While Perth in Carlisle was compelling the Town Clerk to proclaim Charles
Edward, and would accept no prevarication, Mayor Joseph Backhouse had the
distasteful task of delivering the keys to the Prince at Brampton.[135] The victorious
Highlanders began to gather in all livestock and provisions from within a fifteen-
mile radius of Carlisle and gradually to occupy the town. Most of the forces at
Brampton, except the Prince's personal guard, were the next to follow Perth's into
Carlisle, but the heroes of the hour, the Athollmen and the other besiegers, entered
last of all.[136] The beleaguering Atholl brigade were hungry, the villages around
Carlisle having provided little in the way of supplies during the siege, but the
hardships of Lord George's men were not over even when they entered Carlisle.
They were not summoned to their quarters in the town until the evening and were
then lodged in the castle vaults and in a ruined house nearby, without the benefit of
meat, drink, candles or coal for a fire. Lord George put this down to O'Sullivan's
incompetence or malice — he could not decide which quality was uppermost — but
either way it was a poor return for his heroic Athollmen.[137]

At least the Highlanders were now faring better than their putative opponents,
the luckless troops in Wade's army. Wade could hardly have chosen a less
propitious moment for the long-delayed march west from Newcastle, for his soldiers
were now in a truly wretched condition. Many had come over from Flanders
already dejected from an epidemic of dysentery. They had never been used to
campaigning in northerly latitudes and normally spent the harsh months from
October onwards in winter quarters.[138] In Newcastle their camp had been partially
under water. Moreover, half of the army was made up of foreign troops, Swiss,
Dutch and German, to whom it was a matter of utter indifference who sat on the
English throne. The Dutch provoked widespread condemnation by their insolence
and uncooperativeness. The native troops, particularly those who had conferred
with Wade's dragoons, were already more than half convinced of the Highlanders'
invincibility. To make matters worse, Wade at seventy-two had turned into a
notorious miser and his parsimony disastrously affected the health and morale of his
men.[139] This was clearly in evidence during the two-day march to Hexham, when

the troops had to contend with two major enemies without ever catching sight of the Highlanders: the weather and Wade's frugality. They were obliged to lie out at night on an open moor on the night of Saturday the 16th, since their tents could not be pitched because of the hardness of the ground. Floundering knee-deep in snow, sick and dispirited, they would have been an easy prey for the Highlanders. Their deepest disgust was reserved for Wade, who grudged every penny he had to spend on providing bread, fire or straw, and so kept his men on iron rations.[140]

On this Saturday night Wade's pathetic force got as far as Ovington. The Marshal had planned to leave Newcastle at dawn, but the Swiss troops had the van and refused to move out until 10 a.m. Thereafter broken roads, a hard frost and snow three feet deep further retarded progress. In such circumstances the morale-building exercise of Generals Howard and Oglethorpe and Brigadiers Cholmondeley and Mordaunt marching on foot at the head of the infantry was pointless.[141] The seventeen-mile march soon turned into a veritable nightmare; some of the rearguard did not get into Ovington until 9 a.m. the next day. The terribly broken roads cratered with ice and the arctic temperatures meant that sheer fatigue overtook the latter columns and they only managed to join Wade at all because Generals Huske and Oglethorpe sent out parties of country folk with lights and carts to bring them in.[142]

In London meanwhile, the main military development was that Ligonier was ordered up to Lancashire with an army of fifteen foot regiments, three of horse and two of dragoons.[143] Horses were to be changed at Coventry, where Newcastle ordered the Mayor to have fresh mounts ready.[144] The Quakers of London visited Ligonier and his officers and offered to provide at their own expense 10,000 woollen waistcoats for soldiers going with Ligonier on the winter campaign. The Lord Mayor and citizens of London raised a subscription to buy blankets, and George II provided shoes out of the privy purse.[145]

Yet the principal event in the capital this Saturday was the meeting at Lord Gower's house to attempt to resolve domestic political differences and to discuss Pitt's terms for joining the Pelhams. All the luminaries were there: Newcastle, his brother Henry Pelham, Chancellor Hardwicke, the Duke of Bedford, Harrington, Cobham and William Pitt. No better evidence exists of the failure of the Whigs at this stage to comprehend the seriousness of the rebellion than this purely domestic meeting, which was in no way influenced by events at Carlisle, but presupposed an inexorable continuance of the political status quo.[146]

Sunday 17th November

Final preparations were now being made in Carlisle to receive the Prince in a triumphal entry. Ogilvy's regiment moved out from the town to quarters at Butcherby in order to make room for the Prince's guards.[147] Perth issued a declaration to the Mayor of Carlisle, requiring him to proclaim King James at the market place.[148] This Backhouse was forced to do after the usual dissembling and protestation.[149] The surrender of Carlisle was found to have yielded to the Highlanders valuable military supplies: 1500 arms, 160 barrels of powder, 500 grenades and about 120 good horses.[150]

Wade's force, encountering increasingly heavy snowdrifts, struggled on as far as Hexham.[151] The vanguard entered at about 4 p.m. and the rear not until midnight.[152] A participant spoke of the second day of his awful journey as follows: 'It is impossible to give you a detail of our distress . . . at first the most intense frost with perpetual falls of snow which lasted during our march to Hexham . . . either through the bad conduct of our commissariat or the impossibility of his executing his contract in this terrible season, the men upon their coming to their ground very late at night the first and second day's march wanted both straw, firing, forage and meat.'[153] With advance guards thrown out to Hatwhistle and Hayton Bridge, Wade soon learned that his trek was anyway in vain as Carlisle had now fallen.[154] This was just as well, for his men were in no fit state for another day's march. A day of rest on the 18th was therefore ordered.[155] Bitterness towards Wade among his officers was now palpable. Tyrawly complained that all the necessary equipment for the army — bread, straw, carriages, firing, clothes — had been scantily provided because of Wade's meanness. The Marshal was impervious to any advice that did not emanate from his quartermaster or from General Wentworth: 'he is infirm in mind and body, forgetful, irresolute, perplexed, snappish . . . sometimes at the expense of good breeding'.[156]

The Whigs were now apprised of the fall of Carlisle and had to find some way to rationalise this disaster. Writing in ignorance of the true position, Chancellor Hardwicke said that although the surrender of the town was a misfortune, at least the castle would be able to hold out for another eight days, in which case the Highlanders would hardly tarry for a siege but must press on into England.[157] When it was realised that the castle too had fallen, Whig propaganda attributed this to diabolical conduct by the clansmen. It was alleged that they had captured women and children, bound them together in front of the castle, tied hand and foot and chained, while they advanced the trenches and brought up siege ladders. In this way the garrison was rendered impotent and so gave up the fight.[158]

In fact any dishonour attached to the Whig side. Durand in Penrith claimed, contrary to all the evidence, that nothing had been said at the time of Carlisle's capitulation about giving a parole not to serve for a year and a day; he did not therefore feel himself bound by these conditions. Apparently Wade had encouraged Durand in his disingenuous and dishonourable reneging by giving it as his opinion that the terms of the surrender meant only that the captured garrison was prevented from fighting against that particular body of Highlanders which was operating around Carlisle.[159] Since it could always be claimed subsequently that it was uncertain whether the body of Highlanders in the field was the selfsame force that had taken Carlisle, Durand's parole could (conveniently) be construed as meaningless.

None of the Whig commentators could see in the fall of Carlisle anything other than a story of treachery, chicanery or cowardice. It did not occur to any of them that the conduct of the militia was quite reasonable, given the genuine legal and constitutional doubts they entertained about their own status, and it was this, not cowardice, which led to their hesitation and indecision. If there was a villain to be identified, it should have been Wade, but although by the end of the rising most members of the government were utterly disillusioned with him, at this stage only

Chancellor Hardwicke pointed the finger at the Field-Marshal. It is, however, characteristic of the ignorance of local conditions that prevailed in London that Hardwicke pointed, through ignorance of geography, to an option that Wade did not in fact possess: 'Many people think he might march through Durham by Barnard Castle and so over Stainmore which is said to be a good road, by which artillery may pass.'[160] At every point the inadequacy of the administration in London in face of the invasion was becoming daily more evident.

Monday 18th November

This was the day appointed for Charles Edward's triumphal entry into Carlisle, and the clan leaders duly welcomed their Prince into the town whose fall had struck such a blow to Whig confidence. He rode in on a white charger to the skirl of pipes and proceeded to his quarters at the house of Mr. Highmore, an attorney-at-law.[161] This was a large white-fronted house on the west side of English Street. Spirits were high all round: Charles Edward announced that the people of Carlisle had behaved well towards him, while Lord George Murray declared that 'that usurper' (George II) should see how he got Carlisle from them again.[162]

Although Perth had yielded his position as Lieutenant-General to Lord George, he was the Jacobite personality most in evidence in the administration of the occupied town. He ordered that all horses in Carlisle should be brought to the Castle Yard at 2 p.m.; the suspicion prevailed that horses belonging to the militia and other Whig supporters still lay hidden in the town.[163] All who could show proper title would then have their horses returned to them, but the others would be seized by the Highlanders. Moreover, the punishment for concealing horses was death.

Perth also had to deal with matters such as petitions from the prisoners the Jacobites had taken, who complained of ill-treatment and lack of food.[164] But, in contrast to Brampton, he seems to have played little part in the Council that was called immediately after Charles Edward's entry into Carlisle to decide what to do next. Here the continuing tension between those who supported Lord George Murray in wishing to return to Scotland, and those who wanted to follow the Prince and press on into England, was observed once more. There were four possibilities before the Highland leaders: to return to Scotland; to await developments in Carlisle and in particular to see if the English Jacobites would rise; to march against Wade; or to push on through Lancashire to London, so as to remove all possible pretexts for inactivity from both the English Jacobites and the French.[165]

The faction supporting Lord George Murray and arguing against a further advance into England stressed two things: Charles Edward's army was too small to attempt the invasion and therefore reinforcements should be awaited; secondly, there had so far been no signs either of a rising in England or of a French landing. With desertions, plus the garrison that would have to be left behind to secure Carlisle, the Prince would have barely 4,500 effectives to take into England.[166] Moreover, because the tents provided at Edinburgh had been left on the Moffat-Carlisle road, even this small force would have to be divided.[167] Besides, all reports now reaching Carlisle indicated that retreat to Scotland was the most prudent course. There was disquieting news from across the border, especially about the recapture of Edinburgh, and with the build up of strength of the Royal Navy in the Channel, there was now a better chance for a French landing in Scotland than in England.

Charles Edward and his faction countered with three main arguments.[168] First, Lancashire was Jacobite country and just a few days' march away; supporters of the Stuarts should not be allowed to say that only the failure of the Jacobite army to proceed south from Carlisle prevented them from joining. Secondly, if the clansmen withdrew, the French would have an excuse to cancel their plans for a descent on England. Murray of Broughton clinched the argument here by prevailing on the Marquis d'Eguilles to divulge his instructions from the French king.[169] These were to ascertain the true state of affairs in Scotland, the strength of Charles Edward's army, what friends he had in England, and to advise on the feasibility of French assistance in the light of his findings. It was quite clear from all this that a French landing did depend on a credible second front in the north, and this would be shown to be illusory if the army retreated to Scotland. Finally, Murray of Broughton, who was allowed to participate in this Council meeting in order to reveal the finances of the army, pointed out that for pecuniary reasons it was impossible to stay in Carlisle. Since the army depended for its survival on the public monies collected, it was imperative to proceed into England to collect there.

While the chiefs were reeling under the force of the last two arguments, Charles Edward delivered the *coup de grace* to his opponents by claiming to have in his possession letters from his supporters in England in which they promised to join him at Preston.[170] At this, Lord George Murray, who had expressed his opposition to the Prince's proposals very cautiously in view of recent events, declared that if the Prince truly desired an advance into England, he was sure the army would follow him. On the lead from Murray, the clan chiefs concurred. It was agreed that an advance party be sent south immediately and another detachment, Pitsligo's horse, be told off to patrol the Newcastle road beyond Brampton to see what had become of Wade.[171] As for the main army, after a period of rest in Carlisle, during which time the weather might improve, and when accurate intelligence of the enemy had been received, it should move south in two columns about half a day's march between each other. Lord George Murray would take charge of the first division, consisting mainly of the Lowland regiments, with Elcho's Lifeguards thrown out in front. The Prince would command the second division, formed chiefly of the clan regiments and the rest of the cavalry.[172] In addition to agreeing this plan, Charles Edward sent instructions with MacLachlan of MacLachlan to Lord Strathallan at Perth to follow with all his power, orders which Strathallan ignored.[173]

In Penrith one of Lord Lowther's agents wrote early in the morning to the Duke of Devonshire that he did not expect the Highlanders to come further south than Carlisle and strict orders had been issued to them by their leaders not to stray from that town.[174] The words had not been long written when such facile confidence was shattered. In the afternoon Lord Elcho arrived with his Lifeguards. The Jacobite quarter-master immediately demanded quarters for 250 cavalry that night and 8,000 troops on the night of the 19th.[175] In the event, though, Elcho's men alone — about half of the threatened 250 — billeted in Penrith that night.[176] In the town the church plate was hidden on the approach of the Highlanders and the expenses of this exercise charged to the churchwarden's accounts.[177] Intelligence of the Jacobites' presence was quickly relayed to points south, though as yet their intentions could not be inferred; their route could only be known once they reached Appleby, where the Lancashire and Yorkshire roads forked sharply.[178]

Elcho's men spent their time reconnoitring the environs of Penrith and deciding which of the outlying villages were feasible quartering points for the army.[179] Because of the difficult terrain and the distance from Penrith, the villages of Lowther, Graystock and Hulton were immediately struck off the list of possible locales. One thousand bales of hay and ten loads of oats were ordered from each of the great houses in the vicinity: Lowther Hall, Edna Hall, Dalemain, Hutton John, Hutton Hall and Greystoke Castle. All complied with the order except Lowther Hall.[180]

In London the Pelhams held a Council meeting at which the hope was expressed that Wade would be able to defeat the Highlanders before a French invasion.[181] Newcastle's abiding nightmare was to have to fight on two fronts at once. Similar expectations of an imminent encounter were evinced in Carlisle. Jacobite surgeons requisitioned linen for binding wounds in the hoped-for clash with Wade, who in some accounts current that day had got as far as Thurloe Castle, six miles beyond Brampton.[182] Wade, however, was still at Hexham, attempting to see if his army was in a fit state to face the clansmen. Even the Field-Marshal was under no illusions about the wretched condition of his men and the continuing problems of commissariat; the work of all the butchers in Hexham and the import of food in several carts from the surrounding villages sufficed only to provide the army with twenty-four hours' food.[183] Wade therefore decided to hold a Council of War on the 19th and, if conditions had not improved, to order a retreat to Newcastle.

As for the defence of England, desultory detachments were now forming up along the supposed line of Jacobite march. Part of Ligonier's forces arrived in Stone, and Bligh's regiment came into Chester.[184] In the latter town Cholmondeley had sent important advice to Newcastle concerning the bridges over the Weaver and Mersey.[185] He counselled against breaking down Crossford Bridge, on the grounds that it was the principal artery for the linen, cotton and salt trade of Wales and the north-west.[186] Instructions were therefore issued to secure and fortify the bridges rather than break them down. Cholmondeley was assigned the impossible task of holding the line of the Mersey until Ligonier or Cumberland could come up.

Tuesday 19th November

By this time Charles Edward had succeeded in reassuring the people of Carlisle that his men were not looters, rapists or child eaters, and had impressed the Quaker community sufficiently for them to bring him a quantity of beer from their own stocks on his first night in the town.[187] For the bulk of the Highland army the day passed quietly in preparations for the march south.[188] Their exact intentions were not of course divulged. Kilmarnock played along with the belief that their route would take them through Appleby towards Yorkshire by responding positively to a petition from the Mayor and Aldermen of Appleby.[189] He promised them that a formal notice of protection would be issued to them even though they did not need it, as the Jacobite army was tightly disciplined and did not pillage.

At Hexham Wade's Council of War took a unanimous decision to retire to Newcastle, both because the transport system in the army had broken down and because of lack of provisions.[190] Owing to the impediment of the snows and the non-availability of sufficient waggons, there was only three days' supply of food left instead of the eight days' provision originally planned for. The artillery train had been delayed: not all of it had arrived in Hexham even by the morning of the 19th; and there was considerable desertion among the drivers of the waggons.

The decision to return to Tyneside temporarily destroyed even the Duke of Newcastle's faith in Wade, and he made arrangements to receive thenceforth independent assessments and intelligence reports from General Oglethorpe.[191] Wade's army then had to struggle back painfully through the snows to Newcastle, which was reached on Friday the 22nd.[192] Fortunately for them, the troops were well received in that town. There were no sudden increases in prices, such as were common when an army was in town, and the troops were all got under cover, being lodged by the magistrates in public halls, malt houses and empty buildings. The seriously exhausted were even accommodated in private homes.[193]

Another setback for Whig plans was the illness of Ligonier, described by Henry Pelham as 'so altered that I would scarce think him the same man'.[194] Ligonier indeed went so far as to suggest that General Hawley might be given his command. Newcastle, however, determined to persevere with his ailing commander. By now nine of the regiments of foot brought over from Flanders plus Ligonier's horse and the dragoons of Bland's and Ker's were en route for Lancashire.[195] Another six regiments of foot (Bedford's, Montagu's, Granby's, Halifax's, Gore's and Cholmondeley's) had been raised, together with horse battalions commanded by the Dukes of Kingston and Montagu. Dukes Richmond and Anstruther had been named as Lieutenant-Generals under Ligonier. The plan was to intercept the Highlanders at Warrington and Stockport (the immediate destination for, respectively, Kingston's and Montagu's horse), or, if they advanced too fast, at Stone and Macclesfield.[196] It was considered particularly important immediately to strengthen the forces at Chester, especially in the light of persistent rumours of pro-Jacobite insurrections there.[197] By Tuesday the 19th, then, Ligonier's advance guard under General Cornwallis had arrived in Chester via Newport (Shropshire) having, according to Cholmondeley, met an 'extraordinary reception' in every town they passed through (this was certainly true of their entertainment in the city of Oxford).[198]

On this Tuesday the sensation of vulnerability to the southward movement of the Highlanders was felt acutely in two localities. One was the East Riding of Yorkshire, where Sir Conyers d'Arcy, with just 350 militiamen at Richmond, particularly dreaded an incursion since the nature of the country effectively precluded obstruction of the enemy's march.[199] Not only was there an abundant food supply in a county rich in corn and cattle, but there were dozens of different roads and passes available to the invaders and also many points at which the various rivers were fordable. The other area conscious of imminent threat was Liverpool, where Colonel William Graham was given contingency instructions to withdraw to Chester with the Liverpool Blues, should large numbers of Highlanders approach the town.[200]

Wednesday 20th November

This was the day for the first detachment of the Jacobite army under Lord George Murray to move down to Penrith. The advance of the 3,000 or so persons (not all of them combatants) from Carlisle was closely tracked by Whig agents, who reported them trekking through Lord Lonsdale's estates at 2 p.m. and coming into Penrith between 4 p.m. and 9 p.m.[201] Of the effective fighting strength, 600 lay that night at Plumpton Wall and another 600 in Penrith, where pressure on accommodation led to as many as one hundred being billeted in a single house.[202] The Postmaster in Penrith was asked to deliver up the Post Office Accounts but stalled and gained himself twenty-four hours by requesting to wait on the Prince in person.[203]

Lord Irwin's apprehension in Beverley was only partially allayed by news of the advance of the Highlanders to Penrith.[204] At first they were reported at Brough, believed heading for York, but even when this rumour was scotched another sprang up in its place, this time to the effect that the Jacobites' intention was to bypass Wade and head for Leeds.[205]

In Carlisle final preparations were made for the momentous southward dash of the main army. Heavy baggage was to be left at Carlisle castle; no women other than soldiers' wives were to be allowed on the march; horses were allowed only to staff or field officers or such others as their colonel could declare on his honour were unable to march.[206]

In London news of the fall of Carlisle, mixed with reports of Jacobite risings in Wales, Shropshire and Cheshire, in which Sir Watkin Williams Wynn was said to be implicated,[207] led Newcastle to declare: 'The rebellion is far from being over or to be despised. An army of nearly 10,000 desperate men, inured now to fight and fatigue, is actually in England . . . every day shows that this rebellion is by no means a trifle.'[208] In addition to the rising, Newcastle had to contend with an unfriendly House of Commons, hostile to the proposal to send for the remainder of the English troops in Flanders and demanding an inquiry into the causes of the successful progress of the rebellion.[209] Despite further meetings between Henry Pelham and Pitt, the latter still remained aloof, and Prince Frederick's adherents at the rival 'court' of Leicester House intimated that they would only join a government of national unity if the Pelhams got rid of some of their favourites. In foreign affairs Newcastle was faced with the possibility that Holland might make a separate peace with the Bourbon powers; beyond that, he could not see how England could fight both France and Spain with a rebellion at home. Newcastle's remarks to Chesterfield at the very moment the Jacobite army was commencing its epic march show clearly how shaky was the administration that confronted it: 'This [a separate peace by the Dutch] would indeed be reducing ourselves to our wooden walls when we have rebellion at home and the most considerable powers of Europe are at war with us abroad.'[210]

NOTES

1. SP Dom 67/96; 68/23, 24.
2. SP Dom 67/97; 72/95,97.
3. W.O. 71/19 ff. 286-96; SP Dom 70/37.
4. Pattinson to Newcastle, 26 September 1745, SP Dom 69/46.
5. SP Dom 69/111.
6. Newcastle to Gilpin, 19 September 1745, SP Dom 68/68.
7. SP Dom 68/69-70.
8. SP Dom 70/38-41; Jarvis, i. p. 124, 219 et seq; ii. p. 41 et seq.
9. HMC, 10, 1, pp. 129-30.
10. O'Sullivan p. 92.
11. Fergusson, *John Fergusson* p. 108.
12. Lockhart Papers, ii. p. 455.
13. HMC, Various Colls, viii. p. 123.
14. Add. MSS. 35889 f. 41.
15. *Scots Magazine* 1745 pp. 530-34.
16. Pelham to Trevor, 8 November 1745, HMC, 14, ix. p. 133.
17. Fortescue, *British Army*, ii. p. 134.
18. Nicholas pp. 113, 144.
19. Add. MSS. 35889 f. 13.
20. Fitzherbert MSS.
21. SP Dom 73/77.
22. *Orderbook of Lord Ogilvy's Regiment* p. 295.
23. SP Dom 73/78.
24. Mounsey p. 42.
25. W.O. 71/19 f. 296.
26. Mounsey p. 63.
27. SP Dom 73/43.
28. SP Dom 70/96.
29. SP Dom 73/62.
30. Mounsey pp. 42-43.
31. Chevalier de Johnstone p. 56.
32. W.O. 71/19 ff. 286-336.
33. O'Sullivan p. 92.
34. W.O. 71/19 f. 297.
35. *Gentlemen's Magazine* 1745 p. 612.
36. *London Magazine* 1745 p. 565.
37. HMC, V. p. 331; Mounsey p. 63.
38. Chevalier de Johnstone p. 57.
39. Mounsey pp. 42-43.
40. O'Sullivan p. 93.
41. HMC, Various Colls, viii. p. 124.
42. Whitehead, 'Brampton in 1745' pp. 47-54.
43. *Ogilvy's Orderbook* p. 295.
44. Chevalier de Johnstone pp. 58-59.

45. HMC, Various Colls, viii. p. 121.
46. SP Dom 74/1; HMC, Du Cane 77.
47. Jarvis, i. p. 242.
48. Jarvis, ii. p. 48.
49. Yorke, *Hardwicke,* i. pp. 417, 425.
50. HMC, Various Colls, viii. p. 124.
51. Mounsey p. 76.
52. Ibid. p. 64.
53. HMC, Various Colls, viii. p. 124.
54. W.O. 71/19 f. 298.
55. *Ogilvy's Orderbook* p. 295.
56. *Manchester Magazine* 19 November 1745.
57. Staffs CRO. SMS 520.
58. Add. MSS 35889 f. 33; SP Dom 73/17; Brand, *Newcastle,* ii. p. 528.
59. SP Dom 73/99.
60. HMC, 10, i. pp. 286–87.
61. Stuart MSS. 268/5; 269/109.
62. Jarvis, ii. p. 85 et seq.
63. SP Dom 78/39.
64. Maxwell of Kirkconnell p. 62.
65. O'Sullivan p. 93.
66. Chambers, 'Marches' p. 48.
67. Ray pp. 84–95.
68. Mounsey p. 44.
69. Add. MSS. 33050 f. 91.
70. *Ogilvy's Orderbook* p. 295.
71. *Quarterly Review* 1899 pp. 448–49.
72. Whitehead, 'Brampton in 1745' p. 59.
73. SP Dom 79/24.
74. SP Dom 73/106.
75. 'Two Yorkshire Diaries' p. 107.
76. SP Dom 73/106.
77. Hoghton Tower p. 118.
78. HMC, Various Colls, viii. p. 123.
79. Maxwell of Kirkconnell p. 63; Browne, pp. 127–28; *Ogilvy's Orderbook* p. 295.
80. Mounsey p. 45.
81. SP Dom 73/117.
82. Tomasson p. 74.
83. W.O. 71/19 f. 299.
84. HMC, Various Colls, viii. p. 124.
85. Mounsey pp. 64, 76.
86. Vernon Papers pp. 520–21.
87. *Birmingham Gazette* 13 November 1745.
88. Ritchie, loc. cit. pp. 113–19.
89. SP Dom 74/18.
90. Tomasson p. 75.
91. Mounsey p. 47.
92. Elcho p. 313.
93. W.O. 71/19 f. 301.
94. SP Dom 71/60; Jarvis, i. p. 124.
95. W.O. 71/19 ff. 301–03.
96. HMC, Various Colls, viii. p. 124.
97. *Manchester Magazine* 26 November 1745; Harris, *Hardwicke,* ii. p. 189.
98. Mounsey pp. 52–53, 67, 77.

99. L.M. ii. p. 193.
100. Blaikie, *Itinerary* p. 26.
101. W.O. 71/19 ff. 304–05.
102. L.M. ii. p. 193.
103. Tomasson p. 75.
104. O'Sullivan p. 94.
105. Tayler, *Anon. History* p. 99.
106. Elcho p. 313.
107. Staffs CRO, D 798/3/1/1.
108. SP Dom 96 f. 83.
109. Tayler, *Anon. History* p. 99.
110. Earwaker, *Constables Accounts* iii. p. 20; Earwaker (1889) pp. 143–47; Jarvis (1961) p. 80.
111. W.O. 71/19 ff. 306–08.
112. Mounsey p. 79.
113. Ibid. pp. 53, 69.
114. SP Dom 83 ff. 314–18.
115. W.O. 71/19 f. 336.
116. Mounsey p. 54.
117. Elcho p. 314.
118. Tomasson p. 76.
119. Elcho p. 314.
120. Tomasson pp. 76–77.
121. Tomasson pp. 76–83.
122. Ibid. p. 80.
123. Murray of Broughton p. 231.
124. 'John Daniel's Progress' pp. 174–75.
125. Murray of Broughton p. 231.
126. *Chronicles of . . . Atholl,* iii. pp. 81–82.
127. SP Dom 90 f. 228.
128. HMC, Various Colls, viii. p. 125.
129. Simpson, *Derby* p. 242.
130. Add. MSS. 32705 f. 314.
131. HMC, Lothian p. 152.
132. Hughes, *A Plain Narrative* p. 16.
133. HMC, Various Colls, viii. p. 125.
134. SP Dom 73/120.
135. SP Dom 82 f. 84; 74/1; 81 ff. 217–19, 220–23, 224–26.
136. HMC, 12, vii, p. 356; SP Dom 74/35; Mounsey pp. 49–50.
137. Tomasson p. 75.
138. Ray pp. 102–03.
139. SP Dom 74/5.
140. Henderson pp. 57–58.
141. Tayler, *Anon. History* p. 97.
142. SP Dom 73/121.
143. *London Magazine* 1745 p. 566.
144. SP Dom 73/128.
145. *Scots Magazine* 1745 p. 535.
146. Newcastle-Chesterfield p. 80 et seq.
147. *Ogilvy's Orderbook* p. 295.
148. Add. MSS. 30170 ff. 42, 44.
149. SP Dom 76/5; Mounsey p. 56.
150. Fergusson, *John Fergusson* p. 113.
151. Ray pp. 103–04.

152. Henderson p. 58.
153. Yorke, *Hardwicke*, i. pp. 466–68.
154. *Manchester Magazine* 26 November 1745.
155. Simpson, *Derby* pp. 243–44.
156. Ewald, i. p. 280.
157. Add. MSS. 32705 f. 316.
158. 'Two Yorkshire Diaries' p. 108.
159. SP Dom 76/123.
160. Yorke, *Hardwicke*, i. p. 466.
161. Mounsey pp. 50, 101.
162. SP Dom 74/74.
163. Add. MSS. 30170 f. 143.
164. SP Dom 77/80.
165. Elcho p. 323.
166. Maxwell of Kirkconnell p. 67.
167. Ibid. p. 68.
168. Tomasson p. 90.
169. Murray of Broughton p. 435.
170. Chevalier de Johnstone p. 82.
171. *Ogilvy's Orderbook* p. 295.
172. Maxwell of Kirkconnell p. 68.
173. Chevalier de Johnstone p. 82.
174. Simpson, *Derby* p. 243.
175. SP Dom 74/11.
176. SP Dom 74/26.
177. Whitehead, 'Brampton in 1745' p. 50.
178. SP Dom 74/28.
179. HMC, Various Colls, viii pp. 126–27.
180. Fergusson, *Retreat* p. 223.
181. Richmond, ii. p. 177.
182. HMC, Various Colls, viii pp. 126–27.
183. Marchant pp. 226–27.
184. *General Evening Post* No. 1896, 19–21 November 1745; *Manchester Magazine* 19 November 1745.
185. SP Dom 74/32.
186. Jarvis, i. p. 81.
187. O'Sullivan pp. 95–96.
188. Climenson, i. p. 218.
189. SP Dom 74/54.
190. SP Dom 74/19; Jarvis, i. p. 68.
191. SP Dom 74/20.
192. HMC, Various Colls, viii. p. 135.
193. Henderson p. 58.
194. Beresford p. 44.
195. Simpson, *Derby* pp. 244–45.
196. SP Dom 74/17.
197. Add. MSS. 35889 ff. 44–45; *Manchester Magazine* 26 November 1745.
198. SP Dom 74/11; Ward p. 165.
199. HMC, Various Colls, viii. p. 127.
200. Jarvis i. p. 245.
201. SP Dom 74/40 & 54.
202. Fergusson, 'Retreat' p. 223.
203. Simpson, *Derby* p. 244; *Manchester Magazine* 26 November 1745.
204. SP Dom 74/36.

205. Harris, *Hardwicke*, ii. p. 189; HMC, Various Colls, viii. pp. 128–29.
206. *Ogilvy's Orderbook* p. 296.
207. Hardwicke-Herring Correspondence p. 730.
208. Add. MSS. 32705 f. 318.
209. Newcastle-Chesterfield Correspondence pp. 83–86.
210. Ibid p. 83.

4

The Race for the Mersey

AND now it was time for the Highlanders to commence the perilous dash southwards. The day's march was to take the main army to Penrith through hostile territory, lands alienated to the Portlands by William of Orange but formerly crown property of James II.[1] In a different era, of mass political consciousness, support for the Prince might have been expected here from the ordinary people, whose wages were low and conditions miserable. Cumberland's economy at this time was pastoral, based primarily on sheep; poverty was endemic, so that the bulk of the county rates in the 1740s went on vagrant bills.[2]

But if the influence of the Portlands kept the inhabitants unfriendly, a greater obstacle to the army was posed by geography, for the road between Carlisle and Shap was notoriously 'bad country' (in the words of Lady Oxford who had travelled it in May).[3] In 1698 Celia Fiennes had spoken of the 'sixteen long miles' between Carlisle and Penrith and drawn attention to the succession of huts and hovels made of mud walls that one passed on the road.[4]

The scheme for the occupation of Penrith had been decided immediately after the fall of Carlisle. The advance scouting party, the Lifeguards, reached the town on the 18th and moved off next day to Lowther Hall.[5] On the 20th the vanguard arrived — Lord George Murray and the Athollmen, Glenbucket's and John Roy Stewart's regiment. Now on the 21st it was the turn of Penrith to accommodate the main army. The Highlanders' advance displayed that precision and coordination which was to amaze and confound their enemies throughout the invasion of England. The 120 horsemen at Lowther Hall pushed on through heavy snowdrifts in the morning to Shap.[6] Their progress was tracked by Hanoverian agents through Thrimby, where about a dozen of them drank with a government informant, then to Shap and Holt and finally to Kendal itself, where they arrived between 6 and 7 p.m.[7] Ogilvy's regiment meanwhile moved down from Butcherby to take up its station at Clifton, a few miles south of Penrith.[8] Lord George Murray and the vanguard moved down to Shap, fighting against the elements all the way. A profound fall of snow made the going between Penrith and Kendal particularly tough.[9]

The main body moved out of Carlisle in the early morning by the English gate and marched south through Wetherall.[10] Seven miles out from Carlisle the Beacon of Penrith was descried, nine miles away. This was a pillar on a knoll outside the town which could be seen by travellers on the Penrith road from a hill covered with fern and heather, both hill and knoll being landmarks for anyone journeying south from Carlisle.[11] A mile further some of the army battalions detached themselves and went into billets at Heskett, to relieve the expected pressure on Penrith.[12] With Charles Edward on foot at their head, the clan regiments pressed on to Penrith which they began to enter at noon, 'swarming in like bees' as a local inhabitant described them.[13] The Prince himself came into the town at about 3 p.m. and was quartered at the George and Dragon inn in preference to the place that had been set aside for him at the home of Mr. Thomas Simpson.[14]

The behaviour of the townspeople in Penrith was calm. The most exaggerated fears entertained about the Highlanders had been dispelled by their conduct in Carlisle, and indeed the citizens had little reason to complain about the visit from the clansmen. While the common soldiers received board and lodging free, the officers paid for everything they consumed in a rather extravagant fashion to court favour with the local inhabitants; five guineas were disbursed in gratuities to the servants where the Prince lodged.[15] If the burghers had cause for satisfaction, Charles Edward did not, for only one recruit came forward in Penrith, a Mr. Sanderson, and he was not a local, but a Roman Catholic gentleman from Northumberland.

The advance of the Highlanders to Penrith astonished their enemies. Wade had fallen back to Newcastle, certain in his own mind that Charles Edward would not push further into England and thus risk being trapped between his army and Ligonier's, especially with the awful precedent of 1715 to guide him, when the Jacobite force had been caught at Preston between the armies of Wills and Carpenter. Wade was correct in thinking that the existence of two Hanoverian armies would act as a restraint, but this operated not on the clansmen but on the secret supporters of the Stuarts in the north, who in such circumstances were less likely than ever to declare for their prince. Charles Edward himself was not in the least deterred, since on arrival in Penrith he had word from Kilmarnock that Wade had indeed retreated to Newcastle.[16] Wade's return to Tyneside dismayed the optimists among the Whigs, who had confidently predicted that Lord George Murray and the vanguard who had occupied Penrith on the 20th would have to be recalled to Carlisle to deal with the advancing Field-Marshal.[17]

So now there were Highlanders strung out along a line from Kendal to Carlisle. Those left in Carlisle were accused by the townspeople of nothing more remarkable than requisitioning beds and kitchen equipment in the town centre for their use in the castle and obliging butchers to accept their own nominal prices for meat.[18]

The question for the Whig government to answer was where the Jacobite army would go next. When the Scots left Penrith there were those who thought they would make for Yorkshire so as to avoid both Wade and Ligonier (who was moving up to intercept them in Lancashire); if this happened, both the North and East Ridings were under threat.[19] York was much spoken of as a likely target because of the numbers of Catholics there.[20] The Duke of Richmond thought that the destination must be North Wales, for a rendezvous with Sir Watkin Williams Wynn and the Welsh Jacobites.[21] The inhabitants of Whitehaven had their own reasons for fearing a 'visit' from the Highlanders. Apparently, Lochiel had had dealings with the timber merchants of this town and was owed some £1,400 by them, and it was thought that he might take this opportunity to settle accounts with Whitehaven in the bluntest possible way.[22] Whitehaven might have seemed an attractive prize anyway. It was at this time the second or third port in the kingdom owing to its share in the tobacco trade (the lumber business in which Lochiel was involved and which was mainly from Whitehaven to the Baltic had been interrupted since 1742 by the European war).[23] It was a strongly Hanoverian town and by the end of September 1745 had raised 600 volunteers.[24] Militarily it would have presented no obstacle, as it was open on all sides.[25]

All of these conjectures were based on the idea that the Highland army would improvise its objectives and work on a day-to-day *ad hoc* basis. At this stage the strategic ability of Charles Edward was seriously underrated. The response of the London authorities was still muted. Newcastle's main concern on this Thursday seemed to be ordering searches for hidden weapons. The Lord-Lieutenant of Essex, Earl Fitzwalters, was instructed to search Thornton Hall at Brentwood for an alleged concealed cache.[26] The Duke of Devonshire was alerted by Newcastle to the possibility of hidden arms in Lord Norfolk's house at Worksop; in view of the fluid situation, Devonshire himself counselled the captains of the Derbyshire regiments to be ready to march at a moment's notice in any direction.[27] Some of the best intelligence the Secretary of State received this day was in an anonymous letter from an alleged Welsh Catholic, which stated categorically that the Jacobite objective was London.[28] Once there, the Stuart prince would be joined by large numbers of supporters, especially Catholics who 'expect no mercy from you and are determined to show none'.

One matter which should have troubled Newcastle was the apathy of the people in face of the Highlanders' advance. If little enthusiasm was shown for Charles Edward, there was also little determination to oppose him. Although Wade and others had advised the populace to harass the clansmen continually, by sniping at them from behind hedges and cutting off stragglers, no signs of such activity had appeared. One correspondent complained that the Yorkshire Hunters had let slip a good opportunity by failing to harass the Jacobite rear at Carlisle.[29] It was alleged that many in the Jacobite army wanted to desert and would have done so if there had been irregulars in the vicinity to give them succour, but since Carlisle was garrisoned by the Scots there was nowhere for them to desert to. On the whole, though, this was a good day for the Whigs. On the very day William Pitt in a speech in the House of Commons recorded his opinion that the only method of scotching the rebellion was to augment naval forces, so that reinforcements could not arrive from France for the 'Young Pretender', HMS *Sheerness* captured the French ship *Soleil* carrying Lord Derwentwater and French troops to Scotland.[30]

Friday 22nd November

On this Friday 2,846 men of Charles Edward's army spent the day in Penrith, through which another 2,000 had already passed.[31] The principal reason for the sojourn was to allow the rearguard under the Duke of Perth, which was proceeding from Carlisle via Warwick Bridge, to come up with the main army.[32] Further scouting parties were sent out to neighbouring villages like Langwathby to order that bushels of oats be brought into Penrith and to seek fresh billets.[33] From this arose the presumption of the people of Penrith, unaware as they were that the aged Field-Marshal was by now back in Newcastle, that the Highlanders intended to stay and meet Wade somewhere outside their town.

By this time something like a true picture of the exiguous numbers in the Jacobite army had been gained from clandestine counts taken at Eamont and Fallowfield bridges.[34] In an attempt to muddy the clear view thus obtained, the Highlanders gave out that there were great numbers still to come from Scotland. By an interesting irony this story could have turned out to be true, for on this day Lord John Drummond landed from France at Montrose with a force of about 800 men.[35] Drummond badly impaired the chances of success for Charles Edward's invasion by refusing to obey the orders left behind for him by the Prince — they instructed him to join the main force with all speed on arrival. Drummond decided that he would wait until news came of a victory in England before he would make his next definite move.

While Lord Nairne's battalion stood guard over the Prince's quarters in Penrith, the baggage and cannon began to arrive, beginning about 3 p.m.[36] The twelve small field pieces and twenty carriages of baggage, drawn by two or three horses apiece, made a stir as they entered, though the townspeople seemed ultimately more interested in getting a sight of the 'Highland ladies', principally Lady Ogilvy and John Murray's wife. A total of sixty carriages, thirty-one for baggage, and sixteen small cannon had now been transported from Carlisle.[37]

Meanwhile in Kendal the day dawned on a frenetic scene. The advance horse had done their work well and a bellman went round the town before first light, announcing the orders of the Jacobite commissary-general. These were that all public and private houses be made ready to receive the Prince and his army and all should have in supplies of bread and ale.[38] All bakers and butchers were ordered to work, and provisions from surrounding villages were requisitioned. The constable was instructed to have the public money ready and to serve individual notice to all householders about the billeting burden they should bear. Many moderate houses were assigned as billets for groups comprising eight officers, twenty men and six horses.[39] Having achieved all this, Elcho's advance column then moved on towards Lancaster.[40]

For the most part their labour was wasted, for when Lord George Murray and his troops arrived, they refused to be bound by the agreed billeting arrangements and preferred to take their own choice of accommodation.[41] At about two o'clock in the afternoon this vanguard proper began to arrive in Kendal. First to appear were the men of the Atholl brigade, now numbering about 850 according to one count, drawn up three abreast.[42] An hour later came Glenbucket's regiment and then John Roy Stewart's. Later that day Ogilvy's too moved down to Kendal from its station at Clifton.[43] Murray and the van had suffered a gruelling day's travel through roads clogged with snow and ice. Frequent stops had been necessary to rest the horses and to clear the way through snowdrifts.[44] By nightfall about 1200 were bivouacked in the town, mainly quartered in Stricklandgate and Stramongate, with a few in Highgate. Once again the precise co-ordination of the army seems to have impressed the inhabitants. One wrote: 'Such a number of Scotch black cattle I have never seen, except the droves that go into the south for slaughter . . . then come their horses that look as if their masters had made bedding of what they (*sic*) poor beasts should eat.'[45] Great care was taken in Kendal both to sustain the morale of the troops and to avoid giving offence to the town's inhabitants. Ogilvy's regimental order book contained the recommendation that all officers be lodged with their men, 'be much with them', and that great care be taken to pay for everything in their quarters and elsewhere and to avoid all abuses against the citizenry.[46]

In Newcastle Wade's army arrived back exhausted and encamped in private, public and empty houses prior to another gruelling march, this time southwards.[47] Wade himself sent an express to the Yorkshire Hunters at Brough, ordering them to Bishop Auckland via Barnard Castle.[48] Once again there was speculation about the Highlanders' destination. While the men of Kendal knew they were heading for Lancashire and guessed that from there they would proceed to Wales, in London Yorkshire was still the favoured target.[49] York once more figured in government calculations; Yorkshire opinion was that with Ligonier on his way to Lancashire, the Jacobites would cross into their county from Penrith over Stainmoor.[50] At Scarborough defence preparations were made; in Pontefract the officers of the West Riding Companies met to decide military dispositions; at Leeds the West Riding Deputy-Lieutenants hurriedly discussed contingency plans.[51] A panicky tone was evident in Archbishop Herring's letter to Hardwicke this Friday; he thought King George far too casual: 'I should think it the duty of an honest man and good subject to tell him that his crown was in danger of being shaken and that whoever at this juncture could give him contrary advice, either knew nothing as he ought to know or meant to betray him.'[52]

A definite note of apprehension was now in the air. The loyalty of the town of Shrewsbury was considered suspect by Herring.[53] That the growing Whig fears were not groundless can be seen from developments in Lancashire. Despite the confidence in Yorkshire that Ligonier's route to the north-west would bar the way to the Highlanders, Sir Henry Hoghton, as staunch a Whig as any in Lancashire, disbanded the county militia because both Wade's and Ligonier's forces were too far away to help.[54] There was the further confusion about the legal position of the militia that so bedevilled England during the rising; money was not available to keep the militia in being for another fourteen days. And in Scotland events seemed to be turning in Charles Edward's favour, quite apart from the arrival of Drummond. While at Deal the *Sheerness* brought in the prisoners from *Le Soleil* in triumph, a brilliant Jacobite counterstroke was achieved with the daring capture of HMS *Hazard*, which was promptly renamed the *Prince Charles*.[55]

Saturday 23rd November

On this day the most taxing march yet confronted the main part of the Jacobite army, which under Charles Edward intended to get to Kendal by nightfall. In 1729 it had taken one traveller on horseback from noon until 7.30 p.m. riding non-stop to traverse the 'eighteen long miles, on the vilest road up and down hill that can be'.[56] The route lay through enclosed lands for the first few miles and then opened out into what Defoe had described as 'the wildest, most barren and frightful of any that I have passed over in England or even in Wales itself'.[57] A brief pause was made early in the day by the Prince at Lowther Hall, from which later arose an absurd story that he had got drunk there.[58] Certainly the later penchant for alcohol that is sometimes said to have been awakened by this campaign would have served the Prince well on this occasion, for later in the day, on a desolate tract of land between Penrith and Shap, Charles Edward was so overcome by fatigue that he had to take hold of the shoulder belt of one of the men in Ogilvy's regiment (fortuitously left behind at Clifton) to prevent himself from falling down in a faint.[59] Observers claimed that he seemed to walk several miles half-asleep in this manner and his appearance on arrival in Kendal well after dark was a jaded one, though much admiration was elicited from the people of Kendal that he should have walked in his typical Highland dress for the eighteen 'long miles' and through such mountainous country.[60] The citizens of Kendal were indeed much friendlier to the Highlanders than those in Penrith had been but, worryingly, none of them was prepared to join the Stuart army.[61]

While Charles Edward went to his lodgings in Stricklandgate, the erstwhile occupants of the Stricklandgate billets, Lord George Murray and the Atholl brigade, moved south to join Elcho and the guards at Burton, just outside the Lancashire border, leaving the rest of the van in Kendal.[62] The first of Elcho's men were in Burton by 1 p.m. where they ordered quarters for one hundred horses and 700 foot.[63] As the chance of contact with hostile forces increased, the Jacobite army began to bunch up. Well over eighty per cent of the invading force was now in one body in Kendal. Apart from Elcho's and the Atholl brigade, only Perth's regiment was not with Charles Edward. Since its task was to convey the baggage and artillery, Perth's went via Barrowbridge for the night's halt at Orton,with the intention of reaching Kendal on Sunday.[64] The direct route, with its constant hills and pock-marked road, had proved a severe enough test for the infantry, so there was no question of taking the heavy impedimenta of the army that way.[65]

Government intelligence of the progress of the clansmen was first-rate. From the movement of the van south from Kendal, as accurately reported from Hornby Castle, there could no longer be any reasonable doubt that Lancashire was the Jacobite destination.[66] Extremely accurate counts had been taken by government informers of the numbers passing over Eamont bridge south of Penrith, and a precise picture of the resources available to Charles Edward was being formed in London.[67] The largest tally gave 900 horses and 4,700 foot in all, of which it was said there were only 2,000 'good men'.[68] Moreover, the Highland ruse of giving out at each town that another force, composed of the followers of Macleod and Sir Alexander MacDonald of Sleat, was on their heels had now been clearly 'placed' as the wishful thinking it was.[69] As for the ultimate intentions of the Highlanders, a rendezvous with the Welsh Jacobites in North Wales still seemed the most likely objective.[70] The Duke of Richmond reported from Lichfield that the present rate of

Highland advance would carry them well clear of Wade and down into Chester by 27th November, before he (Richmond) and Ligonier could form a viable army.[71] On receiving news of the Jacobite presence in Kendal, Richmond wrote: 'this proves they intend to avoid fighting Marshal Wade and intend to take Chester and get into North Wales or fight us before we are formed into one corps, which cannot be before the 29th or 30th'.[72]

Lord Lonsdale concurred in thinking that the enemy's destination must be Wales, but there were still some sceptics. One view was that the march by the van towards Lancashire was a feint and that the real aim was still Yorkshire, which Charles Edward would approach via Appleby.[73] Tension was still high in Yorkshire: while Lord Irwin in the East Riding intensified his persecution of 'Papists', Earl Malton warned that although his forces could deal with any pro-Stuart riots or risings, he would be unable to defend the city of York against an incursion from the Young Pretender.[74] Further south in the county, in Leeds and Wakefield, something close to panic was in evidence at the prospect of a 'visit' from the Highlanders, though sanguine commentators pointed out that an itinerary taking the Jacobite army through Leeds was most unlikely, as the flooded rivers and narrow valleys to the west of the town would seriously curtail the marching rate the Scots liked to maintain.[75]

In Lancashire the authorities now had to deal not with a vague fear of incursion but the probability, amounting almost to certainty, that the Highlanders would be upon them in a matter of days. At a Council held in Chester on this Saturday by Lord Cholmondeley a decision was taken to break down the Mersey bridges.[76] The bridge at Warrington was partially destroyed to make it unusable to the clansmen, but in such a way that it could easily be repaired later. The Liverpool Blues were the body concerned with implementing this order, which they effected by destroying two arches of Warrington Bridge.[77] In Chester itself Cholmondeley's position was far from secure.[78] The greatest confusion reigned there, with the people who lived in the suburbs bringing their bedding and effects into the town at the same time as the leading families of Chester were doing their best to decamp into the countryside. Some attempt was made to put Chester into a defensive posture by bricking up the city gates, leaving two small wicket gates on the bridge and on the east side, and by fortifying and provisioning the castle. A further threat to Cholmondeley was the uncertain loyalty of many of the citizens of Chester, whose proclivities towards the House of Stuart were well known; in Staffordshire, for example, a strong rumour was current that Chester would be delivered up to the Scots by treachery from within the city walls.[79] In Manchester meanwhile Lord Derby finally concluded that the defence of the town was hopeless and departed southwards, announcing the disbandment of the militia on the following Monday.[80]

In London George II appointed his second son, the Duke of Cumberland, to supreme command of the armies in England and to immediate command of the forces supposedly assembling in Lancashire, adding a reinforcement of two battalions of foot guards.[81] In reality, of course, this army was still in the Midlands: Lord Halifax's regiment was in Northampton, Bligh's, Sempil's and Howard's were in Coventry, where the townspeople entertained them free of charge; the Foot

Guards had been ordered to rendezvous in Leicester; and Ligonier himself had still not departed northward. Horace Walpole in typically sardonic fashion pointed out that, in contrast to the official complacency, symbolised by the loyal address to George II by the entire legal profession (which attended the king this Saturday in 250 coaches), the reality of the situation was that Ligonier was still in Petersham, playing whist with Lord Harrington.[82] So much for the hapless Durand's dispatch of an express to Ligonier at Preston (Ligonier eventually left London this day for Lichfield).[83]

The only fully operational army in the field, that of Wade, was being further impaired by dissension and lack of morale at the decision-making level. At a Council of War held in Newcastle this Saturday, Wade's officers, led by his second-in-command Handyside, opted for an immediate movement southward the next day (Sunday the 24th); the army should be divided into three columns which would unite by day and separate by night to avoid excessive billeting pressure on the towns on the line of march.[84] Wade peremptorily overruled this decision and announced that the whole army would keep together at all times; in order to provide proper victualling, the army would not march until Monday the 25th.[85] Orders were accordingly sent to the Lords Lieutenant and Justices of the Peace of the areas through which the army would march, ordaining that the maximum aid and assistance be provided both for the troops and in the matter of repairing all roads.[86] In disgust Handyside appealed over Wade's head to the Duke of Newcastle;[87] Wade was then obliged to justify his actions to the Secretary of State. Wade explained that there was the greatest reluctance on the part of town authorities in Northumberland and Yorkshire to support him in billeting and victualling his army; he had therefore decided to bivouack his soldiers in one body at night, away from the towns, so as to avoid alienating the townspeople and to prevent pillage.[88] Most of his heavy artillery would have to be left behind in Newcastle, and there was an acute provisioning problem, but he saw no alternative to this method of proceeding. The chances that Wade's army would ever come within hailing distance of the Highlanders were now receding dramatically.

Sunday 24th November

For Charles Edward this Sunday was truly a day of rest. While the Prince remained closeted in his lodgings in Stricklandgate, guarded by one hundred of Glenbucket's men, some 3,000 of his army made preparations for the march into Lancashire next day.[89] That afternoon the cannon and baggage arrived in Kendal, now drawn on sixty-three carriages with two- or three-horse teams.[90] Behind the artillery the rearguard for next day, now composed of Perth's, Ogilvy's and John Roy Stewart's would form up.[91]

For those who spent the day in Kendal, churchgoing was an obvious preoccupation. Many different services were heard in the various Kendal churches, but Charles Edward did not attend any of them, for reasons of protocol officially, because there was no churchman in the town of higher rank than curate, but really so as to provide no grounds for offending anyone's religious susceptibilities.[92] In a clever bid to win the affections of the poor of Kendal, the Prince instructed his officers to contribute liberally to the church collections, and it is said that the sight of gold and silver coins on the pewter alms plate impressed the townspeople favourably. Charles Edward himself was pleased with the efforts of the non-juror minister from Aberdeen, George Law, who preached a rousing sermon to his officers and was rewarded with an invitation to dine that night with the Prince.[93]

Although there were some grumblings about the lack of a proper commissariat in the army, so that the men never knew from one town to the next what provisions they could expect to find, morale in the army remained high. For the majority of the Scots, Sunday 24th November passed quietly enough; for some of them there were the compensations of the King's Arms, which Lady Oxford in May 1745 had found the best inn in the whole north-west.[94] The only extant evidence of administrative activity this day is an order that all estates, houses and effects belonging to the Earl of Suffolk be protected from looting and damage.[95] The cavalrymen spent the day requisitioning fresh supplies of horse: special immunities and privileges were granted to anyone in the environs of Kendal who would bring in horses or provisions of their own accord. This matter of requisitioning horses had consequences that became a vexed issue later on, since many who followed the Jacobite army south of Kendal in the hopes of recovering their mounts often found themselves arrested by the local authorities as stragglers and having to prove their innocence of rebellion at a later date.[96]

Further south, the day was more eventful for the vanguard as it pushed on to Lancaster. About 1800 men left Kendal early, making their way through narrow lanes at first as far as Middleton Park and Leighton Hall, ancient seat of the Catholic Middleton family, and then for the last six miles over steep stony hills to Lancaster.[97] Elcho, heading for Lancaster from Burton, took the indirect route via Hornby Castle in order to check on the distribution of forage.[98] About fifty of Elcho's Lifeguards, led by the young lord himself, came to Hornby Castle at about 11.30 a.m., dined there and pressed on to Lancaster, arriving about 2.30 p.m.[99] Lancaster itself was first entered by about a dozen hussars at 11 a.m., followed by another batch of troops at noon, and a further contingent of about 200 just after 2 p.m.[100] The latter were Athollmen, led by Lord George Murray, who was thus the first senior Jacobite officer to enter Lancaster. The magistrates of the town had at first toyed with the idea of defending the castle, but Murray warned them of the dire consequences if they should attempt anything so foolish.[101]

Elcho and his immediate entourage came into the town at 4 p.m. and rode up Church Street, where they halted outside innkeeper Isaac Rawlinson's house and demanded billets.[102] About an hour later the rest of Elcho's men, who had remained drawn up in the street until billets were found, dispersed to their various quarters while their leader was shown into a parlour below stairs in the back part of Rawlinson's house. Shortly afterwards Elcho was joined in his quarters by Lord George Murray, and together they worked on the orders to be issued to the townspeople.[103] The public money was of course demanded, and in addition it was commanded that all butchers, bakers and farmers should bring in provisions from the country around Lancaster under pain of military execution. Lord George, whose pleas for an intelligence network had so far gone unheeded, procured two agents in Lancaster, one of whom was sent to Yorkshire to get news of Wade and the other to Staffordshire to gain intelligence of Ligonier and Cumberland. Henceforth Murray was always to maintain his own cadre of agents.

Most of the men expected in Lancaster that night had arrived by 5 p.m. so a 9 p.m. curfew was proclaimed. The going from Kendal to Lancaster had been so much easier than from Penrith to Kendal, and this was in line with the usual experience — Skene accomplished the journey in 1729 in five and a half hours, including a stop at Burton — so that there was no question this time of troops straggling all night.[104] To some in Lancaster the curfew seemed a punitive measure and the town did indeed have some reason to be nervous about the coming of the Jacobite army. The authorities had taken a clear pro-Hanoverian line on the outbreak of the rising, having sent in a loyal address to George II and imprisoned likely Jacobites and suspected priests.[105] For this reason the magistrates had hoped for succour from Wade, but he had told them firmly he could do nothing for them; they should either harass the Jacobite army by using the militia as snipers to prevent the clansmen's dispersing into small foraging groups, or, if this proved impracticable, the militia should be disbanded.[106] At this stage, then, the most the town authorities could hope for was that Wade would march for Manchester via Halifax and Rochdale and intercept the Scots there. The Whig propensities of the magistrates in Lancaster may account also for the harsh tone of the Jacobite proclamations and the peremptory nature of some of their actions; for instance, all those in prison at Lancaster Castle for debt were instantly set free.[107]

The townspeople were clearly more sympathetic than their leaders. Elcho's guards were described as 'all brave men, poorly mounted and in good spirits . . . they are dressed with two pistols on each side, a musket slung over their shoulder and a broadsword. They have plenty of money, principally French guineas.'[108]

Sunday 24th November also saw the start of an incident that was to become a *cause célèbre* — the involvement of Dr. John Burton (later immortalised as Dr. Slop by Sterne in *Tristram Shandy*) with the Jacobites. For reasons of his own (but which clearly originated in his own enthusiasm for the Stuart cause) Dr. Burton permitted the tenants of his Yorkshire estate to go to Kendal to view the Highland army while he himself went to Hornby Castle and presented a letter of introduction to the Duke of Perth.[109] Since it was Elcho and not Perth who was at Hornby, the former read the letter and, suspecting Burton of being a Whig agent, sent two of his men to place him under arrest.[110] After an unsatisfactory cross-examination, Elcho took Burton with him to Lancaster. However, on arrival in Lancaster, Burton was no longer double-guarded but seemed to be under no restraint and to have retained his sword and pistols.[111] Several witnesses testified to a change of attitude towards Burton by Elcho once Lord George Murray had spoken to the doctor. Elcho then simply extracted from Burton his parole not to leave Lancaster without authorisation.[112] The doctor's later experiences in Lancaster, especially when Charles Edward arrived, were to provide the basis for a prosecution against him after the rising.

By the night of the 24th the Camerons, MacDonalds (of Keppoch, Glencoe, and

Glengarry), the Appin Stewarts, assorted MacGregors and Mackinnons and Pitsligo's horse had also joined Elcho and Lord George Murray in Lancaster. In London the question still uppermost was, what was the Highlanders' destination? While North Wales still remained the favourite conjecture, speculation had hardened around the town of Shrewsbury as a likely springboard for the Jacobite entry into Wales. The reasons for this were alleged to be several: first, that the country around Shrewsbury 'abounded' with provisions and the farmers could not be persuaded to remove their stock until the danger was so near that such action would be too late; secondly, that the Shropshire countryside, though presently quiet, would manifest its latent disaffection with the approach of the Highlanders; thirdly, and most importantly, seizure of the hundred-ton ships on the Severn at Shrewsbury that plied there from Worcester and Bridgnorth would enable the entire Jacobite army to become riverborne.[113] Between Shrewsbury and Bridgnorth there were at least 140 vessels, each capable of transporting 300 men with all their baggage. One of Newcastle's correspondents recommended the destruction or removal of all ships on the River Severn between Welshpool and Worcester, with compensation offered to the owners.[114]

On the other hand, there were still those who feared an incursion into Yorkshire, particularly in the West Riding. One report gave Kirkby Lonsdale as the Jacobite objective; from this undoubtedly arose the rumour that the Highlanders would march to Settle and proceed south by the valleys to the west of Leeds.[115] If so, this would at least bring them within theoretical range of Wade, from whom the government in London had by now heard the disconcerting news of the dissension in the Council of War and the dismal intelligence of the proposed slow progress of his whole and undivided army through Chester-le-Street to Durham.[116] All now seemed to depend on the army that Ligonier and Cumberland were assembling. Newcastle could do little or nothing except take comfort from the reports of continuing vigilance in the loyal counties, of searches for arms in Derbyshire, the examination of Lord Norfolk's servants, and most of all from the heartening manifestations of loyalty in Oxfordshire, usually considered a disaffected county.[117] This Sunday the vicar of Burford in Oxfordshire, Francis Potter, sounded a counterblast to the sermons being preached in Kendal by taking as his text: 'For the children of Israel have only provoked me to anger with the work of their heads, saith the Lord' (Jeremaiah XXII, 30) — the clear implication being that erring Israel was the University of Oxford, and the substance of the discourse being that only with the defeat of the Stuarts was the Church of England safe.[118]

Monday 25th November

With the main army moving down this Monday to Lancaster, Lancashire itself now lay apparently at Charles Edward's mercy. The speed of the Highlanders' advance had confounded their enemies, so that earlier plans to intercept the 'Young Pretender' in Lancashire had had to be abandoned. No effective military force remained in the county to oppose the clansmen. The Blues had retreated from Bury to Liverpool and the county militia had disbanded, in theory on a legal technicality, which seemed to raise the issue of the status of the militia as a legal entity, but in reality because Lord Derby, the Lieutenant-General, realised that no aid would be forthcoming from Wade and that therefore the militia would have to confront the Highlanders alone — something they had no stomach for.[119]

Since Lancashire was par excellence the Catholic county, much was expected of the Catholic gentry by Charles Edward. In this expectation the Prince was particularly encouraged by his Irish officers, who did not realise that Catholicism and Jacobitism had by now parted company. The Catholic clergy's advice to the faithful was not to become involved in the rising, since this would have the effect of reversing all the concessions made by the authorities to the Catholic religion since 1715 and would lead to rigid enforcement of anti-Catholic legislation.[120] So although Sir John MacDonald was heard to grumble about Sheridan that he had not established any contacts with Catholic priests in Lancashire, it is doubtful that, even if he had, such contact would have brought any specific benefit to Charles Edward.[121]

So, with Cumberland's forces assembling at Meriden Common near Coventry, Wade's army still on Tyneside, and the county militia disbanded, the Jacobites could look forward to a triumphant progress through Lancashire. Only the Liverpool Blues remained as an irritant — they would never appear in the field but could do valuable work for the government in breaking down the Mersey bridges.

Much discussion had already taken place between the authorities in London and the Whig aristocracy in the county about the likelihood of Lancashire's declaring decisively for the Stuarts. It was well appreciated that the behaviour of the county was crucial and might even decide the outcome of the rebellion. Newcastle's brother Henry Pelham thought that Lancashire did not provide as favourable a prospect for the Jacobites as it had done in 1715.[122] Newcastle himself was less sanguine. Endorsing the Deputy-Lieutenants' search for arms among the Roman Catholics of the county, he remarked: 'As . . . it is possible they [the Jacobites] may soon attempt to come into Lancashire there cannot be too great attention given to the conduct and behaviour of the Roman Catholics in that county.'[123] A similar divergence of opinion can be seen within the ranks of the north-western Whigs. While Sir Thomas Mostyn of Mostyn dismissed the idea that Charles Edward's cause would find any echo among Lancashire Catholics, Sir Henry Hoghton of Hoghton Tower opined: 'our enemies are as strong as then [1715] and I know of no converts to be depended on'.[124] Jacobite sources later claimed that only uncertainty about French intentions prevented a general rising in their favour during the closing days of November.[125]

On this Monday morning Charles Edward and the main column — comprising John Roy Stewart's, Cluny MacPherson's, Perth's, part of the Atholl Brigade and Glenbucket's — quit Kendal and passed by way of Farleton knot, 'a pretty high hill of continuous bare rock',[126] to Burton, where the townspeople had the reputation of being 'most obliging'. Defoe had earlier described this particular stretch of road as being 'locked in between the hills on one side, high as the clouds and prodigiously higher, and the sea on the other, and the sea itself seemed desolate and wild, for it was a sea without ships, here being no sea port or place of trade, especially for merchants; so that except colliers passing between Ireland and Whitehaven with coals, the people told us they should not see a ship under sail for many weeks together'.[127] Then it was on to Lancaster, which was entered by way of the bridge and up Bridge Lane. A few miles out of Lancaster, Charles Edward was joined on the march by one Dr. Henry Bracken, who described the Prince as looking most dejected.[128] Bracken's testimony has to be treated with circumspection, for here was no Dr. Burton but rather the opposite, one who, while professing friendship for the Stuart prince, was sending reports to Newcastle, whose agent he was.

The Prince then led his army through China Lane and onto the Market Place, where King James was proclaimed at about four in the afternoon. This procamation particularly affected Lord Balmerino, whose emotions were later minutely described by witnesses at his trial, but seemed to have little impact on the Lancaster populace.[129] Mindful of how they had risen too soon in 1715, and determined not to become involved this time, they looked on in silence. The only recruit the Prince found here was Charles Douglas, Lord Mordlington, who accompanied the Highlanders on their passage through Lancashire and was later taken prisoner by Hoghton's men.[130] Nevertheless the rumour began here that several hundred Lancastrians had joined the Jacobite army. Hence the 500 Lancaster men incorrectly described as having joined Charles Edward in Graham's verse history of the rebellion (*An Impartial History* (1774) p. 31).

Immediately on being conveyed to his quarters in Church Street (later the Conservative Club)[131] the Prince had to deal with the problem of Dr. Burton. The latter's behaviour on the entry of the Stuart hero into Lancaster provided the circumstantial evidence which was to lead Newcastle to order an inquiry into his conduct.[132] Apparently the landlord at the Red Lion inn at Bridge End (an inn that had received Lady's Oxford's 'imprimatur' on her visit in June)[133] had rented out space in an upstairs room, from which interested parties could observe the entry of the main Jacobite army by the bridge.[134] Thomas Jackson and his wife were one couple to take advantage of this, and on entering the room descried an unguarded Burton at the window with a loaded gun. Burton told them he had seen Wade's army at Durham, where the Field Marshal's officers had informed him that they would only fight the Highlanders if they had odds of three to one in their favour.[135] While the advance contingents of the main army were trickling into town, Burton and the Jacksons were joined by John Parkinson. Burton now proceeded to claim knowledge of Jacobite intentions. They would make for Wales, where they would be joined by 20-30,000 men; Ligonier's army would consequently either be destroyed or avoided. If the latter, the 30,000 would quickly grow in to a force of 100,000 with recruits from South Wales; with this army they would either march on London or await an expeditionary force from France or Spain.[136]

When about one-quarter of the Prince's men from Kendal had crossed the bridge, Burton caught sight of Charles Edward himself with his entourage. Crying 'there's the Prince', he gestured to the royal guards and in his eagerness to be seen he blocked the others' view from the window. On being remonstrated with, he warned his companions not to look out of the window, lest they be taken for spies. As soon as Charles Edward was past the window, Burton went downstairs to find him.[137]

Once arrived at the Prince's lodgings, he explained his mission to John Murray of Broughton, who brought him before his royal master. Closeted with the Prince, Burton pledged his loyalty and told him that if he had marched through Yorkshire, he would have been joined by very many supporters there.[138]

A long interview left the Prince perplexed as to Burton's reliability.[139] Burton repeated that the Duke of Perth knew him and could vouch for him, so that in the end Murray of Broughton agreed with his royal master that they should leave the matter of how to deal with the troublesome doctor until Perth could be found.[140] Burton then spent two hours trudging the streets of Lancaster in search of the Duke.[141] He was recognised in the street by a Scottish Catholic named Maxfield, who had known him in York and could verify his Jacobite sympathies.[142] Soon after acquiring his referee, Burton encountered Perth himself. The whole affair was explained to John Murray, Burton's good faith guaranteed, and the good doctor given unconditional liberty and informed that a pass signed by Perth would be prepared for him in the morning.[143] Burton then made his way to the Post Office to order horses from the Post-Mistress (the Master having decamped).[144] It was fortunate for Burton that the Jacobites had suspected him, for the undeniable fact that he had not been received by them with open arms introduced an ambiguous note into the story of his sojourn at Lancaster, which probably saved him from the gallows after the rising. When Burton received his pass and departed for Yorkshire the next day, he exited from the story of the '45 but achieved a niche in history through the *cause célèbre* of his later trial and through being immortalised by Sterne.

It was particularly dangerous for Burton that he spent much of the day with Bracken, for the latter was compiling a detailed dossier on the Jacobites for Newcastle.[145] In his report he claimed that one-third of all Jacobite forces in Lancaster were either old men over sixty or boys under seventeen. He counted 624 horses but described them as 'out of order and slender shaped'.[146] This concentration on physical appearance also marked his description of the soldiers; they were 'low in stature . . . in general well armed but very few of the common men have pistols'. According to Bracken, only about a thousand of the Scots were really impressive in appearance, and most of these were veterans of Sheriffmuir. However unprepossessing to Henry Bracken, the Jacobites were performing a most efficient job of collecting the public monies. Altogether £158-12-8¾ was collected in excise, representing taxes on brewers and victuallers, candles, hides and malt.[147]

The atmosphere in the town seemed much to the liking of the troops, and after all Lancaster in 1745 as a country market town presented a most pleasing aspect. Apart from the castle, from which most of the prisoners had now been released, Lancaster possessed both a commodious church in a splendid situation and a harbour into which seaborne craft could discharge cargo. Symptomatic of the high morale in the army was a conversation reported by the Whitehaven gypsy James Ray at the Sun inn; on complaining of the unsatisfactory nature of his horse, one Lowland gentleman was informed by his friend that there were good horses in plenty in London, where they would soon be.[148] And there is evidence that the townspeople of Lancaster, though drawing the line at joining Charles Edward's army, were by no means unsympathetic to his cause. Alderman William Bryer sought an interview

with the Prince at ten that night and was seen in conclave with him, accompanied
by just two Highland guards, in circumstances that later led to his being
investigated for Jacobite sympathies.[149]

Bracken too got an opportunity to observe the Prince at close quarters in the
evening. While Lord Balmerino was dining with Charles Edward in Church Street
that night, he recognised Bracken through the window as someone he had met in
Paris and who had the reputation there of being an English surgeon of high
standing. For the second time that day Bracken was close to the centre of the stage
and was thus able to record a somewhat farcical panic that arose when Charles went
into the garden for a while without notifying his bodyguard. On realising that the
Prince was out of their sight, the guards overreacted nervously, thinking that
'Tearlach' [Gaelic: 'Charlie'] had been the victim of kidnap or silent assassination.[150]

On this Monday night, then, the Jacobite army lay stretched along a line from
Burton to Garstang, with the bulk in Lancaster under the Prince's standard which
Clanranald's held this day.[151] The vanguard was in Garstang, about 2,000 in
number, where another £30-13-8¼ in public money was collected, while Ogilvy's
regiment brought up the rear in Burton.[152]

In Dublin, Lord-Lieutenant Chesterfield wrote a letter to Newcastle, brimming
with confidence about the outcome of the rising, even if it were supported by an
invasion from abroad.[153] In Chesterfield's opinion, the army in England and the
fleets around it were more than sufficient to deal with both the rebellion and the
French. In London, Newcastle, in closer touch with events, could not be so
eupeptic. He stepped up his programme of anti-Catholic searches and seizures in
Yorkshire and Essex (this time the principal target was Lord Petrie's house), but
until either Wade or Cumberland made a decisive move, the Secretary of State
could only wait the drift of events.[154] Already the authorities in the Midlands were
beginning to grow alarmed at the Highlanders' rate of approach. In Derbyshire a
meeting took place in Ashbourne at the Blackamoor's Head between the Duke of
Devonshire and his Deputy-Lieutenants and Justices of the Peace to discuss means
of impeding the Jacobites' progress, but nothing of significance emerged.[155] The
most worrying news came from south Lancashire in the line of the Highlanders'
march. A body of about two hundred Jacobite sympathisers assembled in the night
at Ormskirk, plying for volunteers at drumbeat and proclaiming King James.[156]
Even though this mob was dispersed by the Ormskirk burghers and about a dozen
made prisoner, at this stage in the invasion the 'Ormskirk insurrection' was an
ominous development.

One man under no illusions about the seriousness of the Jacobite inroads was
William, Duke of Cumberland, who on this day received the formal royal orders
from his father.[157] These stressed the need to co-ordinate with Wade and contained
the instruction that in the event of a junction of the two armies, Cumberland was to
take command over Wade. What most perturbed Cumberland was the Jacobites'
astonishing rate of advance.[158] Learning to his relief that the Liverpool Blues had
broken down the bridge at Warrington, he ordered the most northerly regiment of
dragoons, stationed at Stone, to move towards Warrington. In the meantime, all
roads towards Chester were to be repaired and detailed planning undertaken for
forced marches and the cantonment of a large number of troops.[159]

As for Wade, he seemed more than ever out of the reckoning, despite Chesterfield's hope that by the time Newcastle read his dispatch of 25th November, the ageing Marshal would have annihilated the enemy. While in Newcastle, Wade was lobbied by the Lowther faction in Cumberland, led by Walter Ludgridge of Whitehaven, to move across the Pennines and relieve Carlisle now that the main Jacobite army had gone south.[160] Ludgridge enlisted the support of Generals Mordaunt and Howard and gained an interview with Wade, but derived little consolation from it. Wade stressed that the overriding military objective remained the destruction of the enemy forces, from which their evacuation of Carlisle would naturally flow. With a concentrated pursuit southwards now commencing, he could spare no troops for the relief of Carlisle.

Yet on one matter Wade had had second thoughts. The final orders issued for the southward march of his army embraced the plan urged by Handyside and other senior officers at the Council of War on 23rd November. Wade's forces were now to proceed south in three columns to avoid the necessity of making camp at night.[161] The first column would march on the 25th to Durham, to Darlington the next day and then on successive days to Northallerton, Boroughbridge and Allerton, where it would halt and await the arrival of the second and third columns, pursuing the same itinerary. The second and third columns were scheduled to leave Newcastle on Tuesday the 26th and Wednesday the 27th.

Tuesday 26th November

Since leaving Carlisle, the main army and the vanguard had been about a day's march apart, with the consequence that Charles Edward had seen nothing of his Lieutenant-General, Lord George Murray. Now it was planned to bring almost the entire army together at Preston. Murray and Elcho therefore set off early from Garstang with 2,000 men quartered there.[162] Elcho's horse was first into Preston, between 11 a.m. and noon.[163] Then Lord George with the main body of the vanguard marched straight through Preston and occupied Ribble Bridge on the south side of the town; he quartered the troops in the villages south of Preston to make room in the town for the main force accompanying Charles Edward.[164] Murray had a twofold reason for the occupation of Ribble Bridge. First, he had to have regard to the strategic and tactical implications of the whole army's being quartered in and around Preston. In 1648 Cromwell had pulled off a military *tour de force* by his surprise march on Preston from the east. To prevent the descent of a Hanoverian force on the unsuspecting Highlanders, Murray had to secure all the approaches to the town, and the most important of these was Ribble Bridge. Secondly, the Scots entertained a superstitious dread of Preston after their defeats there in 1648 and 1715, and Murray, with his well-known sensitivity to the feelings of his men, had to find some way of exorcising these ghosts.[165] This he did by marching the vanguard through Preston and out to the other side, so that it could not be said, as Murray of Broughton expressed it, that the town would be 'their *ne plus ultra* for a third time'.[166]

In reaching Ribble Bridge and then turning back with most of his forces after placing a guard, Lord George Murray unwittingly started a rumour that was soon seriously to distort the news received in London about the Highlanders' progress. Various reports began to circulate in the capital that the 'rebels' had retreated to Preston, had withdrawn northwards from Preston, or were hemmed in by besieging forces in Preston. Apparently they were all based on a single report emanating from Warrington, which simply recorded the withdrawal of most of Lord George's men into Preston after securing Ribble Bridge.[167]

In Lancaster Charles Edward and the main force departed early in the morning in good spirits, for it was well known that the twenty miles from Lancaster to Preston was the best stretch of road between Carlisle and Manchester. As the Highlanders filed out of Lancaster, Dr. Burton, preparing for his journey to York,[168] was asked by his servants to identify the Prince and the Duke of Perth, which he did. The other doctor in the story, Henry Bracken, soon revealed his true colours. After having smilingly acknowledged Lord Balmerino's wave as he galloped out of Lancaster, Bracken got together with the town magistrates and laid a plan for interception of the stragglers. First, however, they had to await the passage of the rearguard under Lord Ogilvy, whose orders on this Tuesday were to move down from Burton to Garstang.[169] Ogilvy's stayed just long enough in Lancaster to eat some bread and cheese, standing in the street, and then were gone again; the last Scot quit Lancaster about noon.[170] Immediately Bracken armed some thirty mounted volunteers and set off in pursuit to pick off stragglers. In this way he was able to take eight prisoners before Ogilvy's halted for the night at Garstang.[171] (In James Ray's history of the rebellion, the author rewrote the incident so as to cast himself in the 'heroic' Bracken role.)

Charles Edward meanwhile was enjoying the first, albeit meagre, fruits of Lancashire's attachment to the House of Stuart. Much was expected of Preston, where Jacobite sympathy was traditionally strong. In 1715 the town was an unquestioned stronghold of both Jacobitism and Catholicism; indeed the former Anglican vicar of Preston, Samuel Peploe, owed his rapid elevation in the Church to his staunch Hanoverianism in the teeth of this opposition. The representation of Preston in Parliament also supported the view of the town as a Jacobite redoubt. Both Henry Fleetwood (MP from 1708-22) and Thomas Hesketh (MP from 1722-27) had been members of the Jacobite club in Preston.[172] As if to confirm Lancashire's Jacobitism, the first sign of recruits began to appear on the road from Lancaster to Preston. The best-known of these to historians was John Daniel, author of a valuable memoir of the '45 who described his enlistment under the Stuart banner as follows: 'The first time I saw this loyal army was betwixt Lancaster and Garstang; the brave prince marching on foot at their head like a Cyrus or Trojan hero, drawing admiration and love from all those who beheld him, raising their long-dejected hearts, and solacing their minds with the happy prospect of another golden age.'[173] Daniel raised about thirty recruits for Perth's regiment, to which he was assigned. His brother, Rev. Edward Daniel, joined too and was commissioned by Perth to take blank commissions to likely members of the Lancashire gentry. This proved a dangerous mission, and when the Highland army moved on, Lancashire Whigs attempted to murder him. In terror Edward Daniel fled from his house at night and went into hiding until after Culloden.[174]

Another important recruit was Francis Townley, who was later to command the Manchester regiment. Townley had seen service in the French army and was a devout Roman Catholic.[175] When the Jacobite army lay at Lancaster Townley visited his friends the Shuttleworths at Gawthorpe Hall near Burnley and tried unsuccessfully to persuade them to join him. As a precaution against the failure of the rising, Townley then hid at Gawthorpe Hall a hoard of coins worth about £160, before departing for Preston. The Townleys of Townley Hall were one of the few Lancashire Catholic families whose loyalties had remained as firm as ever since the '15. Another such family was the Tyldesleys: James Tyldesley served in the 1745 rising as Edward Tyldesley had done in 1715.[176]

Yet another volunteer who joined at Preston was the Welsh lawyer David Morgan, who had been legal adviser to the Jacobite Duke of Beaufort and intimate of Sir Watkin Williams Wynn.[177] Morgan was the author of the pamphlets 'The Country Bard' and 'The Christian Test' which attacked Walpole and corruption in the name of 'Country' ideology. Morgan and his servant John Barry set out from Monmouthshire to meet the Prince's army at Preston. About a mile south of the town they left their mounts behind and walked into the town so as not to arouse suspicion. They then presented themselves to the Prince.[178]

In every way this day's events were the most heartening yet for Charles Edward. The road to Preston was an easy one — from Lancaster to Garstang there was a village placed almost uniformly at one-mile intervals — and the Stuart prince was more than ever aware of reliving history as he passed through Garstang, which had been a night's halting-place for the ill-fated Jacobite army in 1715. One incident alone soured the passage through Garstang. A treasure box was stolen from a waggon and hidden in a field which lay behind and a little to the south of the Town Hall. Severe retaliation had to be threatened before the townspeople returned the money.[179] Beyond Garstang, at Newsham Chapel, Newhouse, the Rev. John Carter sought and received from the Prince personal assurances that neither he nor his chapel would be harmed.[180] Orders were also dispatched to the steward at Walton Hall to deliver forage and hay to the army at Preston. Similar requisitions were laid on Sir Henry Hoghton of Hoghton Tower (1500 tons of hay, 200 bushels of oats and ten carts of straw under pain of military execution), but by this time Sir Henry had fled to his relatives in Yorkshire.[181] Hoghton had frustrated the Highlanders in another way, by his order on the 5th of November that all gunpowder held at Preston should be sent to Liverpool.[182]

In Preston itself the Prince made a triumphant entry. After the customary proclamation of King James, his elder son rode out of the town with his guards to view the dispositions on Ribble Bridge, before returning for another procession through the town and what was described as 'the loudest acclamation of the people you can imagine'.[183] Charles Edward then went to his lodgings on the north side of Mitre Court, by the entry to Strait Shambles.

At about the same time, in the late evening of Tuesday the 26th, Cholmondeley in Chester received orders to prevent 'by all possible means' the crossing of the Mersey by the Jacobite army. He was ordered to break down Barton bridge, eight miles north of Warrington on the Manchester road, and accordingly the Liverpool

Blues were told off for the task. The Blues now commenced a mammoth bridge-breaking exercise, for, in addition to Barton bridge, they demolished Carrington and Holmes bridges and, most important of all, Crossford Bridge at Stretford, which cut the main road between Manchester and Chester.[184] They were also instructed to destroy Salford Bridge at the entrance to Manchester, but this was not done. Reports from Manchester make it clear that opposition from 'the mob' when they heard Salford Bridge was next in line for demolition, after Stockport and Barton bridges, prevented the operation.

Manchester was of course the next obvious target for the Jacobites, and the consequence was a mass exodus from the town, except for the not inconsiderable rump of Jacobite supporters.[185] All shops and warehouses were closed or empty, and although a bellman went round the town forbidding the sending of effects and provisions out of Manchester, this had little effect.[186] A meeting was held between James Cheetham and Robert Booth, the Justices of the Peace for the County of Lancashire, and the two Manchester constables to decide what, if anything, they could do in the face of the Jacobite threat. While this conference took place at Dangerous Corner, other meetings of the principal inhabitants of Manchester went on at the three chief inns in town — the Bull's Head, the Angel and the Old Coffee House, where the burghers were entertained at official expense. Both conferences had to bow to the inevitable, since it was clearly out of the question for either Wade's army or the Ligonier/Cumberland force to reach them in time. Wade's troops were a hundred miles away, at Chester-le-Street, having accomplished the march from Newcastle thanks to extremely favourable weather.[187] In any case, their effectiveness as a fighting force was in doubt. Tyrawly, one of Wade's deputies, wrote despondently to Newcastle that he doubted that there would be an army left by the time they got to Wetherby, since no care had been taken to provide the troops with meat, straw or forage: 'I really begin to suspect we are afraid of those scoundrels [the Highlanders] . . . the Marshal knows best what he is about, for my own part I don't pretend to it.'[188] The one positive action Wade took this Tuesday was to despatch General Oglethorpe's cavalry regiment to link up with Ligonier.[189]

As for Ligonier, Cholmondeley's news that the Highlanders were at Lancaster and that he had no confidence in the troops at Chester, who were raw and poorly armed, confirmed him (Ligonier) in the belief that it was foolish to concentrate his army too far forward. He had always intended to assemble his infantry at Lichfield as the most northerly feasible point. There was also the strong suspicion attaching to Ligonier that he did not want to carry out the original instructions to proceed to Lancashire, as this might mean coming under the orders of Wade, of whom Ligonier had no very high opinion.[190] Accordingly, Ligonier now ordered all regiments in the west of England to concentrate at Lichfield, while to give a semblance of adhering to the original instructions he pushed out a cavalry screen to the Mersey and strengthened it with some of the new battalions raised at Chester.

Ligonier's successor as commander-in-chief of the sourthern army, the Duke of Cumberland, left the Palace of St. James for Lichfield on this day[191] amid a general feeling that the Jacobite options had now narrowed to two: they would either have to press on into North Wales or advance to Lichfield to give battle. Although the numbers in the army were known, there was still considerable apprehension about the outcome of such a clash. As one Whig in the inner circle of decision-making remarked: 'It will sound oddly abroad to have the whole force of this kingdom employed in opposing the progress of 5 or 6,000 Highlanders (for our last and best counts reduce them to the former number) but we can't afford another échec.'[192]

The Duke of Newcastle continued to have reports of panic dinned at him (this time from Nottinghamshire, where the roads were said to be clogged with refugees) and to be urged to take strong action against the English Jacobite leaders like Sir Watkin Williams Wynn, currently said to be conspiring with other Jacobite notables at the Somerset coffee house.[193] Newcastle correctly analysed that matters like this were a bagatelle; what was really worrying was the military situation in the North. His particular concern at this juncture was the number of Scots deserters from Dutch regiments who were crossing England to serve in Charles Edward's army. Orders were transmitted to the commissioners of customs in the northern ports of England to keep a special watch for such soldiers and to detain them.[194] In the case of men arriving from Holland it was ordained that they be stopped and searched even if they had all the correct discharge papers and passes from their Dutch regiments.

Wednesday 27th November

With the whole army present in Preston and its environs, including even Ogilvy's rearguard regiment and the baggage, which arrived from Garstang, the first opportunity had arisen for the chiefs of the army to confer together since Carlisle.[195] There were two main issues to discuss at the Council in Preston this Wednesday: one was the route the army should take, and the other was the likely support to be received from within England and outside.[196] There was no dispute over the objective of the march; this was, as it had always been, London, despite Whig conjectures that the army was heading for North Wales. The question was rather what the itinerary should be on the way to London. Lord George Murray proposed marching on Liverpool with one column, even though Warrington Bridge was down.[197] After collecting the public monies there, his column would rejoin the main army at Macclesfield. Murray's main aim was to supplement the Highland treasury. Word had reached him that the citizens of Liverpool were engaged in a wholesale process of packing their money and goods on board ship in the Mersey, and he reckoned that they would pay a good deal to prevent a visit from the clansmen. Murray's plan was, however, vetoed. The failure of the Scots to descend on Liverpool led, then and later, to the construction of the most absurd hypotheses to explain their non-appearance. One of Chancellor Waugh's correspondents thought their bypassing Liverpool attributable to a desire not to be 'enclosed between two armies (!) and the sea'.[198] Even O'Sullivan, who should have known better but is, alas, totally unreliable in his reminiscences, later wrote that the Prince's original intention was to proceed through Liverpool and Chester but that he went to Manchester instead when he heard the Mersey bridges were broken down.[199] The story of the broken bridges and their impediment to a westerly march was also used to explain the Jacobite army's failure to turn south-west from Manchester on

Sunday 1st December, and taken up and used by Smollett in his history of England.[200]

When the other chiefs overruled Murray's plan as lacking any tactical or strategic point, Lord George retorted that his main purpose in proposing it had been to keep the enemy guessing as to the ultimate Jacobite destination. However, this end could still be achieved by turning to advantage the destruction of the Mersey bridges. It was essential to keep up the pretence that the itinerary was to North Wales, and this could be achieved by giving out that the intended route was via Altrincham and Northwich and, moreover, that the army would already have turned south-west at Warrington if the bridges had not been destroyed. In normal circumstances the Jacobites would have had to show their hand at this point, since an army marching to Wales would turn south-west at Preston, or at the very latest at Wigan, and bypass Manchester altogether. The brilliance of Lord George's scheme was that he could now appear to be carried out of his way towards Manchester when that was his true route anyway.[201]

On the other issue, that of reinforcements for the tiny Jacobite army, both Charles Edward and the Marquis d'Eguilles had recourse to 'expedient exaggeration' to silence the sceptics among the chiefs. The Prince claimed that he had letters from English Jacobites who pledged themselves to join him at a later stage in the campaign. In particular he claimed to have a letter from Sir Watkin Williams Wynn, brought to him by Sir Watkin's servant Meredith, which informed him of preparations being made by the Welsh Jacobites in the Cycle of the Red Rose to equip a regiment of 300 horse; with these and Williams Wynn's armed tenants, a junction would be effected with the Jacobite army between Macclesfield and Derby.[202] The Duke of Beaufort would meanwhile raise South Wales and seize Bristol.

Whether Charles Edward had such a letter is doubtful though not impossible but at this stage the Prince was not, as later in Derby, asked to produce documentary evidence of the promises from his supporters. Nevertheless, either in order to brazen the matter out or in response to a genuine message received from Wynnstay (Williams Wynn's country seat), Charles Edward indited a famous letter to Williams Wynn, acquainting him with the success achieved by the Jacobite army so far and urging him to join them with all his power: 'The particular character I have heard of you makes me hope to see you among the first.'[203] In a covering letter the Duke of Perth amplified some details. Sir Watkin was to have *carte blanche* to raise men and grant commissions which the Prince would confirm. He was not to worry unduly about numbers: 'It will be looked upon as a battalion if it come to the number of 4 or 500 men or upwards. But whatever numbers you bring will be acceptable, though they were below that and even though they were very small.'[204] Also sent to Williams Wynn, verbally, was the message that he should join the Prince at Ashbourne. But as with the earlier letter to Barrymore, these communications never reached their destination; the bearer was intercepted by one of Cumberland's agents.

As for the likelihood of French assistance, M. d'Eguilles offered to lay bets that his countrymen had either landed already in the south of England or would do so in a few days' time. It was decided in the Council to bruit it about that a French landing was imminent and that the Jacobite itinerary was through Wales. The upshot of this can be seen in a communication from Lord Lonsdale to Newcastle: 'they have one with them they call the French ambassador . . . and they express in general great expectations of assistance from France when they get into Wales, where they also expect numbers to join them. They talk likewise of reinforcements that are following them from Scotland.'[205]

The final item on the Council's agenda was a consideration of the reports from Lord George Murray's spies, who had now returned from their missions. Wade was reported to be marching south to Doncaster, but there was still the possibility that he might cut across the Pennines into Lancashire. Ligonier was still raising his army around Coventry and Lichfield.[206] Murray had also acquired a new agent at Preston, a Mr. Danvers, who was given the mission of reconnoitring and reporting on the dispositions the new commander Cumberland would make.[207]

Despite the feeling among some who were present at the Council that the real problems had merely been shelved, the enthusiasm of the citizens of Preston for the Stuart cause and the very high state of morale in the army affected even the pessimists.[208] The propensity of Preston to Jacobitism was particularly pleasing, since a couple of decades before Defoe had passed this judgement on the town: 'There is a good deal of good company but not as much as before the '15 — many of the families here and hereabout were affected by it and will not soon recover.'[209] The rank and file of the army particularly appreciated Preston after marching seventy miles in three days.[210] After the snow and ice of Cumbria the weather had turned mild and the accommodation provided for the troops in Preston was the best yet.[211] The town at this time was by common consent a beautiful and picturesque place, where many of the neighbouring gentry had their winter houses. Almost no trade or manufacture was carried on there and the best represented profession was that of lawyer.[212] Preston's two broad main streets were extremely well-paved with the finest of small stones.[213] The Jacobite soldier Rollo Anderson, who breakfasted on the 27th with a couple of Welsh Jacobite recruits, described Preston as 'the prettiest by far of any [town] I have yet seen in England and where we have found the best friends'.[214]

There could be no doubting the friendliness of the inhabitants and their enthusiasm for the Stuart cause. When the manifestos of James and Charles were read, the people asked for copies and seemed keen to read them. When the Prince himself made a point of riding through the town in Lowland dress, to contrast with his normal practice of going everywhere on foot clad in Highland plaid, the gesture was well received by the inhabitants, who invoked blessings on him as he passed by.[215] One of the tasks for the day was to get the army properly shod, and no objection was raised to the provision of thousands of pairs of shoes; Charles Edward himself had a pair made for him by a suitably deferential Preston cobbler.[216]

While rest and recreation was the (literal) order of the day (though we are not told whether the Highlanders utilised the notorious red-light district — the prostitutes walked in the churchyard every night between nine and midnight),[217] Charles

Edward rode out with his entourage to inspect the battlefields of 1648 and 1715. A discussion took place with the veterans of the '15 (including Lord George Murray) about the conduct of the battle, during which the Prince sharply criticised General Wells's tactics on that occasion.[218]

Only one incident impaired the general euphoria of the day. Sir Francis Geoghan and Captain Brown of Lally's regiment, who had come over with the Marquis d'Eguilles in October, were given commissions to raise a Lancashire regiment. Some misgivings were voiced to the Prince even at this stage, since it was felt that for propaganda reasons it would be better if the raising of volunteers were done by Protestants. These reservations were compounded when Geoghan and Brown began to parade the streets to the sound of drums, arrayed in their French uniforms with the Catholic Order of St. Louis prominently displayed on their breasts.[219] It was this incident that decided the Prince to give the command of the Lancashire regiment he expected to form to somebody less obviously identified with France.

Although Preston did not, as Rollo Anderson asserted, provide large numbers of recruits, it was an important source of revenue. Apart from the £169-5-2¾ collected in excise duties, several hundred pounds were raised by Mrs. Grimshaw, wife of the county under-sheriff, and handed over to the Jacobite chiefs at the Bull inn, ostensibly as the price of public safety. It has to be emphasised that this was a covert contribution to the Stuart cause and in no way a levy.[220]

A few of the cavalrymen posted in the village of Walton-le-Dale, south-east of Preston, were detached to order billets at the next town of call, which was to be Wigan.[221] About ten of them arrived in Wigan that night and the same number in Leigh.[222] Another scouting party was thrown out to Chorley and Bolton in the hopes of drumming up support among the leading Catholic families, but what they found was most discouraging. The mansions of many traditional Jacobite families lay deserted, in the charge of old retainers, while the owners had decamped to Liverpool when the Blues retreated there from Bury.[223] Clearly they neither wanted to join Charles Edward nor to undergo the tribulation of telling this in person to his officers. These scouting parties, and particularly those to Wigan and Leigh, seriously confused the Lancashire Whigs. A dispatch arrived in Liverpool from the Mayor of Preston in the evening, informing the Earl of Derby that a party of Highlanders was on its way to take possession of the partly destroyed Warrington bridge.[224] This led to further panic in Liverpool. All shipping cleared into the Mersey Channel and all valuables were laden on board, while the leading citizens sent their wives and children over the river to the Wirral.[225]

While the Highlanders in Wigan gave a taste of requisition to come by borrowing a cart for the baggage, reports came in from nearby Warrington of divided loyalties in that town.[226] On the one hand, the house of one John Cheshyre was reported fitted out with tapestries so as to serve as a temporary court for the Stuart prince if his route lay that way.[227] On the other, there were also tidings of a mass secreting of plate and valuables in a cellar with a secret entrance in one of the houses in the Corn Market. In Manchester the canard was rife that the clansmen were burning down Salford, and many people flocked in from the eastern areas of Manchester to learn the truth of this.[228] The Manchester postmaster quit the town for London with the monies he held to prevent their falling into the hands of the Jacobites, and all members of the militia still in the town were formally discharged and sent home.[229] And in Stockport Manchester citizens were reported arriving with their goods, chattels and 'best effects'.

Far to the north in Cumbria, a serious clash had taken place between the local inhabitants and part of the force left in Carlisle. This Wednesday morning about forty men left Carlisle under the command of the Earl of Kilmarnock's son, to join the main army and bring intelligence from Scotland. When they reached Penrith a palpable hostility towards them on the part of the townspeople was discernible. Somewhat apprehensive about their position should the town make common cause against them, the Jacobites gave out that another thousand men were following and ordered billets for them. This attempted ruse served only to infuriate the citizenry, and eventually the horsemen galloped off to Lowther Hall. Here supper was ordered of Lord Lonsdale's stewards, but one of them slipped away and got back to Penrith, whence he returned accompanied by a large force of townsmen. A brief but fierce exchange between this contingent and Jacobite cavalry resulted in losses to the latter of one dead, two seriously wounded and eleven prisoners, who were at once sent under guard to Wade.[230]

Had news of this development, which seemed to threaten communications in the rear, reached Preston, it might have put a damper on the high spirits in evidence that night. The Duke of Perth had, like his colleague Lord George Murray, found a seemingly reliable secret agent, one Barnabas Matthews, whose mission was to convey messages to Sir Howland Stanley, to post three letters to Jacobite contacts in Liverpool and Chester, and to inform the Mayor of Liverpool that his rightful Prince would not be troubling him with a visit.[231] Both Perth and the Prince shook Matthews by the hand and wished him well on his venture; Perth prepared a special warrant, giving unimpeded access to the bearer on the Prince's business.[232]

Meanwhile Lord Elcho was dining with David Morgan at the Joiners' Arms and finding him congenial company. Morgan discussed Elcho's ride ahead of the army all the way from Carlisle and suggested to him that, if he were given vanguard duty again, he should beat up for volunteers as soon as he came into a town instead of waiting for the infantry to arrive, since the uniforms of his Lifeguards made so much greater an impression than the somewhat tatterdemalion Highland foot soldiers arriving later.[233] The conversation then turned to the Prince. Morgan asked Elcho what Charles Edward's true religious beliefs were; Elcho shook his head and said that it was hard to tell, but he believed his religion was 'to seek'.[234] This dialogue later became famous when Mr. Tew, a native of Preston who waited on their table, repeated it at Morgan's trial.[235]

In another inn, the Black Bull, normally impossibly thronged with travellers, other officers expressed an eagerness for battle, the sooner the better. The reality of an impending clash and the stern task faced by Cumberland's army seemed to be realised in London, where a subscription was opened by the Lord Mayor and others for the relief of soldiers employed on the winter campaign. And although Chesterfield in Dublin penned another sanguine letter, claiming that 49,000 were sure to beat 8,000 (his figures were less than accurate), a weary Cumberland arriving at night in Lichfield knew that the outcome was by no means a foregone conclusion.[236]

NOTES

1. SP Dom 74/68-70.
2. Hughes, ii. p. 6.
3. HMC, Portland, vi. p. 190.
4. Fiennes p. 202.
5. SP Dom 74/55.
6. *Manchester Magazine* 26 November 1745.
7. SP Dom 76/56.
8. Ogilvy's Orderbook p. 296
9. SP Dom 74/52
10. SP Dom 74/74.
11. Skene p. 127.
12. SP Dom 74/74.
13. HMC, Various Colls, viii, p. 128.
14. Ibid. p. 131.
15. HMC, 13 vi. p. 162.
16. Maxwell of Kirkconnell p. 68.
17. SP Dom 74/55.
18. SP Dom 77/63.
19. Collyer, loc. cit. pp. 90-91.
20. Add. MSS. 35889 f. 44.
21. Richmond to Newcastle, 21 November 1745, Add. MSS. 32705 f. 338.
22. Ray p. 98; Jarvis (1954) p. 51.
23. Hughes, ii. p. 49.
24. SP Dom 79/24.
25. SP Dom 69/121.
26. SP Dom 74/45.
27. SP Dom 74/47 & 48.
28. SP Dom 73/101.
29. HMC, Various Colls, viii. pp. 133-34.
30. V.P. pp. 533-34.
31. HMC, Various Colls, viii. p. 132.
32. Elcho p. 324.
33. Ferguson, 'Retreat' p. 223.
34. Jarvis, ii. pp. 15, 62-63.
35. Elcho p. 318; Blaikie, *Itinerary* p. 27.
36. O'Sullivan p. 98.
37. HMC, Various Colls, viii. p. 131.
38. Ibid. pp. 129-31.
39. SP Dom 74/63.
40. SP Dom 74/65.
41. SP Dom 74/74.
42. HMC, Various Colls, viii. p. 129.
43. Ogilvy's Orderbook p. 296.
44. Tomasson p. 62.
45. HMC, Various Colls, viii. p. 129.
46. Ogilvy's Orderbook p. 296.
47. HMC, Laing, ii. p. 384.
48. HMC, Various Colls, viii. pp. 129-30.
49. Collyer pp. 91-92.
50. HMC, 13 vi. p. 162; Add. MSS. 32705 ff. 346-47.
51. Ray pp. 139-40.
52. Herring-Hardwicke p. 731.

53. Ibid.
54. Miller p. 119.
55. Ray pp. 117, 120-21, 168-70; Marchant pp. 185-86.
56. Skene p. 128.
57. Defoe, ii. p. 270.
58. Harris, ii. p. 128.
59. Chambers p. 182.
60. SP Dom 75/8.
61. Elcho p. 235.
62. SP Dom 76/56.
63. *Derby Mercury* 29 November 1745.
64. Elcho p. 325.
65. SP Dom 74/83.
66. *Manchester Magazine* 26 November 1745.
67. Newcastle to Chesterfield, 30 November 1745, SP Ireland 408/241; Jarvis ii. p. 15.
68. SP Dom 75/57; HMC Various Colls, viii. p. 135.
69. *Manchester Magazine* 26 November 1745.
70. SP Dom 75/8.
71. Richmond to Newcastle, 23 November 1745, Add. MSS. 32705 f.354.
72. Ibid.
73. SP Dom 74/76.
74. SP Dom 74/81; Herring-Hardwicke p. 732.
75. 'Two Yorkshire Diaries' p. 108; HMC, Various Colls, viii. p. 136.
76. Jarvis i. pp. 83-84.
77. Jarvis i. pp. 245.
78. SP Dom 74/84.
79. Staffs CRO D/798/3/1/1.
80. Earwaker p. 144.
81. *Manchester Magazine* 26 November 1745.
82. *London Magazine* 1745 pp. 566-67.
83. SP Dom 74/76.
84. SP Dom 74/74.
85. SP Dom 75/30.
86. SP Dom 74/76.
87. SP Dom 75/3.
88. Wade to Newcastle, 28 November 1745, SP Dom 75/49.
89. HMC, Various Colls, vii. pp. 132-33.
90. Ray pp. 118-19; Ogilvy's Orderbook p. 297.
91. SP Dom 75/16.
92. SP Dom 75/35.
93. Allardyce Papers ii. p. 406; Tayler, *Jacobites of Banff* p. 324.
94. HMC, Portland vi. p. 190.
95. HMC, 10 iv. p. 346.
96. Ewald i. pp. 280-81.
97. HMC, Various Colls, viii. pp. 132-33.
98. SP Dom 76/56.
99. SP Dom 79/89.
100. *Manchester Magazine* 26 November 1745.
101. Nicholas pp. 141-43.
102. SP Dom 83 f. 375.
103. Tomasson p. 93.
104. Skene p. 128; Harrison p. 113.
105. SP Dom 70/23; 72/125.
106. Jarvis i. p. 82.

107. Nicholas p. 144.
108. SP Dom 76/48.
109. HMC, 12 vii. p. 356.
110. SP Dom 83 ff. 210-11.
111. SP Dom 81 ff. 249-50.
112. Murray of Broughton p. 436.
113. SP Dom 74/90.
114. Ibid.
115. Collyer pp. 91-92.
116. HMC, Laing ii. p. 354.
117. SP Dom 75/4; Jarvis ii. pp. 311-12.
118. Ward p. 167.
119. Jarvis i. pp. 125-35; ii. pp. 318-19.
120. SP Dom 74/66.
121. Murray of Broughton pp. 245, 436.
122. Miller p. 116.
123. SP Dom 74/24.
124. Miller pp. 116-18.
125. Stuart MSS. 272/92A.
126. Skene pp. 128-29.
127. Defoe ii. p. 269.
128. SP Dom 76/46.
129. Howell, *State Trials* 18 p. 478.
130. Miller p. 119.
131. VCH, Lancs, viii. p. 19
132. SP Dom 76/48.
133. HMC Portland vi. p. 190.
134. SP Dom 81 ff. 146-47.
135. SP Dom 85 f. 108.
136. SP Dom 84 f. 109.
137. SP Dom 76/70.
138. SP Dom 83 f. 376.
139. SP Dom 76/9.
140. SP Dom 83 ff. 208-15.
141. SP Dom 83 ff. 287-91; 343-46.
142. HMC, 12 vii. p. 356.
143. SP Dom 83 ff. 27-28, 51-52, 106.
144. SP Dom 81 ff. 252-54.
145. SP Dom 81 ff. 249-50.
146. Mahon iii, Appendix lxxii.
147. Jarvis i. p. 177.
148. Ray p. 131
149. SP Dom 77/62.
150. Mahon, ibid.
151. Ogilvy's Orderbook pp. 297-98.
152. SP Dom 76/56; Elcho p. 326.
153. Add. MSS 32705 f. 379; Newcastle-Chesterfield Correspondence p. 87.
154. SP Dom 75/70; Jarvis ii. pp. 309-10.
155. Simpson (1826) pp. 246-49.
156. SP Dom 76/2; *London Magazine* 1745 p. 608; Marchant p. 193.
157. SP Dom 75/5.
158. SP Dom 75/7.
159. SP Dom 75/16.
160. HMC, 13 vii. p. 126.

161. HMC, Various Colls, viii. p. 133.
162. SP Dom 75/14.
163. SP Dom 75/16.
164. Elcho p. 326.
165. Tomasson p. 97.
166. Murray of Broughton p. 245.
167. Jarvis (1941) loc. cit; *General Evening Post* No. 1900, 28-30 November 1745.
168. SP Dom 83 f. 376.
169. Ogilvy's Orderbook p. 298; SP Dom 75/79.
170. Roper p. 88.
171. Ibid. pp. 86-89.
172. Clemesha p. 199; Hardwick, *Preston* p. 252.
173. Blaikie, 'John Daniel's Progress' p. 168.
174. Tayler, *Jacobite Epilogue* p. 149.
175. Harland pp. 227-28.
176. Blundell ii. p. 166.
177. Howell, *State Trials* 18 p. 372.
178. Allardyce, ii. pp. 450-51.
179. Fishwick, *Garstang* p. 74.
180. Blundell, ii. p. 161.
181. Miller p. 119.
182. Ibid. p. 118.
183. SP Dom 76/56.
184. Jarvis i. p. 85.
185. Earwaker, *Constable Accounts* iii. p. 21.
186. Talon p. 226.
187. HMC, Laing, ii. p. 354.
188. HMC, Various Colls, viii. p. 132.
189. SP Dom 75/25.
190. Whitworth p. 111.
191. Cumberland p. 305.
192. HMC,14 ix. p. 134.
193. SP Dom 75/22-23.
194. Jarvis i. p. 201.
195. Elcho p. 237; Ogilvy's Orderbook p. 298.
196. Chevalier de Johnstone pp. 62-63.
197. Chambers, 'Marches' p. 52.
198. Musgrave to Waugh, 30 November 1745, Mounsey p. 115.
199. O'Sullivan p. 98.
200. Smollett xi. p. 225.
201. Jarvis i. p. 87.
202. *Quarterly Review* 1899.
203. HMC, iii. pp. 255-56.
204. Ibid. p. 256.
205. Lonsdale to Newcastle, 27 November 1745, SP Dom 75/46.
206. Elcho pp. 328-29.
207. SP Dom 97 f. 146.
208. O'Sullivan p. 98.
209. Defoe ii. p. 268.
210. SP Dom 75/44; 76/69.
211. SP Dom 75/43.
212. HMC, Portland, vi. p. 190; Ray pp. 126-27.
213. Skene p. 132.
214. SP Dom 75/42.

215. Elcho pp. 327-29.
216. Mahon, iii. p. 265.
217. Skene p. 130.
218. Murray of Broughton p. 246.
219. Elcho p. 328.
220. Whittle ii. p. 243.
221. Ibid. ii. p. 53.
222. HMC, 10, i. p. 288.
223. Williamson p. 61.
224. Ibid.
225. Jarvis ii. pp. 16, 21.
226. Jarvis (1941) p. 141.
227. Beaumont, loc. cit. p. 185.
228. 'Two Yorkshire Diaries' p. 109; Bowman p. 271.
229. Talon pp. 226-27.
230. Mounsey p. 116; Ray pp. 197-99; Jarvis (1954) pp. 47, 52; Gordon & Arnot i. pp. 134-35.
231. SP Dom 75/127.
232. SP Dom 75/36.
233. *British Magazine* 1746 p. 230.
234. *Scots Magazine* 1746 pp. 324-25.
235. Elcho p. 85; Howell, *State Trials* 18 p. 371.
236. Mahon, iii. Appendix lxix.

5

Interlude in Manchester

Thursday 28th November

ON this Thursday Charles Edward and the main army experienced a short and easy day's march. When Celia Fiennes traversed the twelve miles of this road in the 1690s she described it as the worst stretch of her entire journey, but since 1726 the Preston-Wigan road had been turnpiked and the new sixteen-mile road posed few problems for the traveller.[1] Past the country seat of Sir Roger Bradshaw and into the small market town of Wigan, built of brick and stone, the Jacobite army marched. The road between Preston and Wigan was lined with onlookers who stood at their doors to watch the Scots go by. Most of them wished the Prince success but declined to fight when offered arms, on the grounds of lack of training.[2] This was no more than prudence, for even to be seen on the same road as the Jacobite army on a given day would later be argued as an incriminating circumstance. A certain Mr. Fletcher, who was employed by a neighbour to recover impressed carts and horses, and therefore followed the Highlanders into Wigan this Thursday, was later arraigned as a traitor and sustained his innocence only with difficulty.[3]

There was much overt and covert support for the Stuarts in this part of Lancashire — after all Wigan itself was in the palm of Lord Barrymore — but recruits continued depressingly few. The only one of note in Wigan was Christopher Taylor, later an ensign in the Manchester regiment, who had been educated in France and had returned to his father's estate near Wigan just before the rebellion.[4] Once in the town, the Prince found accommodation in the Old Manor House in Bishopsgate, close to the parish church, where the absent squire's wife was paid ten guineas for the night's lodging. Quarters were demanded for 8,000 men, Warrington announced as the next stop on the itinerary, and the comparatively large sum of £129-19-1 collected in public money.[5]

While the main force refreshed itself at the few good inns in the town like the Eagle and Child, the vanguard proper (Ogilvy's, John Roy Stewart's and Elcho's) went on to Leigh.[6] A party of these was at Chorley before daybreak (between 6 and 7 a.m.), where a brief pause was made at the Bull's Head to collect the public money, amounting to £22-16-11.[7] The detachment in Leigh, as well as taking up £37-13-6 in public money, almost entirely from the town brewers and victuallers, also involved the constable for Higher Pennington, Mr. Lowe, in expenses of £13 — heavy disbursements on the scale he was used to — being £8 and £5 for two horses which he was required to purchase for the cavalry.[8] The other constable, in Lower Pennington, Richard Buck, expended £1-5-5 on billets for the troops, a large

89

number of whom were lodged with James Keel and William Boydell, the local luminaries. The Leigh constables also took the precaution of spending extra money on fires at the watch house and extra guards to keep the peace in the town and make sure that no offence was given to the occupiers. All in all about 800 men lay that night in and around Leigh.[9]

By far the most dramatic exploit of the day was that of Sergeant Dickson, who went on ahead even of the advance horse to beat up for recruits in Manchester. Dickson set out from Preston on the night of the 27th with the blessing of Lord George Murray's aide-de-camp Chevalier de Johnstone, accompanied only by his mistress and a drummer.[10] Dickson's arrival in Manchester was thought at first to be the harbinger of the main army but, when his exposed position was realised, some of the Whigs in the town tried to take him prisoner. Dickson threatened to blow out the brains of the first to lay hands on him and, while his enemies hesitated, he was rescued by the large Jacobite faction in the town.[11] He was immediately joined by James Brettargh, Thomas Deacon, Thomas Syddal and George Fletcher, all later officers in the Manchester regiment (and all executed for rebellion in 1746).[12]

Hard on the heels of the intrepid Dickson came Pitsligo's horse, more than a hundred strong. Between 6 and 7 p.m. they were spotted passing Four End Lane on their way to Manchester.[13] At about 8 p.m. Pitsligo and his men arrived there in the most auspicious circumstances, heralded by a fine moonlit night and greeted by about eighty volunteers.[14] The mob which had assembled to greet the Prince received the cavalrymen very well and showed an inclination to join the army.[15] The two Manchester constables, Thomas Walley and William Fowden, were summoned to appear before Pitsligo. Fowden lay low in his house and tried to avoid contact with the incoming Highlanders by cautioning the townspeople to say they did not know where he was. But it did not take long in such a friendly town as this to discover his house. A party of Scots appeared there and marched him down to the Bull's Head. So eventually and grudgingly both constables were forced to obey the summons. The more foolhardy of the two, Fowden, then made so bold as to ask Pitsligo by what authority he summoned and commanded him. Pitsligo clapped his hand on his sword, drew it partly out of its scabbard and said: 'By that!'. He added that the Prince's orders must be carried out on pain of military execution. Not surprisingly, the constables did not demur.[16]

Meanwhile, since Warrington Bridge was down, south-west Lancashire continued fearful of a descent by the Highlanders en route to North Wales. Their most likely path was by way of Warrington and Liverpool: from Wigan to Warrington the road was turnpiked, and again from Prescot to Liverpool (the Prescot-Warrington section was turnpiked in 1753).[17] This seemed to make Warrington a certain Jacobite destination. As it turned out, this town, which had been originally designated as the place where Ligonier's army would confront the clansmen, did not even receive a visit from the roving cavalry to collect the excise.[18] The advanced columns of the army, in fact making for Leigh, were reported on a common about a mile from Warrington between 3 and 4 p.m. This alleged vanguard consisted of two men detached from the army to order provisions at Warrington as a camouflage.[19] The two were taken prisoner by the Liverpool Blues, who had already performed such valuable services for the Whigs in the matter of Warrington Bridge, and confined at the Town Hall.[20] Considerable unease was evinced in Warrington this day and throughout the Highlanders' sojourn at Manchester. The lords of Bensey Hall, Atherton Hall and Marbury Hall in the environs of Warrington were known Jacobite sympathisers, and there was pro-Stuart feeling in the town too.[21] When a Jacobite slogan was raised and a toast drunk to Charles Edward in the Old Coffee House, the result was a riot in the horse market. The inmates of the town's workhouse decamped to take service with one side or the other. The master of the Red Lion inn was reportedly tried and sentenced to be hanged later for blatant Jacobitism.[22]

Liverpool, too, could still not be sure it would be spared an incursion, especially since Perth's envoy Barnabas Matthews was on this morning attempting to find recruits for the Prince as close as Maghull.[23] Indeed in France Charles Edward was confidently reported to have entered Liverpool in triumph.[24] The most lurid of such reports managed to combine Ligonier, Cumberland, Liverpool and Chester in one communiqué. Having defeated Ligonier in battle, it was alleged, the Stuart prince took Cumberland prisoner and incarcerated him in Liverpool; he then went on from Liverpool to take Chester![25] Though untouched except by rumour, Chester too contained its quota of worried Whigs. Persistant whispers continued to be heard about an imminent *coup de main* by the Welsh Jacobites on Chester castle, even though Cholmondeley insisted as vehemently that this citadel was impregnable to an enemy without heavy artillery.[26]

Cholmondeley was being exhorted by Cumberland at this very moment to remain sanguine and to hold the castle at any cost. Cumberland, fatigued with his arduous journey to Lichfield, now attempted to block the routes either to Chester or Derby.[27] He informed Newcastle that with his cavalry cantoned from Tamworth to Stafford, and a flying squadron as a screen at Newcastle-under-Lyme, he was ready to move in either direction (Chester or Derby) to force the Highlanders to an engagement. Wade was apprised of his intentions and urged by the Duke to send his cavalry ahead to harass the Jacobites.[28] Wade, who was now at Newbridge with the expectation of being at Boroughbridge on Monday the 2nd of December and Wetherby the next day, had of course already detached Oglethorpe.[29]

Cumberland's plans were based on the assumption that the Jacobite captains would give him a breathing space by remaining for a few days more at Preston; he misread the day's halt on the 27th as nervousness, considered an advance on Manchester would be madness, and ridiculed the enemy for their vacillation. As yet he had clearly not taken his opponent's measure. Nor for that matter had Ligonier, whom Cumberland had found at Lichfield a sick man 'low and dispirited' from a raging fever.[30] This did not prevent the general from endorsing Cumberland's optimism at all points. Ligonier's view was that Charles Edward had missed his opportunity by failing to cross the Mersey and attacking the van of his (Ligonier's) troops while his rear was still some distance away. He shared Cumberland's opinion that the Highlanders had wasted their time in Preston, and if they would just stay there until Sunday (1st December), Cumberland could go over onto the offensive.[31] The other favourable factor that made it in his view impossible for the Jacobites to stay long in Lancashire was that Oglethorpe (at Pierce Bridge on the 28th and expected in Richmond on the 29th) and the dragoons were closing fast on them, and Wade himself was only six days' march from Manchester.

The one snag, as Ligonier saw it, was that unless the Duke of Devonshire and his militiamen could make the road to Derby impassable, it was possible for the Jacobite commanders to bypass Cumberland.[32] This was because of 'the Bow Hills, a ridge of impracticable hills', dividing Derbyshire and Staffordshire and stretching from Stockport to the western side of Macclesfield. If Cumberland moved up to the Mersey, the Highlanders could get to Stockport, and thence to Derby via Buxton, since it would then be impossible to intercept them unless by some miracle an army could be thrown across the Bow Hills. Nevertheless, Ligonier considered a thrust into Derbyshire by the Jacobite generals unlikely, and he ended his euphoric *tour d'horizon* by recommending his friends to buy shares, in the confident expectation of a successful outcome to the campaign.

Friday 29th November

While Pitsligo's awaited the advent of the main army in Manchester, the rearguard began to close up once again — always a sign of the imminence of momentous decisions. Ogilvy's and John Roy Stewart's left Preston at 6 a.m., proceeded eight miles along the road to Wigan, and then veered off to the left to strike across country to the night's quarters at Leigh.[33] Charles Edward and the main force meanwhile set out along the fourteen-mile road from Wigan to Manchester, another bad stretch of highway.[34]

Hopes were high for a considerable accession of fighting strength in Manchester, which was reported to have rejoiced openly at news of the Jacobite victory at Prestonpans.[35] The town was well known to possess at least three distinct coteries of adherents to the House of Stuart. There were the leading members of the gentry (such as the Townleys, Byroms and Dickensons); the High Church clergy of the collegiate church; and the important group of Non-Juror followers of Dr. Thomas Deacon. The attitudes of many of the most important citizens of Manchester towards the rising are known to us in some detail. Some of this evidence suggests that the Manchester Jacobites joined Charles Edward more out of reluctant conviction than from any hope that his rebellion could ultimately be successful. Dr. Robert Hopwood, a physician and member of the Royal College of Surgeons, later testified that on his return to Hopwood Hall (near Manchester) from London about the time of the outbreak of the rising, Dr. Thomas Deacon tried to recruit him for the Jacobite cause.[36] He in turn tried, early in November, to persuade Dr. Deacon not to join the Stuart prince. Deacon replied that the rebellion could not possibly succeed and even if it did, he personally would not be a shilling better off, but that if the Highlanders came to Manchester he would feel obliged in conscience to join them if he could not get a dispensation from his superior on account of his large family. When Hopwood asked him who his superior was, Deacon replied 'the Prince himself'.

A similar ambivalence characterised the attitude of many other Jacobites from the intellectual and professional classes. Richard Edward Hall, later surgeon extraordinary, was a convinced Jacobite, yet when the Prince came he was not prepared to risk life and property on his behalf and kept a low profile during his true prince's stay in Manchester.[37] For example, he was not even mentioned as having been present at the reception for the Prince at Mr. Dickenson's. For all this, apart from Dr. Peter Mainwaring, later physician extraordinary at the Manchester Infirmary, the only Whigs of note in the town were Henry Brooke, the high master of the grammar school, and Warden Peploe, the well-known Whit prelate, although naturally the merchant class in general did not share the fervid enthusiasm for Jacobitism of the gentry.[38] Many people engaged in commerce had already quit Manchester in alarm at the wilder rumours of rapine that had earlier been rife, and this fear was compounded by the exaggerated estimate of the clansmen's numbers. Since they would not put their goods on board ship like the people of Liverpool or send their families to a place of safety like the Wirral, large numbers of the prosperous middle sectors had already left town with their effects.[39]

Those who remained by and large displayed considerable enthusiasm for the main Jacobite army as it began to enter town about 11 a.m. Charles Edward himself reached Salford around 2 p.m. and the centre of Manchester about an hour later.[40] As he rode through Salford, the Rev. John Clayton of Salford Grammar School bowed to him 'upon one or both knees' (in the words of an eyewitness). The Prince waved his bonnet at him, whereat Clayton replied: 'God bless your Royal Highness Prince Charles'. On Clayton's embracing a friend of his, Hugh Stirling, who had just joined the ranks of the army, Charles Edward drew his sword and made a complimentary gesture in Clayton's direction. At this the crowd took to calling, 'Long live Parson Clayton.'[41]

The first man into Manchester proper this Friday was the immensely tall Andrew Hay (described as being seven feet high), later an exile in France.[42] The first officer to be generally recognised in this main column was the aged Glenbucket.[43] Everywhere the Highlanders were well received. The town was illuminated, bells were rung and several people kissed the Prince's hand and cheered him all the way to his lodgings.[44] A bonfire was lit by a Mr. Cotterel.

The only people conspicuously not to take part in the celebrations were the Manchester constables, Thomas Walley and William Fowden. Early that morning, at about nine, Pitsligo summoned Walley to the Bull's Head.[45] He ordered him to go out of town with his fellow constable, bearing the staves of office, there to await the Prince and conduct him into Manchester. Walley replied that the constables' jurisdiction did not extend beyond Salford Bridge.[46] Similar evasions were employed by Walley and Fowden to escape all the tasks laid upon them. When ordered to ring the bells, Walley replied that this formed no part of the prerogative of a constable; this lay in the power of the churchwardens. Similarly, in order to confuse the issue, when Walley was ordered to attend O'Sullivan at the Saracen's Head to arrange billets for the army, he contrived to 'misunderstand' his instructions and arranged the billeting with Hugh Stirling and another Jacobite officer before going to his interview with O'Sullivan at the Saracen's Head.[47] When O'Sullivan heard what had happened he flew into a rage and told Walley that his arrangements were null and void — the army would now distribute its own billets. A long delay before the churchwardens could be found further infuriated Pitsligo, so that when Walley attempted further evasions in the reading of the proclamation of 'King James' at the Market Cross, the Scottish chiefs were in no mood to humour him.[48]

The reading of the Jacobite proclamation at the Market Cross was of course the thing the constables most wanted to avoid. When this was insisted on and, at about 4 p.m., Walley and Fowden were taken to the Cross under armed guard, what ensued was closer to farce than anything yet in the campaign. First, Fowden claimed he could not read the proclamation since he had left his spectacles at home. Then Walley pleaded he could not read it either since he had a speech impediment. The Highland chiefs cut through this impasse by making Fowden repeat aloud the phrases in the proclamation after they had been read to him.[49]

After the proclamation the Jacobite leaders dispersed to their quarters, the Prince to the house of John Dickenson in Market Street Lane, Tullibardine to Mr. Marsden's and the Duke of Perth to Mr. Gartside's, there to take stock of the situation. One less than satisfactory development was that the Jacobite demand for public money had to be repeated peremptorily after the proclamation; James Waller, a prominent local citizen, was made the reluctant instrument for conveying the demand to the relevant parties under pain of military execution.[50] Nevertheless there was much to cheer a Jacobite heart in Manchester and the Prince was in good spirits that night. In his room at Dickenson's house he had a list of those who had subscribed to the defence of George II and an accurate inventory of horses in Manchester, which he began to work on. To celebrate his arrival the Rev. Clayton preached an address in the Collegiate Church. Another clergyman, the young Mr. Coppoch, so impressed the Prince that he received the appointment of royal chaplain and was to become a familiar figure for the rest of the campaign by praying for the Stuarts and the success of their army in every town the Highlanders passed through. Another of the fellows of the Collegiate Church, the Rev. Cattel, demonstrated his commitment by lavish hospitality to a captain in John Roy Stewart's regiment.[51] Not only did the captain receive better hospitality than he had ever had in his life but on leaving he was presented by his host with a powder flask.

The atmosphere in Manchester this Friday night is well conveyed by the experience of John Taylor of Hopwood, who travelled the five miles to Manchester to see the Jacobite army. On his way out of the Boar's Head in Milnegate Street he was accosted by two clansmen who accused him of being a militiaman. He was led at gunpoint to a Highland colonel in Fennol Street, but after questioning him the colonel decided he was innocent of espionage and gave him 2/- to drink the Prince's health.[52] Taylor was then taken to Dr. Thomas Deacon's house, which was next door to the place of his interrogation. Deacon opened the door in person, offered rum all round and drank 'good health and success to you all', thinking that Taylor was a new recruit. Deacon then continued in high spirits: 'don't be afraid, young man, your cause is good — a great many have joined them'.

The same kind of euphoria was everywhere in evidence. At the Prince's lodgings the talk was all about how he should enter London, whether on foot or on horseback, and in what dress. The clansmen meanwhile dined well on the best the town's inns could provide, apart from the Bull's Head and the Saracen's Head, the Sign of the Anchor in Cockpit Hill and the Golden Goose in Key Street being the most popular venues. The luckless constables did not fare well, however. Fowden had already been told that morning that if he refused any commands given him in the Prince's name he was a dead man. Upon Fowden's replying that he had taken an oath of loyalty to George II, the Jacobite officer with him at the Saracen's Head retorted angrily: 'If you mention George of Hanover in my presence, I'll stab you dead'. He was therefore in no mood to remonstrate when Murray of Broughton addressed an order to the High Constable (which Walley and Fowden had to carry out under pain of military execution) for the provision of corn, hay and other forage for the army. Next the two constables were sent for by the officer commanding the artillery train who ordered them to press 180 horses with carriages for the park, an order which once more they tried to evade on the grounds that there were not that many horses and carriages in Manchester. Finally, at ten that night the constables were involved in a further imbroglio, this time to do with the casting of bullets, when the gunsmith James Evans tried to avoid this task laid on him by the Highlanders. The constables were pressed into service to find the men to make bullets; these arrived the next morning at Evans's house and were held to their task until the clansmen's departure on Sunday morning.[53]

While the aplomb of the Jacobites in Manchester contrasted with the despondency of Whit officialdom, elsewhere in south-east Lancashire roving parties of Jacobite outriders continued to levy the public monies in the major towns. A party of them came to the Swan inn in Bolton and collected £35-6-4 in excise plus the tiny sum of £1-12-0 in Bury:[54] little else was uplifted in the latter town, since all valuables had been concealed by the people there, who, hearing of the strong press for horses, had also hidden their mounts in the remote country areas.[55] Another party rode through the village of Lees to Oldham, where they arrived about 9 p.m. Their guide was John Whitefoord, a local Jacobite, who directed the Scots to the likely hiding places for arms and put them on the scent of a party of Whig soldiers said to be in the vicinity.[56] Links between Oldham and Manchester were particularly strong at this juncture, and it is related that after the later Jacobite levy on Manchester, Oldham's weavers accepted a temporary reduction in the prices of their fabrics.[57]

On their way to Oldham the Highlanders had searched Chamber Hall and Middleton Hall for horses. Chamber Hall was the seat of Edward Gregge, who was away serving in the militia; his servants had spirited all his horses away, so the Scots came away empty-handed here.[58] In Middleton they had more luck, being helped by Jeffrey Batterby (shoemaker to the Hopwoods) to levy the excise. Another scouting party moved down close to Warrington, where one of their number crossed the Mersey, was seized by the ever-vigilant Liverpool Blues and was sent to prison in Chester.[59] The Blues had set out that morning from Liverpool under the command of Col. Campbell and arrived in Warrington in the evening. Passing over Sankey Common at twilight, their vanguard, understandably jittery, mistook a flock of geese for a Highland patrol and opened fire on them.[60]

Meanwhile at Lichfield divided counsels prevailed in the Hanoverian army. From the intelligence Ligonier had on the morning of the 29th about the Jacobite advance as far as Leigh and Wigan, Cumberland still considered that Liverpool was the target, and his secretary Sir Everard Fawkener wrote to the people of the town to keep all their effects on board ship in the Mersey estuary in anticipation of a Jacobite descent.[61] When it dawned on Ligonier and Cumberland that Manchester was the objective, the Lord Lieutenant of Derbyshire, the Duke of Devonshire (who was in Lichfield) was drawn into strategic discussions. He promised Cumberland that the road between Buxton and Derby would be broken up by nightfall, which the Duke thought would preclude an enemy advance that way.[62] To get advance intelligence of Jacobite movements, a subaltern and fifteen men were despatched to Macclesfield to report on any move towards Stockport, and similar parties were sent to Knutsford and Nantwich, to act under the immediate orders of the Duke of Kingston, based at Congleton.[63] Cumberland's problem this Friday was that he wanted to wait until all his forces were in one body before risking a battle. Ligonier forecast that all would be ready on Saturday with the arrival of the Guards, when battle would in any case be imminent, given the Jacobites' rate of advance.[64] Despite slight worries over the condition of the troops through lack of straw, Ligonier confided to his Major-General, Jack Roper, that he expected the rebellion to be ended soon.

Cumberland with Skelton's and Bedford's plus the Guards and artillery intended to move up on the 30th to Stafford, where Johnson's, Sempill's and Douglas's were stationed. A few miles to the north, at Stone, another infantry regiment would be located, together with Ligonier's horse.[65] Even though this seemed to provide a credible fighting force all told, Cumberland's army was still widely dispersed. Of the infantry, Howard's was at Tamworth and would not reach Stafford until Sunday, Granby's was in Warwick en route to Walsall, Halifax's in Shrewsbury and Handyside's in Coventry. Kingston's horse was scattered in Cheadle, Uttoxeter and Congleton, Mark Kerr's in Stoke and at Darlaston, and Montagu's in Burton-on-Trent, while Cobham's had only just reached Northampton.[66] Another problem for Cumberland was that his orders to break up the Buxton-Derby road would on his own reckoning force the Jacobites to bend their steps towards North Wales, but Chester which would then be on their itinerary was dangerously exposed. Only Cholmondeley's, Bligh's and Gower's stood between the Jacobites and the town.[67] All in all, Cumberland was now betting heavily on something that was far from certain — that the Jacobites would consent to join battle with him somewhere just to the north of Stafford.

One other possible Jacobite itinerary did not cross Cumberland's mind but was taken very seriously in Yorkshire. This was the idea that Charles Edward might yet cross into Yorkshire to deal first with the threat from Wade.[68] Since a possible route from Lancashire to Yorkshire might lie through Woodhead and over Holm Moss, the local militia pulled up the Holm Causeway. An irruption into Yorkshire seemed even more likely the next day when Jacobite outriders came to Rochdale and the people of Halifax began to fear the worst.[69]

Wade's army was still far away in Piercebridge, despite having encountered fairly good weather.[70] Wade's tripartite division of his forces was into horse, dragoons and infantry. His plan was that the foot should advance through Catterick, Bedale and Boroughbridge so as to arrive in Wetherby on 3rd December. The cavalry should aim to arrive the same day at Tadcaster via Northallerton, Thirsk and York, while the dragoons should proceed no further than Ripley and Knaresborough, pending further orders.[71] It was clear at this stage that the immediate danger to the Jacobites did not come from Wade but from the south.

Saturday 30th November

This Saturday proved an eventful and memorable St. Andrew's Day for all parties in Manchester. Once again, most heavily involved in the day's activities were Walley and Fowden, the constables. Walley was summoned early to the timber yard in order to expedite the dispatch of planks to Crossford to repair the bridge there.[72] He was obliged to authorise payment for the labourers, their drink and equipment (torches, chains, nails, ropes etc) and for others of them to attend the artillery park. Fowden meanwhile was forced to issue orders even more incriminating which later led to his being arraigned on treason charges. These included issuing warrants for forage and horses, ordering all horses sent 'out of town' to be brought back, having bullets made and providing carts for their transport, having a drummer beat up for recruits, and procuring militia weapons for the Highlanders. The most important matter was the casting of some 50,000 bullets for which William Middleton and Thomas Tipping were pressed unwillingly into service.[73] The Scottish leaders, now alive to the evasive tactics of Walley and Fowden, made them take a bible with them so as to swear the persons they approached to obey the Prince's orders (it was a particular cause for animus against the constables later that they had allowed the term 'the Prince' to be used on all their warrants).[74]

Finally, in the afternoon, O'Sullivan summoned Walley and Fowden and asked them to take in hand the billeting arrangements. On Friday the Highlanders had arranged this themselves, with the result that some of the townspeople were inundated with clansmen in their homes while others had none. Walley and Fowden were ordered to work out a system that provided a more equitable distribution among the houses. Fowden then arranged billets in Market Street Lane and King Street, and Walley did the same in Market Square, Ridgefield and Deansgate.[75] The chief driving force and harrier of the recalcitrant constables was David Morgan, who was tireless in using Stuart warrants for requisitioning horses and arms. Morgan's particular target was the JP Robert Dukinfield, who on the Highlanders' arrival had fled the town with a quantity of arms.[76] Morgan persuaded Lord Pitsligo that Dukinfield had a big enough cache of arms to make him a prize worth bringing in, so Pitsligo's horse set off to search for him at his country seat — only to find that he had fled from there as well.

The Prince mounted his horse at noon outside George Fletcher's house and proceeded to ride around Manchester with his bodyguard, in hopes of impressing the people.[77] The incident was described by Miss 'Beppy' Byrom, daughter of the fervent Jacobite John Byrom, whose womenfolk had spent most of Friday night and

Saturday morning making 'St. Andrew's crosses' for the troops: 'We went to Mr. Fletcher's and saw him [the Prince] get a-horseback, and a noble sight it is, I would not have missed it for a great deal of money; his horse had stood an hour in the court without stirring, and as soon as he gat on he began a-dancing and capering as if he was proud of the burden, and when he rid out of the court he was received with as much joy and shouting almost as if he had been king without any dispute.'[78] On his tour of Manchester Charles Edward was easily distinguishable from his officers by having a white rose in the top centre of his bonnet, as opposed to their cockades worn on the side.[79] Though well received and cheered wherever he went, the Prince did not have quite the effect intended by his presence, since by now the two or three hundred recruits were enrolled in the army and no more were forthcoming. And it seems that though the crowd was suitably impressed by the cavalry (not surprisingly, as these were Elcho's blue-uniformed Lifeguards), it was somewhat taken aback by the unprepossessing and slatternly appearance of the infantry, many of whom were described as 'diminutive creatures'.[80]

Charles Edward's most swashbuckling action was to issue a proclamation in which he declared that since the Mersey bridges had been broken down he would repair them, particularly Crossford Bridge, which, however, he did not intend to use. Perhaps, he added, the bridge could be of service to General Wade when he arrived.[81] This proclamation was of a piece with the Jacobite strategy of keeping the enemy guessing and inculcating the idea that after Manchester (to which, on this version, they had only come because of the destruction of bridges further down the Mersey) the army would turn south-west into Wales.[82] Despite the cavalier tone in both this communication and another, about the indefeasible rights of his father James, the Prince had experienced considerable difficulty in having the broadsheets printed. The problem was to find a printer prepared to undertake such 'treasonable' work. As soon as the van arrived in Manchester, an officer had been sent to see the printer Berry but for some reason he was not given the work. The most obvious candidate, Robert Whitworth, a staunch Hanoverian who published the *Manchester Magazine*, had fled the town at the Jacobites' approach. His apprentice Thomas Bradbury was prevailed on to do the work under duress but proceeded so slowly that Captain Thomas Deacon twice went over to hurry him up and on the second occasion took with him a company of armed men who threatened to burn down the printing works if the proclamations were not produced more speedily.[83]

In the afternoon services were held in various churches in Manchester. At one of these, attended by the Byroms, chaplain Shrigley prayed for the 'King and the Prince' but named no names. Coppoch, now Charles Edward's chaplain, preached two sermons this day: one was on the text 'The Lord is King, the Earth may be glad thereof'; the other was on the theme 'Render unto Caesar the things that are Caesar's'.[84] Then, while civilian Jacobites enjoyed viewing the artillery in Camp Field, the army leaders faced the serious business of another plenary Council meeting.

It was at this meeting that the strength of opinion favouring a retreat to Scotland first fully manifested itself. Elcho pointed out that only about two hundred volunteers had been obtained in Manchester out of a total population of 30,000, and this in the town that was supposed to be the most committed Jacobite stronghold in England.[85] Of these recruits, only two were genuine members of the gentry and about twenty were merchants, while the rest, Elcho declared, were derelicts with no means of subsistence; they had indeed told him that they had long since resolved to join the first army to enter town. In general, Elcho opined, Charles Edward was sadly deceived by the bells and the bonfires.[86]

O'Sullivan agreed that retreat was the best course: 'according to all rules of war and prudence it was the only party (*sic*) to be taken'.[87] It was clear that there was no real support for the Prince in England and there was no sign of the French. Charles Edward countered by arguing that the cause of the former was the latter — the only reason for the failure of the English Jacobites to rise hitherto was the non-appearance of the French. However, he had just received a letter from his brother Henry in Paris, stating that a French invasion was a certainty and that a landing on the south coast of England would be made on the 9th of December.[88] At this Lord Nairne spoke in favour of going on, and Morgan, whom the Prince had co-opted onto the Council as an alleged expert on the English Jacobites, urged the chiefs to head for Wales.[89] A compromise route was suggested: the itinerary would be through Stafford, Birmingham, Warwickshire and Oxford to London, so as to tap Jacobite support in Staffordshire and the West Midlands and to sweep up all students at Oxford University who supported the Stuarts. There was the added consideration that if the University students joined in large numbers, their families would be forced to attach themselves also to the Jacobites.[90]

Seeing that the Council was swinging in favour of pushing on southwards, but recognising the strategic uselessness of the alternative itineraries, Lord George Murray intervened and suggested that before coming to a final decision on retreat, the army should march the length of Derbyshire, so as to give more time for the French and the English Jacobites to make a move.[91] This proposal was eagerly seized on by the opposing factions. Before the Council adjourned, however, a decision had to be taken on who should command the new regiment of Manchester volunteers, to be called the 'Manchester regiment'. Elcho sardonically suggested that, given the low calibre of the recruits, Captain Brown, who was used to commanding 'banditti', should be given the post.[92] But it soon became clear that the Manchester recruits wanted nothing to do with the Irish officers Geoghan and Brown. The volunteers at least agreed with Elcho on one point, which he had expressed with some vehemence at this meeting, that the career officers of the king of France risked nothing more than imprisonment if they were taken by the enemy. The Manchester men wanted a more committed figure as their leader. It was d'Eguilles who first suggested Francis Townley as the colonel: in a report to France d'Eguilles described him as follows: 'of all the men who surround the Prince he has the greatest intelligence and prudence'.[93] In the end it was decided to leave the election of a leader to the recruits themselves. At a meeting held by the men later at the Dog inn in Acres Court, the command was at first offered to David Morgan, on the ground of his being a confidant of the Prince. Morgan turned the offer down and suggested that Townley would be more suitable.[94] Townley was accordingly chosen but did not prove a popular choice. James Bradshaw, an important volunteer, immediately quarrelled with him and was transferred to the Lifeguards, while Townley's brusque treatment of Samuel Maddock was eventually to cost him his life.[95]

Despite Elcho's strictures, many of those who enlisted for the Manchester regiment were of high calibre. John Holker was perhaps the best of them and certainly the luckiest.[96] Unlike the others he was not taken prisoner at Carlisle at the end of December 1745 and served until Culloden, when he went on to a glorious future as a captain of industry in France.[97] Another person clearly of high ability was John Sanderson, made captain in the regiment. He was formerly employed as an overseer in the Northumberland coalworks and was in some ways the classically unlucky younger son under primogeniture, since he had no estate of his own whereas his eldest brother had considerable property in the North-East. Sanderson was particularly esteemed by Charles Edward and was often seen in his company. He was described as 'always near the Pretender's person, as much to the fore as the Duke of Perth or any other of the Pretender's great men'.[98]

The other luminaries in the Manchester regiment all suffered execution in 1746 (except for Samuel Maddock who turned King's evidence). Thomas Syddall, barber and peruke maker, had accumulated a fortune of £2,000 and at the age of thirty-six now purchased a commission as an ensign in Captain Thomas Deacon's company. Syddall was described by the same agent who had offered the analysis of Sanderson as 'always at the head of the Pretender's advance guard' and was later much in evidence at Derby.[99] Thomas Deacon himself was the eldest son of the non-juring divine Dr. Thomas Deacon. He sat at the table of the Bull in Manchester, took down the names of enlisters, gave them a shilling, and when not writing employed himself making the white and blue ribbons into favours which he gave to those who joined the Jacobite army.[100] Another interesting recruit was James Dawson, a former student of St. John's College, Cambridge, who was present at the meeting to decide the regimental leadership in the Dog inn and paid £150 for his captain's commission. Afterwards he took his turn at the recruiting table at the Bull's Head.[101] The Rev. Thomas Coppoch (who has already been mentioned) was promised the bishopric of Carlisle in addition to being appointed regimental chaplain.[102] George Fletcher, a linen draper from Salford, was given the rank of captain in the regiment but only after refusing a gift of £1,000 from his mother, who hated the Highlanders, if he would desist from this course.[103] Thomas Deacon's two brothers were also in the regiment, Charles as an ensign and Robert as a lieutenant (of the three brothers only Charles survived the rising).[104]

Other recruits were less impressive. Lieutenant John Berwick, a relative of the Byroms, almost certainly joined through being in debt, while Samuel Maddock, an apprentice to William Pennington in Manchester, was later to save his own skin by testifying against his former comrades.[105] Other names that occur frequently in the records of the Manchester regiment are those of William Brettargh and William Crosby, both later taken in Carlisle.[106] Many of those who enlisted in the regiment were weavers. James Strocking and Peter Morris of Salford were both Dutch loom weavers who joined the Prince and later escaped to Dublin. Two other weavers, Hugh Johnston and Matthew Matthews, only escaped execution later — they were transported instead — through having physical infirmities, Johnston being blind in one eye and Matthews deaf.[107]

Perhaps even more risk was run by those inhabitants of Manchester who did not join the regiment but openly revealed their Jacobitism. Such a man was the barber-surgeon Whitlock, who from 2 p.m. this Saturday was engaged in cutting Charles Edward's printed declarations, still wet from the presses, in two (there were two copies on each sheet) and throwing them out of the window of the Bull's Head to passers by.[108] Later Whitlock was seen helping Jeremy Dawson make up blue and white cockades and taking the names of the enlisted men. It was his large family that prevented him from marching on to Derby with the Jacobites.

The atmosphere in Manchester on this Saturday evening was very like that of the night before, with Jacobite optimism, euphoria and good spirits everywhere evident.[109] Charles Edward held a reception in his headquarters to which the principal Manchester Jacobites were invited, the Byroms, Dickensons, Deacons, the Revs. Clayton and Catell and others.[110] This was after the Prince had given a private supper party, of which we know only that the Welsh Jacobites Morgan and Vaughan dined with John Murray of Broughton. Lord Elcho meanwhile invited his entire body of Lifeguards to sup with him in honour of St. Andrew's Day and a toast was drunk to all their friends in Scotland.[111]

Apart from the public money collected, some £300 had been subscribed in Manchester by private 'donations'. A favourite Jacobite ploy was to force those who had subscribed to the associations for the defence of George II to contribute an equal amount to Charles Edward. Mr. Robert Jebb, who had subscribed £10 to George II, was brought from his house under armed guard at 11 p.m. and taken to the Prince's quarters at John Dickenson's house, where an equal amount was demanded for the Jacobite cause.[112] He produced £4-15-0 but the clansmen wanted more, referring to his reputed fortune of £10,000. He was only able to make good his retreat to his own house when John Dickenson accepted his promissory note and paid the remaining five guineas for him.

While these preparations went on in Manchester, parties were despatched thence in all directions for a variety of purposes: to collect the public money, beat up for recruits, commandeer horses and weapons, order billets, reconnoitre enemy movements, or simply to confuse Cumberland. One large party of two hundred or more visited Altrincham; fifty-five men went out to Cheadle via Gatley Ford and returned to Manchester by Cheadle Ford; ten riders came to Stockport and announced the imminent arrival of the army.[113] A small party even pressed on as far as Macclesfield, where leaflets were distributed at the Market Cross. A speech was delivered to the crowd, promising religious toleration and liberty in the event of a Stuart restoration, but this was not well received and the Highlanders, meeting no encouragement in their efforts to recruit for the Jacobite cause, returned northwards.[114]

Shortly afterwards, a company of Cumberland's Royal Dragoons entered Macclesfield and sent a Macclesfield man, Samson Salt, to get intelligence of the Scots. Salt's adventures thereafter were of the 'stranger than fiction' kind. First he was captured by a Jacobite patrol but managed to escape. Then he made his way to

Cumberland at Stone only to be imprisoned on suspicion of being a Jacobite spy. No sooner had he cleared himself and got back to Macclesfield on Sunday (1 December) than he heard of Charles Edward's approach. This news finally precipitated a heart attack.[115]

Most of the activity of the Highland patrols on this Saturday, however, took place north of Manchester. Twenty-three cavalrymen rode into Rochdale, having travelled the very good road from Manchester, and stayed three hours, where they recruited Valentine Holt, later hanged at Penrith.[116] Apart from the £15-7-2 in public money collected from the brewers and victuallers, the main objective here was weapons. The constables were compelled to hand over all arms previously earmarked for the Lancashire militia.[117] In general the burghers of Rochdale had little reason to complain of this visit. The Highlanders behaved well and did not plunder, and so scrupulous was their conduct that when one of the cavalrymen appropriated a horse, its owner was able to regain it by application to the officer in charge of the patrol. The principal consequence of the Highlanders' sojourn in Rochdale was indirect. News of their presence there caused the inhabitants of York to conclude that Charles Edward had at last responded to the entreaties of Yorkshire Jacobites to bend his line of march into their county.[118] Messengers were immediately sent out from Doncaster to Rochdale to learn the further Jacobite intentions.[119] The principal worry was the wool and cloth trade. Manchester lay in a line of traffic and trade that ran through Oldham, Ashton-under-Lyne and Rochdale to the clothing towns of Bradford, Leeds, Wakefield, Huddersfield and Halifax, and was thus directly linked with the Yorkshire wool merchants. Clothiers in Yorkshire had already commenced special journeys to the Lancashire border to bring away their cloth so as to prevent its being despoiled or stolen by looting 'rebels', and similar measures were on foot in Huddersfield, thought to be the likely first target for the Jacobites if they moved into Yorkshire.[120]

The party that had reached Oldham on Friday stayed there overnight and was joined by other patrols next day. Among the new arrivals was the giant Andrew Hay, who was seen in company with the Oldham Jacobite John Whitehead.[121] Oldham seemed disposed to favour the Jacobites. A Mr. Ogdon, who kept a warehouse in Manchester and a private residence in Oldham, was invaluable in showing the Scots the lie of the land in this town.[122] Even more overtly pro-Stuart was Joshua Winterbotham, who handed over the militia weapons to the clansmen and was seen to drink with them as they were drawn up outside Mr. Ogdon's house, openly to rejoice at their coming, and, a little later, to sing 'My Bonny Highland Laddie'.[123]

Other groups of Highlanders were seen at Mottram and Saddleworth, Lees, Crossbank and Hey. An altercation was reported from Lees concerning the driving off by the locals of their cattle and horses.[124] The patrol in Hey made a brief stop at The Grapes before an overnight stay at Taylor Green (Crossbank), seat of the staunchly pro-Stuart Mayall family, who provided hospitality that night and guides through the confusing lanes next morning. A large party was also in Ashton-under-Lyne from about 4.30 a.m. on Saturday.[125] In the teeth of driving rain, foragers from this group searched Lime Ditch Farm and Street Farm near the Woodhouses border. At the first of these they were met with some initial resistance from the pitchfork-wielding farmer and his sons, but at Street Farm they did better and uncovered a quantity of malt hidden away by the old mistress.[126] In Ashton itself the Highlanders' searches were mainly directed by the local labourer John Appleton. As a result Thomas Worthington was summoned to attend the Scots at the house of Mrs. Finlow (who kept the Excise office) and ordered to convoke all excise payers in town.[127] Like the Manchester constables, Worthington feigned physical disability — this time the excuse was lameness — but was ordered to sit down in Mrs. Finlow's while the Highlanders collected the excise (they took up £26-3-1).

Appleton demonstrated further (and perhaps excessive) Jacobite zeal in the hunt for horses. Joseph Wardle, a servant of the local squire, was reduced to tears by Appleton when the latter threatened to shoot him for denying knowledge of the whereabouts of his master's colt. This so enraged Appleton that he then threatened in turn to shoot Wardle for his tears. Matters threatened to escalate when Henry Andrew, a local collier, called out: 'Damn thee Appleton and God bless King George'.[128] This now brought him a threat of death from Appleton, and the clansmen, enraged by the reference to the 'Elector of Hanover', also drew their swords. Only the intervention of their commanding officer prevented the clansmen from dispensing an immediate rough justice. Back in Manchester at the Sign of Seven Stars inn, Appleton revealed the fundamental pragmatism behind his apparent fanaticism.[129] To a group of Scots he revealed that his father had been dispossessed by the Whigs of estates which he, the son, was now trying to regain. At the same time he hedged his bets with the Ashton populace by telling them that he had diverted the Highlanders from their horses' hiding places purely through friendship for his fellow-citizens.

More serious issues were being discussed at Cumberland's headquarters in Staffordshire, where the Duke still could not decide what the Jacobite objective was. The apparent importance attached to the repair of Crossford Bridge, on the way to Sale, Altrincham, Knutsford and the west, rather than the route through Stockport or Cheadle to Derby and London completely deceived the Whigs, though more sagacious leaders might have wondered whether the Jacobites, in so frequently giving it out that they were bound by Crossford Bridge, were not really headed elsewhere. Further confirmation that the Jacobites' destination lay in the west seemed to come from a report that a party of them was at Warrington; this tended to suggest that the movement towards Manchester was either a feint pure and simple or a recruiting diversion.[130] Cumberland, to be sure, continued to feel intuitively that the Jacobites would try to give him the slip by a forced march through Derbyshire and Nottinghamshire, but also thought that they could be prevented from implementing this plan if the necessary roads were broken up.[131] By now Devonshire had confirmed to him that the turnpike between Whaley Bridge and Buxton through Chapel-en-le-Frith was completely destroyed, and this led Devonshire to conjecture that the Jacobites might respond to this with an attempt to get into Nottinghamshire by way of Woodhead (in northern Derbyshire) and Sheffield.[132] Cumberland's main reason for considering that in principle the Jacobites favoured the Derbyshire/Nottinghamshire route was that he imagined they would not want to face his army, though in truth his own military plans were not working out as well as he had hoped. The new regiments which joined him this Saturday were virtually useless for combat and the Duke of Bedford's regiment, which arrived this day in Lichfield, was a particular disappointment. Besides, as the Duke of Richmond pointed out to Newcastle: 'We are not all yet so cleverly together as I could wish . . . there is a great distance between this and our avant porte (*sic*) which is now at Congleton, above forty miles off.'[133]

Undoubtedly Richmond's was the best military mind on Cumberland's staff. As he analysed it, there were five options open to the Jacobites in descending order of advantage to the Whigs. These were: to engage Cumberland's army when it was united; to march into Derbyshire — which would enable the Duke to intercept them by the good southern road to Derbyshire and Nottinghamshire while they laboured over the turnpikes that Devonshire had broken up, and thus sandwich them between his own army and Wade's; to march to Chester and lay siege to it; to proceed into North Wales without attacking Chester — which would mean that Cumberland could not overtake them; and, the worst possibility of all for the Whigs, to retreat to Scotland.[134]

Scotland was now once more beginning to worry Newcastle too. He was particularly apprehensive about the second army forming there for Charles Edward. It was imperative for Cumberland to defeat the 'Young Pretender' so that Wade could proceed north to deal with this second force in Scotland.[135] Since the aim of the Jacobites must logically be London, Newcastle cautioned Cumberland against complacency and particularly about thinking that the enemy would necessarily be deterred by the destruction of the roads in Derbyshire. At all costs, he wrote to Cumberland, you must always be between the enemy and London.

The legendary ambiguity and ambivalence of Newcastle nowhere showed itself more clearly than in his correspondence on this day, for having delivered this dour lesson to Cumberland, almost in the same breath he wrote to Chesterfield: 'nothing material has happened . . . in our interior affairs' and went on to talk entirely about Pitt, Bedford, Gower and London politics.[136] No such ambiguity characterised his brother Henry Pelham, whose letter to Lord Irwin this Saturday contained a distinct note of real apprehension and amazement at the progress of the 'rebels'.[137]

The only incident in the campaign on St. Andrew's Day completely unaffected by developments in Manchester was at Carlisle. In reprisal for the Lowther Hall incident the Jacobite garrison in Carlisle carried off the principal gentlemen in the town and kept them prisoner overnight in the castle, only releasing them next day on their parole not to serve in *any* capacity against any member of the garrison.[138]

Sunday 1st December

The main aim of the Jacobite leaders this morning was to conceal their true destination, Macclesfield. Accordingly, several different detachments were sent by different routes to the west, while the main body prepared to cross the Mersey at Stockport. To confuse the issue still further John Hay of Restalrig summoned

Walley and demanded a guide to take the Jacobites over Barlow Ford to Altrincham.[139] The constables were also commanded to have another 50,000 bullets made and sent on after the army.[140]

The troops began marching out of Manchester at 4 a.m. and the last of the infantry left around 10.30 a.m. Charles Edward himself was seen departing up Market Street Lane at about 6 a.m.[141] The main army crossed the river at Stockport, then a pretty market town noted for its trade in thread-buttons;[142] the Prince was observed fording the river here at about 3 p.m. with water up to his middle and 'looking very dejected'.[143] The artillery and baggage pursued a different route, via Didsbury and Cheadle. The road to Didsbury lay through Jacobite country, past Slade Hall, Heaton Wood (owned by the Fletchers) and by Syddall's house.[144] Then the route lay directly down Didsbury High Street and through the marshes to Gatley Ford, where a bridge was built. Poplar trees were felled and dragged down to the river. Other trees were laid on top of them and planks fastened across, the interstices being filled with sods and clay.[145] All local carts and horses were requisitioned, but even with Pitsligo's hard driving the bridge was not ready to take artillery and baggage until about 3 p.m. Even so, the delicate operation of getting these items safely into Cheshire was not over. The dangers and difficulties of getting the baggage waggons down the swampy lane to Gatley Ford and up again on the other side of the river were as great as those involved in the actual passage by the ford, and a sudden storm could well have swept everything away.[146] Pitsligo's operation, conducted with just fifty-five men, was a considerable triumph. It was no wonder that his men were described as crossing the Mersey 'with as much eagerness as a dog after a duck but with less concern' and that when they emerged from the river they walked on again 'at a prodigious rate', obviously proud of their pontoon engineering feat.[147]

The advance guard of Charles Edward's main column began to enter Macclesfield just after 10 a.m.[148] The army's route into the town took it through low-lying ground by Woodford and Prestbury close to Lyme, the seat of the leading Cheshire Tory Peter Legh. A faint attempt had been made by the more adventurous Tory squires of Cheshire to raise the Stuart standard, but at a meeting of the revived Cheshire Club in Lyme, Legh cast the decisive vote against any pro-Jacobite actions being taken.[149] So there was little encouragement from the day's march to set against the evident hostility of the people of Macclesfield.

Most of the citizens of Macclesfield were at church when news of the clansmen's approach was received. Hearing the tidings, Cumberland's dragoons made off at full speed, not even tarrying to finish the breakfast they were taking with the Mayoress. On hearing the hallooing and general uproar the people in church ran out before the service was over to view the 'Young Pretender' and his men.[150] The first to enter were twenty or so quartermasters who rode to the Market Cross and enquired for the constables. Next they located Sir Peter Davenport's house, looked it over and placed a sign on it which said 'Prince'.[151] About noon a regiment of horse came in. Mayor Thomas Cooper was forced to attend with his officers and the other aldermen at Market Cross to proclaim King James.[152] There they received orders to illuminate the town on pain of military execution. The Mayor went through the motions of raising a cheer but the true feeling of Macclesfield was revealed a little later when the bells were rung backwards by five confused bellringers.

After five regiments had entered the town, the Prince himself finally arrived on foot, in Highland dress and with a bodyguard of some forty men.[153] His secretary John Murray immediately placed the unfortunate Samuel Salt under close guard and ordered that at 4 p.m. on Monday three guides and fifty pioneers with spades and pickaxes were to be delivered over by the townspeople to work under the direction of the captain of the artillery park.[154] The appearance of the Scots seemed no more prepossessing to the people here than elsewhere. The numbers of old men and boys armed with knives (to hamstring the Hanoverian cavalry) were remarked on, and the sight of old Glenbucket bent almost double on horseback did not help to improve the image of the army. Dusk had long fallen before the artillery came in, and though it was difficult to estimate numbers in the dark, the men of Macclesfield figured that there were at most 6,000 Scots in the town. As soon as all forces scheduled to do so had arrived this Sunday night, and all arrangements in Sir Peter Davenport's house were completed to the Prince's satisfaction, it was decided to hold another Council meeting next day as soon as the diversionary forces, such as Elcho's, had come in.[155]

The remaining Jacobite fighting men, all of whom had left Manchester by 12.30 at the latest (except one hundred men in the rearguard), were occupied in camouflage tactics to mask the march on Macclesfield. Elcho's Lifeguards and the Manchester regiment made a very early start for the newly repaired Crossford Bridge.[156] The Manchester regiment was drawn up in St. Ann's Square, where Dr. Deacon came to give his son a farewell blessing before he moved out.[157] Then, following Elcho's, the Manchester men marched up Deansgate through Stretford and over the new Crossford Bridge to Altrincham. On the way they passed through Sale Moor and appropriated the Rector of Sale's horses which were grazing there.[158] The snow lay thick on the ground as the Jacobites entered Altrincham at daybreak. Quarters were ordered for 10,000 men and the excise demanded.[159] Refreshment was taken at the Red Lion inn and one man in Well Lane (now Victoria Street) was deprived of his shoes. Both Elcho's and the Manchester regiment then pushed on to Wilmslow, where they spent the night.[160]

Two smaller parties departed from Manchester in a south-westerly direction as part of the general smokescreen. One of these camped out at night at Chorlton while the other crossed the Mersey at Barlow Ford.[161] It was a party from one of these groups that rode through Knutsford and frightened the congregation as it emerged from Sunday service.[162] Elcho had originally intended to include Knutsford on his route but changed his mind when he heard that 2,000 of Cumberland's men were there. Nevertheless, Knutsford did furnish one recruit: John Cupid crossed over to Wilmslow to see his friend Captain Moss and was persuaded to go with the Manchester regiment on being provided with a horse.[163] Smaller parties also called at Nantwich, Middlewich and Northwich and the first shots fired in this campaign between Cumberland's men and Charles Edward's were exchanged as a result, when two of the Duke of Kingston's advance party came within musket range of the

Jacobites. After a quick fusillade Kingston's men made off with the important news of an apparently imminent engagement with the enemy.[164]

Cumberland, who this Sunday moved his headquarters from Michael Rawlins's house in Lichfield up to Stafford,[165] seemed bemused by the conflicting intelligence coming in from Altrincham, Knutsford and Stockport, which indicated no very clear intention on the part of the Jacobites. The odds still seemed to be on a movement west to Chester or North Wales, but Derby was still a possible destination for the Scots, since thereby they could avoid combat both with Cumberland's and Wade's army.[166] However, Cumberland was still obsessed with the idea that a march to Derby could only take place via Buxton, using the turnpike between Manchester and the Peak district constructed in 1725.[167] Since this was now broken up, the westerly route seemed much the more likely. Only Lord Derby pointed out at this stage that the Jacobites could easily move down through Derbyshire by other routes.[168]

In London all intelligence inclined towards a march on the capital, which Lord Chancellor Hardwicke described as 'a very extravagant and desperate scheme', although here too the obsession with an itinerary via Buxton could be discerned.[169] Insofar as an alternative scenario was entertained, it was thought that the destruction of the Buxton turnpike might force the Jacobites to proceed via Sheffield and onto the Great North Road before turning south for London. On Tuesday 3rd December Newcastle wrote to Cumberland: 'I have had several very positive accounts that they were actually on Saturday last at Sheffield and the whole country believed it so much that the Duke and Duchess of Norfolk and some of the gentlemen of Nottinghamshire have left the county upon it.'[170] The source of this belief undoubtedly lay in the strong rumour that the Highlanders were marching from Manchester to Sheffield.[171] This in turn originated in the story that two Highland officers had entered Sheffield on Friday the 29th and ordered billets for the army. It turned out that the two 'Highland officers' were Scottish merchants in trade at Liverpool, who had been dealing with Wade's army and were actually en route to Cumberland's HQ.[172] Such was the panic caused by the appearance of these two harmless Scots in Sheffield that the wildest rumours were engendered. One canard was to the effect that Lord Ogilvy and Elcho had quit the Jacobite army and fled to Sheffield in disguise.[173] Even more confusion was caused by a quite separate rumour that the Jacobite van was at Sheffield. The inhabitants were reported in great confusion, removing their effects from the town since 'Highland drums had been heard coming over the moors'.[174] Another report said that Jacobite outriders had actually reached Sheffield and that another five hundred would be appearing there that night (Sunday). This in turn led to the gloss on Jacobite intentions that they would proceed via Sheffield and Chesterfield to Worksop and thence to the Newark road, getting clear of the Hanoverian armies, before striking south.[175]

Newcastle spent long hours this Sunday at home in conclave with his brother Henry Pelham.[176] One of the subjects they discussed was a possible fifth column in the south of England. There were fears that the workers in the dockyards were crypto-Jacobites and would support the threatened French invasion by setting fire to the dock stores.[177] Newcastle issued instructions to the governor of Portsmouth to be particularly on his guard against this. The other problem was Wade, whose tardiness was now provoking open criticism — as for instance from Chancellor Hardwicke's son Joseph.[178] Newcastle sent a sharply worded reminder to Wade that speed was essential since the Highlanders' intention now clearly seemed to be to press on to London by forced marches.[179]

Meanwhile in the far north the Mayor of Whitehaven, Walter Luttridge, emboldened by the events at Lowther Hall, called on the Lowthers to take some action against the garrison at Carlisle. He suggested the use of troops from either Ireland or Edinburgh in conjunction with the heavy cannon in Whitehaven.[180]

NOTES

1. Bailey (both articles); Harrison p. 112.
2. Elcho p.330; Maxwell of Kirkconnell p. 70.
3. SP Dom 97 f. 146.
4. Gordon & Arnot, ii. p. 17.
5. SP Dom 75/51.
6. Elcho p. 330.
7. SP Dom 81 ff. 167–68; 319–20.
8. Rose pp. 102–03.
9. Lunn, *Leigh* p. 60.
10. SP Dom 75/58.
11. Talon p. 227.
12. Ibid. p. 228.
13. HMC, Various Colls, viii. p. 134.
14. SP Dom 75/58.
15. Chambers, 'Marches' p. 185.
16. Earwaker (1889) p. 150.
17. Bailey p. 159.
18. Lord Gower to Chetwynd, 16 November 1745, Staffs CRO, SMS 520; Jarvis i. p. 246; Jarvis (1941) p. 145.
19. *London Magazine* 1745 p. 607.
20. Beaumont, loc. cit p. 190.
21. Ibid. p. 199.
22. *General Evening Post* No. 1902, 3–5 December 1745.
23. SP Dom 75/127.
24. Stuart MSS. 271/111–114.
25. Stuart MSS. 272/23.
26. SP Dom 75/31, 64, 65.
27. SP Dom 75/53.
28. SP Dom 75/52.
29. HMC, 10, i. p. 288.
30. Whitworth p. 111.
31. HMC, 10, i. p. 287.
32. Ibid.
33. SP Dom 75/57; 81 ff. 167–68; *Ogilvy's Orderbook* p. 298.
34. HMC, Portland, vi. p. 191.
35. SP Dom 70/88; 71/28; Williamson p. 37.
36. SP Dom 81 ff. 159–60.
37. Mumford pp. 6–7.

38. Ibid. p. 161.
39. Jarvis i. p. 21.
40. Chambers, 'Marches' p. 186.
41. SP Dom 82 ff. 62–68.
42. Add. MSS. 35886 f. 100.
43. Add. MSS. 35886 f. 82.
44. Talon pp. 230–44.
45. Earwaker (1889) pp. 151–55.
46. Jarvis ii. pp. 237–54.
47. SP Dom 97/143.
48. Talon pp. 243–44.
49. HMC, 14, iv. p. 478 et seq.
50. SP Dom 81 ff. 168–69.
51. SP Dom 82 f. 70.
52. SP Dom 81 ff. 156–57.
53. HMC, 14, iv. p. 478; Earwaker (1889); Jarvis ii. pp. 237–54.
54. SP Dom 81 f. 321.
55. *Palatine Notebook,* iv. p. 20.
56. SP Dom 81 f. 311; 82 f. 10, 31.
57. Hartley & Bateson pp. 60–64.
58. MacDonald, *Hopwood Hall* p. 28.
59. SP Dom 76/20.
60. Williamson pp. 62–63.
61. *London Magazine* 1745 p. 608; Marchant pp. 190–91.
62. HMC, 10, i. pp. 439–40.
63. SP Dom 75/58; Add.MSS. 32705 f. 395.
64. HMC, 10, i. pp. 288, 440.
65. SP Dom 75/57.
66. Ibid.
67. Staffs CRO D.1413/1.
68. 'Two Yorkshire Diaries' p. 109.
69. Jarvis (1941) p. 147.
70. Ray p. 139.
71. HMC, Laing ii. pp. 354–55.
72. Jarvis ii. pp. 237–54.
73. SP Dom 97 f. 143.
74. Fitzherbert MSS.
75. Earwaker, *Constables' Accounts* iii. p. 21.
76. Allardyce, ii. p. 448.
77. HMC, II p. 287.
78. Talon pp. 230–31.
79. SP Dom 81 ff. 157–58; Boyse p. 103.
80. SP Dom 75/75.
81. Chambers p. 187; *Ogilvy's Orderbook* p. 300.
82. Jarvis i. pp. 86–89.
83. *Palatine Notebook* iv. pp. 71–72.
84. Elcho p. 331; *London Magazine* 1746 p. 477; Gordon & Arnot ii. pp. 128–30.
85. Elcho p. 331; Chevalier de Johnstone p. 66.
86. Elcho p. 332.
87. O'Sullivan p.99.
88. Ewald i. pp. 278–79.
89. Williamson pp. 64–65.
90. Howell, *State Trials* 18, pp. 375–77.
91. Chambers, 'Marches' pp. 52–53.

92. Elcho p. 333.
93. *Revue Retrospective* p. 124.
94. *Gentlemen's Magazine* 1746 p. 399.
95. Gordon & Arnot ii. pp. 46–47.
96. *Palatine Notebook* ii. pp. 48–49, 111–16.
97. Remond, *John Holker.*
98. SP Dom 81 ff. 165–66.
99. SP Dom 81 ff. 164–65.
100. Gordon & Arnot ii. pp. 150–51.
101. Stott (1929) pp. 5–8.
102. Barnes p. 75; Gordon & Arnot ii. pp. 128–30.
103. *Gentlemen's Magazine* 1746 p. 398; *British Magazine* 1746 p. 230; *Manchester Magazine* 26 August 1746.
104. SP Dom 77/126; Gordon & Arnot ii. pp. 148–49.
105. Add. MSS. 35886 f. 68; Howell, *State Trials,* 18 p. 370.
106. *Palatine Notebook* ii. p. 18; iii. p. 245; iv. p. 19.
107. Gordon & Arnot ii. p. 234.
108. SP Dom 82 ff. 97–98.
109. SP Dom 81 ff. 210–12.
110. SP Dom 80 ff. 226–28.
111. SP Dom 76/56.
112. SP Dom 81 ff. 158–59.
113. Hibbert-Ware ii. p. 104.
114. Davies p. 107.
115. Ibid. p. 111.
116. Fishwick, *Rochdale* pp. 57–58.
117. Mattley p. 6.
118. Ray pp. 134–35.
119. Tomlinson p. 230.
120. Bowman p. 270; 'Two Yorkshire Diaries' pp. 110–11.
121. SP Dom 82 f. 53.
122. SP Dom 97 f. 145.
123. SP Dom 81 f. 297; 82 f. 54; 82 f. 244.
124. Bowman p. 271.
125. SP Dom 81 ff. 180–81.
126. Bowman p. 272.
127. SP Dom 81 ff. 180–81.
128. SP Dom 81 ff. 208–09.
129. SP Dom 81 ff. 187–88.
130. Harris, *Hardwicke* ii. p. 197.
131. SP Dom 75/75.
132. SP Dom 75/73.
133. Richmond to Newcastle, 30 November 1745, Add. MSS. 32705 f. 400.
134. Ibid.
135. SP Dom 76/2.
136. Add. MSS. 32705 f. 393.
137. HMC, Various Colls, viii. p. 134.
138. Add. MSS. 35889 f. 59.
139. *Palatine Notebook* ii. p. 155.
140. HMC, 13 vi. p. 166.
141. Add. MSS. 35889 f. 57.
142. HMC, Portland vi. p. 191.
143. Hibbert-Ware ii. p.105.
144. Moss pp. 74–75; Registers of Church of St. James, Didsbury, i. Pt. 2. p. 38.

145. SP Dom 76/20.
146. Moss p. 77; Shercliff p. 133.
147. HMC, 13 vi. p. 163.
148. Davies pp. 107–08.
149. Newton pp. 388–89.
150. Staffs CRO SMS 49/53/44; Davies pp. 107–08.
151. Richards p. 111; Coward pp. 364–65.
152. Davies p. 108.
153. HMC, Various Colls, viii. pp. 136–37.
154. Davies p. 111.
155. Chambers p. 188.
156. Lloyd pp. 62–63.
157. Stott (1924) p. 2.
158. Ingham p. 138.
159. Ibid; Jarvis ii. p. 35.
160. Elcho p. 334; Howell, *State Trials*, 18 pp. 335, 338, 360–61.
161. Lloyd pp. 62–63.
162. Green p. 69.
163. SP Dom 82 f. 173.
164. SP Dom 76/20.
165. Shaw i. p. 321.
166. Add. MSS. 32705 f. 401.
167. Bailey, loc. cit.
168. SP Dom 76/28.
169. Yorke i. p. 472.
170. SP Dom 76/28.
171. HMC, Various Colls, viii. p. 137.
172. SP Dom 76/8.
173. *Birmingham Gazette* 9 December 1745.
174. SP Dom 76/13.
175. SP Dom 76/13, 17.
176. Bradstreet p. 116.
177. SP Dom 76/1.
178. Yorke i. p. 472.
179. SP Dom 75/72.
180. HMC, 13, vii. p. 126.

6

Decision at Derby

WELL before dawn Elcho's Lifeguards and the Manchester regiment arrived at Macclesfield, having travelled from Wilmslow over Alderley Edge and through Prestbury.[1] So good was their intelligence on likely sources of arms on this route that when they called at the house of Colonel Lee at Adlington they were able to mention the exact place in his home where a store of muskets and pistols could be found. Only two casualties had been sustained on the way from Manchester, two of Elcho's having been wounded by civilian sniper fire near Hale.[2]

The Manchester regiment was now drawn up in Macclesfield churchyard, and weapons were distributed to those who were poorly or inadequately armed.[3] A few men, among them Thomas Deacon, were immediately told off to form part of the scouting party that would set off shortly for Derby.[4] But if Deacon set off with a will, elsewhere in the Manchester regiment morale had suffered in the twenty-four hours since leaving Manchester. Samuel Maddock was dispirited both by the lack of zeal shown by citizens encountered on the march from Manchester and by the apparently chaotic disposition of the Jacobite forces in Macclesfield; as a result he announced his intention to quit the regiment. At this Francis Townley flew into a rage and threatened to knock his brains out. Maddock then confided to Fletcher that since he was not allowed to leave freely, he would desert. Fletcher, fearing the effect such a desertion would have on the morale of the other members of the regiment, offered him a bribe to stay on.[5] Thus placated, Maddock remained, but he bore a profound grudge thereafter against Townley, which he was to indulge in deadly fashion at the treason trials in 1746.

On the other hand Dan Cupid, the friend of Captain Moss, was given every encouragement to remain with the army. On arrival in Macclesfield he was introduced to the Prince, given a glass of wine by the Duke of Perth, and then spent an hour in their company while Highland officers pored over detailed road maps.[6] Cupid offered to join the ranks of the Manchester regiment but was informed that he was destined for a better post, so stayed with the army until Tuesday morning. Another band of volunteers to arrive was Edward Graves and his friends from Newark, who had left their horses behind at Chapel-en-le-Frith and proceeded on foot to Macclesfield where they arrived at 4 a.m.[7] This coterie was not able later to use the excuse of being pressed, as argued by another man seen this day in the Highland ranks, Alexander Love. At his investigation in 1746 Love claimed that he had been pressed at Carlisle to attend the Jacobite baggage, though witnesses testified that he was under no constraint at Macclesfield and so could have deserted.[8]

With the arrival of Elcho and Townley, the urgent business of the Council could be attended to. The question of Wales was once more raised at the Council, but this time a novel argument was adduced to quash the suggestion — namely, that Wales was so mountainous that an itinerary from Macclesfield to there was impracticable.[9] A firm decision was taken that there must be no swerving from the objective of London and that the aim of the army should be to get between Cumberland's army and the capital.[10] Marching orders for Leek and Ashbourne had already been issued when Colonel Ker of Graden, who had been on a scouting mission in the west, arrived with news that Cumberland's forces were cantoned in such a way that they could move to intercept the Jacobites whichever direction they took, whether to Wales or Derby.[11] At this Lord George Murray suggested that the only way to force Cumberland to commit himself was to make a feinting movement in strength towards the west, so as to convince the Hanoverian commander that Wales was the objective.[12] Accordingly it was decided that Murray should move towards Congleton with about half the army while the Prince and the rest remained in Macclesfield for the day to await the outcome of the manoeuvre.[13]

While Lord George Murray's column moved out westwards, the rest of the army remained in Macclesfield, in expectation of an imminent encounter.[14] Monday was spent scaling, firing, and putting in order all musket pieces and in repairing the road about five miles out towards Leek, which was not in a fit state to take the artillery.[15] The sullen and hostile attitude of the people of Macclesfield, large numbers of whom had by now absconded from the town, was still remarked on.[16] The atmosphere is well conveyed in the diary of Mr. John Stafford, a Macclesfield lawyer, who had several officers billeted on him at his house on the corner of Jordangate and Cumberland Street. On visiting the quarters of the ordinary soldiers on Monday morning he found fifty men, women and boys lying on straw in his barn 'like a kennel of hounds, some of 'em stark naked'.[17] When Stafford heard that the Jacobites were to stay another day in town, he was so apprehensive about the prospect of fighting between the Highlanders and the townspeople that he took his wife and some other ladies to the house of a friend in the country.

The hapless Mayor of Macclesfield was commanded by royal Stuart decree to have a quantity of bread ready in every house, to be delivered up that night under pain of military execution.[18] As for the official bakers, they were warned through the constables that if they procrastinated in the fulfilment of these orders for bread, they would have their houses burned down around them. All provisions in Macclesfield and environs — bread, corn, hay and other edibles — were swept up in a vast commissariat drive, in which the Leghs of Adlington particularly suffered through being entirely denuded of hay and corn by foraging parties.[19]

Lord George Murray's column — consisting of Elcho's Lifeguards, Kilmarnock's horse and the Atholl brigade, a total force of about 1,200 men — were reported passing through Gawsforth at about 10 a.m. and arrived at Congleton between three and four in the afternoon.[20] The Duke of Kingston had been there but half an hour before. On hearing of the Highlanders' approach he fled precipitately, leaving a dinner on the table of his quarters which Lord George Murray enjoyed.[21] In Congleton the Scots immediately announced that their prince would join them that night, proclaimed King James, and ordered billets, food and arms. Little support was forthcoming, for though Congleton had been 'disaffected' at the time of George I's accession in 1714, it was now strongly pro-Hanoverian, and in October the town council had contributed ten guineas towards the cost of raising and paying the soldiers at Chester 'for the defence of His Majesty and his government'.[22] The townspeople took careful note of any distinctive Jacobite officers, and this evidence was later used against them: one was George Lockhart, described as 'brandishing a broadsword';[23] another was Major Nairne of Aldie.[24] Any other activity by the burghers would be fraught with danger. An Astbury schoolmaster named Bullen happened to pick up a manifesto distributed by Murray's men at Congleton, and when it was later found in his rooms he was lodged in Stafford gaol as a Jacobite agent.[25]

Hearing of Kingston's rapid departure, Murray decided to send a patrol of some fifty men towards Newcastle (under-Lyme) with orders to proceed as far as Astbury and gather the most precise intelligence about Cumberland.[26] This mixed detachment of foot and horse commanded by Kilmarnock, with Ker of Graden as his deputy, came within an ace of capturing a large party of dragoons at the Red Lion in Talke, six miles north of Newcastle, and would have done so if the infantry had been sent into the village ahead of the horsemen.[27] As it was, the dragoons were alerted by the clatter of horses' hoofs and fled in panic, some hurling themselves through windows to escape. Even so, Cumberland's top agent, Vere, was captured. Vere had been tracking the Jacobite army for some time, keeping within ten miles of it and sending back highly accurate information. Now, brought before Murray at Congleton, he provided the intelligence that Cumberland's cavalry and two regiments of foot were at Newcastle and the bulk of the army with Cumberland at Stafford.[28] According to Vere, the forces at the Duke's disposal totalled 8,250 foot and 2,200 foot.

Murray realised the importance of his catch and had him escorted back to Macclesfield under the personal supervision of Kilmarnock. On arrival the latter advised the Prince to hang him forthwith and bluntly informed Vere that he must prepare to die immediately.[29] Vere attempted to bluster and said that if so much as a hair of his head was hurt, all the friends of those responsible for the injury presently held in government gaols would be executed in reprisal. This served only to enrage the clan leaders further, and the Scots to a man clamoured for the noose.[30] This was opposed by Sheridan and the Irish, and their views prevailed with the Prince — a piece of misguided clemency since Vere's testimony was later to send many a Jacobite to the gallows. Among his interrogators Vere was able to identify Donald Cameron of Lochiel and John Murray of Broughton.[31] When reprieved by Charles Edward, Vere simply took to circumspect intelligence gathering, so that he was later able to testify to having seen John Hay of Restalrig at Peter Davenport's house on the morning of Tuesday the 3rd.[32]

At Cumberland's HQ, Lord George Murray's feint succeeded perfectly in its aim. The Duke of Richmond inferred from this movement and another reported at Leek (in reality the advance scouting party headed for Derby) that the Jacobite intention was to cut off Cumberland's artillery and the three artillery battalions at Stone from the rest of the army. The enemy could not, he thought, be advancing to offer battle at Newcastle since 'there is not one spot of ground except just out of the town, where a squadron can be drawn up between this [Newcastle] and Congleton, the whole country being nothing but small enclosures, very deep and all the lanes narrow "defiles" '.[33]

For once Richmond's acumen had failed him, and the man who read the situation correctly was Cumberland's secretary Sir Everard Fawkener. He still maintained that Cumberland should keep a sizeable force at Lichfield to intercept any movement towards Derby; he took it for granted that the road from Buxton to Derby was impassable, since 'it is so broke that a large number of hands could not in two days render it practicable'.[34] True, all the reports of a large number of Highlanders going by Broken Cross to the west and south-west of Macclesfield, seemingly bound for Nantwich and Wales, seemed to show that this was indeed the itinerary, but Fawkener maintained that this contingency was catered for by existing dispositions: 'If they go to Wales they must pass not very far from our advanced post at Congleton [he was unaware of Kingston's withdrawal] . . . if the motion west was a feint then indeed we shall by our advancing be less in reach of keeping them out of Derbyshire. What is most apt to perplex is that often people who give intelligence mistake a small party for the body.'[35]

Cumberland, who was still beset by a variety of logistical problems, had already decided that the way to bring the crisis to a head was by offering battle. He rode up to Stone from Stafford and reconnoitred a battlefield (this was on Monday afternoon) and on return to Stafford had just finished his dinner when he learned of the thrust towards Congleton.[36] Convinced that the entire Jacobite force would be there that night, he moved his army up from Rugeley and Lichfield to Stone, to which he proceeded himself at eleven on Monday night. Cumberland felt that he could overcome the problems of morale and fatigue in his own army if the Highlanders could be tempted to battle. These problems were considerable. The Duke of Kingston's men had had only six hours' sleep since they left Cheadle on Saturday 30th November.[37] Over and above this, Cumberland's troops were irked by the notorious Jacobitism of Staffordshire. One of his guards described Stafford thus: 'This is a damned Popish town — the people here make no bones of telling us they would rather see the Highlanders among them than the King's troops — the rogues use us very ill but we will be even with them.'[38] The weakness of Cumberland's strategy, however, was that almost the only contingency plan he had laid in the event that his reading of the campaign was wrong was to send sixteen men to Leek to inform him when any Scots arrived (if they had not already done so) and to put their effects 'out of the way'.[39]

As for Wade, his marches subsisted more in the imagination of others than in reality. The Manchester constables paid the expenses of Mr. John Shaw to travel through Bradford and Leeds with an express for Wade, to tell him that the Jacobites had now quit Manchester on their way south.[40] But this attempt to locate the Marshal was soon confused with the rumour that Wade was actually at Rochdale.

This news encouraged the anti-Jacobite mob in Manchester to rampage through the town, threatening to pull down the houses of all known Jacobites. When Dr. Deacon's lamp and windows were broken, the Manchester Jacobites felt constrained to form a vigilante committee as the only way of keeping the peace.[41]

Tuesday 3rd December

When Lord George Murray learned of Cumberland's movements towards Stone, he realised that his feint had been a magnificent success and sent a messenger to Charles Edward at Macclesfield to report that the way to Derby was now clear.[42] December 3rd, which Cumberland had hoped would see the decisive battle of Stone, effectively altered the entire campaign though not a single shot was fired.

Following the information brought from Murray, Charles Edward's main army assembled at Macclesfield at 4 a.m. and prepared for the march to Leek.[43] Since an engagement could now be expected almost hourly, all regimental colonels were ordered to have a two-day supply of bread and cheese provided for their men. The utmost care was to be taken with stragglers: an officer was to stay in the rear of each regiment with a detachment of horse to prevent casual losses.[44] Even so, the Jacobites lost one man even before they cleared Macclesfield. A young Scots boy was stabbed and his assailant escaped through the Angel inn, at which there were heard vociferous threats that the town would be burnt down. Since the attacker could not be found, the landlord of the Angel was taken along as a hostage to guarantee Macclesfield's continuing good behaviour.[45]

The march towards Leek was led by fifty of Pitsligo's horse followed by Lord Ogilvy's contingent. Roy Stewart's and Perth's came next and then the six Swedish cannon with its ammunition. Behind the cannon marched the clansmen of Lochiel, Cluny and Glengarry, followed by the rest of the MacDonalds. Finally came the rest of the artillery, the baggage and the artillery and baggage horses, guarded by the Appin Stewarts, with a rearguard formed by Glenbucket's (amid whom at this point was Lochgarry in personal possession of the royal standard) and the rest of Pitsligo's horse.[46] James Drummond was in command of the money cart and Lord Nairne had been appointed brigadier for the entire march from Macclesfield to Derby.[47]

The road between Macclesfield and Leek via Bosley and Winde was a particularly difficult one, so that whereas the vanguard of Charles Edward's army entered Winde by about 11 a.m., it was 6 p.m. before the entire train of baggage and artillery had all arrived.[48] Much swifter progress had of course been made by Lord George Murray's column, which left Congleton early in the morning and reached Leek via the Cloud (one section by way of Mossley and Dane Enshaw) about nine on Tuesday morning, 'seeming lame from their march' according to one observer.[49] Murray's force then pressed on to Ashbourne via the Bridestones and Rudyard Lake, reached the town between 2 and 3 p.m. and halted there for the night, with small detachments thrown out to Warslow and Okeover Hall (among these being Edward Grave's party from Newark) and some outriders as far away as Wirksworth.[50]

Since many of Charles Edward's soldiers were struggling along the Leek road from Macclesfield at the very time Murray entered Ashbourne with his request for billets for 3,000 men, there clearly existed the danger that Cumberland, had he known the true dispositions of his enemy, could have cut the road between the two columns.[51] The danger was perhaps even greater on Tuesday night, when Cumberland began to realise that the Highlanders would not after all come to Stone to join battle, since in theory by a night march he could have got between Murray and Charles Edward. In fact of course his men were much too exhausted for such a manoeuvre.[52]

The bulk of Charles Edward's force, including the Prince himself, entered Leek in the late afternoon, about six or eight abreast and described as 'marching in tolerable order'.[53] Careful note was taken of their numbers and of the fifty ammunition waggons by a largely hostile population; Elcho indeed made a point of noting in his journal the dislike and apprehension of the people between Macclesfield and Ashbourne, who crowded the tops of hills with men on horseback but made off when approached.[54] A general attempt was made to evade the requests for provisions, forage, horses and livestock which the Jacobites imposed on the town of Leek. The farmers at Swythamley and Heaton drove their cattle into a concealed ravine rather than comply; the local JP William Marshall was taken prisoner in reprisal for the inhabitants' non-cooperation and had to pay £300 to be released.[55]

Nevertheless the Jacobites enjoyed some good fortune in Leek. Cumberland's chief scout Joshua Ball, who should have ridden back to Stone to acquaint his master with developments in North Staffordshire, was made drunk by Jacobite sympathisers and arrived back at Cumberland's HQ far too late for his intelligence to be of any use.[56] And at Hareygate the Quaker Mr. Toft invited a contingent of clansmen to his home for a meal of boiled beef.

While the Prince rested at Mr. Mills's house on the north side of the Market Place, his men spent most of the remaining hours until the march to Ashbourne using the old Norman crosses in Leek churchyard for target practice.[57] There was only one recruit for the army in Leek, a Warslow attorney named Goole.[58] The plan was that both columns — Murray's and the Prince's — should reunite at Ashbourne on the morning of Wednesday the 4th.[59]

By the time Charles Edward was leaving Macclesfield this Tuesday morning, Cumberland had united most of his army at Stone.[60] He drew up his men in battle order on a vast open tract of land just outside the town, called Stonefield, which he and Ligonier had reconnoitred, and there he waited from 4 a.m. until 11 a.m. for the decisive battle which never happened.[61] Cumberland had managed just a few minutes' sleep on a bed of straw in a small room at Mr. Hinkley's house in Stone, while his soldiers crammed the rest of the tiny town. The inhabitants of Stone were greatly alarmed at the thought of the impending battle and some of them took flight, bearing away stories of the booming of great guns at Stonefield.[62] By the afternoon Cumberland began to realise that he had been duped and left his position on the would-be battlefield.

Cumberland had at least demonstrated that he felt prepared to meet the clansmen, but elsewhere in England on this day the same spirit of defiance to the 'Pretender' was little in evidence. Wade's army was now at Boroughbridge, resting for the day 'because of the long march and great fatigue of the troops'.[63] Wade intended to proceed on Wednesday the 4th to Wetherby but his heart was not in the task; he looked forward to the time when his army would be proceeding northwards again, for surely, he thought, the Jacobites would not risk getting between two armies and so would soon commence their retreat.[64]

General Oglethorpe meanwhile had reached York, where he breakfasted with Archbishop Herring, who made great play of making Oglethorpe's hussars 'prodigiously welcome' with ale, bread and cheese.[65] Oglethorpe displayed great animus towards the Dutch, whom he accused of delaying tactics and a general intransigence that had made the march from Newcastle to Hexham a disaster and prevented a direct cavalry pursuit south from Hexham through Durham. There were even worse developments in Derbyshire. On the morning of Tuesday the 3rd the entire body of troops in the county were reviewed by the Duke of Devonshire, the Lord Lieutenant, and went through their exercises to the satisfaction of all present.[66] But an hour later came news that the Jacobite vanguard was entering Ashbourne. In the afternoon the thousand or so irregulars were drawn up again and a decision taken to withdraw in the face of the enemy. At about 10 p.m. the Duke of Devonshire led his Derbyshire Blues away to Nottingham and eternal ridicule.[67]

Tuesday 3rd December had not been a good day for the Whigs. Henry Pelham in London continued to harbour the illusion that the Highlanders would not come towards London. Writing to Lord Hartington he stated: 'It seems out of doubt that they intend for Wales.'[68] Pelham was also concerned about lack of news from Lord Tweeddale, Secretary of State for Scotland, which made it impossible for him to know if Jacobite reinforcements had landed from France: 'a fine way for a Minister to support a prince, when one part of the administration does not acquaint the other with what passes, even in a rebellion'.[69] The general atmosphere of gloom is conveyed in a letter from Lady Irwin to Earl Morton on the 3rd: 'The whole country is in a consternation which I never remember; stocks are low, credit is much hurt, many people break . . . the idea we have conceived of the Highlanders makes everybody tremble; they are now in Lancashire dispersed in bodies from Preston to Manchester; the government is yet ignorant of their numbers, no care having been taken for proper intelligence.'[70] Such was the situation when Charles Edward commenced shortly after midnight his historic march to Derby.

Wednesday 4th December

At about 1 a.m. Charles Edward's army moved out of Leek towards Ashbourne where Lord George Murray's detachment awaited them.[71] Fifty of Pitsligo's horse formed the van, with Cluny MacPherson's the first of the foot. The order of march then took in successively Glengarry's, the rest of Clan Donald, the Appin Stewarts, the Camerons, Glenbucket's, the artillery and baggage, the Manchester regiment, Roy Stewart's, Perth's, Ogilvy's with the remainder of Pitsligo's bringing up the rear.[72] With some of Cumberland's men reported only four miles distant, the tension on this night march was very great, as reflected in the orders of the day, which admonished all officers to be supremely vigilant.[73] For some the strain of an imminent encounter was too great. William Brettargh actually tried to leave the Manchester regiment but was compelled by Townley to go on with it to Ashbourne.[74]

The army had the benefit of a fine moonlit night and was assisted also by the thick frost:[75] the road from Leek to Ashbourne (which was not turnpiked until 1760) was a difficult one and would normally have posed extreme problems for the artillery and baggage waggons, but the frost provided an easy surface for them to travel on.[76] On arrival at Ashbourne at daybreak Charles Edward joined Murray for the march on Derby, and the Stuarts were proclaimed at the Market Cross. Considerable hostility to the Highlanders was in evidence at Ashbourne. The previous evening when Murray's detachment arrived there had been an altercation between a soldier and the keeper of a liquor store who denied his occupation for fear of plunder. Murray had had the storekeeper court-martialled and sentenced to be shot, but on the intercession of the culprit's wife Charles Edward once more displayed his (somewhat misplaced) magnanimity by releasing him.[77]

The united army now made for Derby in close order on a good stretch of road which completed the main Buxton–Derby turnpike.[78] The probable route lay through Bradley, Hulland Ward, Mugginton, Weston Underwood and Kedleston.[79] Only one incident disturbed the tenor of this march. At about 11 a.m. 'troops' were seen on the hills around the road, at which the army drew up in battle order. The 'troops' proved to be little more than inquisitive local gentry with their retainers; following this false alarm the march was resumed and completed without further interruption.[80]

All that afternoon the Jacobite army was entering Derby. The harbinger of the Highlanders was a couple of officers who arrived at 11 a.m. and after demanding billets for 9,000 men entered the George inn.[81] Shortly afterwards a party of thirty hussars under Lord Balmerino came in and, in the words of the contemporary chronicler Hutton, 'bells, bonfires and proclamations were as usual the first orders; horses, arms and the delivery of public money were the next'.[82] The hussars sat silently on horseback in the Market Place for nearly three hours until at 3 p.m. Lord Elcho and his Lifeguards, always the most splendidly attired, made their entry; although their horses were jaded, they themselves were acknowledged to be 'fine figures'.[83] When the main army appeared on foot, marching six or eight abreast, a white standard with red crosses displayed above each regiment, their motley aspect contrasted strikingly with that of the Lifeguards.[84] One observer described them as 'a mixture of every rank, from childhood to old age, from the dwarf to the giant'.[85] The impression was also formed (rightly) that the infantry were entering in discrete batches to make counting them more difficult.[86]

The most efficient billeting arrangements yet were contrived, partly owing to the large numbers of gentry residing in Derby: Tullibardine lodged with Thomas Gisborne at Bridgegate, Perth at Miss Rivett's, Elcho with Mr. Storer, Lord George Murray with Mr. Heathcote, Lord Pitsligo at Mr. Meynell's and so on.[87] Alderman Cooper, who was lame and thus not so fleet of foot as his colleagues, was this time the unfortunate official forced to proclaim Charles Edward Stuart.[88] The Prince himself did not come in until after dusk, having turned aside to visit German

Pole, a leading Tory squire, at Radbourne Hall.[89] The omens there were not propitious: an expected sum of money from Stuart partisans in Leicestershire and the South Midlands had not arrived, and all Pole and his fellow Tories could offer was sympathy and verbal zeal. Nonetheless, it seems that the Prince was not at this stage cast down but was more impressed, to Lord George Murray's irritation, with the bells and bonfires of Derby than with the continuing non-appearance of the English Jacobites.[90] His father James had already been proclaimed by Lord George's orders when, about 6 p.m., Charles Edward rode down Friar Gate, into Queen Street, down Iron Gate and across the Market Place into Full Street, where his lodgings in Exeter House had been prepared.[91]

What was the attitude of Derby and environs to the Highlanders? As always, studied ambivalence was the principal attitude in evidence. As Hutton caustically put it: 'The English were extremely loyal to the House of Stuart when warmed by a good fire and good liquor; but the warmth of their fire, their liquor and their loyalty evaporated together.'[92] There is, however, much circumstantial evidence of the relatively favourable attitude of Derbyshire. On the march into Derby signs of friendliness were displayed by Squire Meynell of Bradley Hall (though there are clear signs that his motive was prudential) and the villagers of Kirk Langley, both of whom had prepared meals for the passing Scots.[93] In Derby itself the high morale of the Jacobite army was palpable. This too is usually attributed to their friendly reception in the town, but could easily have been simple euphoria at reaching a well-provisioned town after having marched, in the case of most of them, since one that morning.[94] The juxtaposition of sentiments in the case of one Scottish correspondent is perhaps significant: 'This Derby is a fine town . . . we are just now going to attack a fine piece of roast beef.'[95]

The reasonably enthusiastic reception given the Highlanders was almost certainly due in part to the realisation in Derby that the Scots were not the barbarians Whig propaganda had made them out to be and, instead of a horde of murderers, rapists and child eaters, were a disciplined force.[96] Certainly John Daniel's account makes clear that the alleged anthropophagous propensity of the clansmen was initially taken very seriously in Derby, and it was that kind of rumour that had already led many townspeople to flee.[97]

On the other hand, the Jacobites enjoyed their usual lack of success when it came to recruiting. Although they beat up for volunteers with a guaranteed five shillings immediately as bait, and a further five guineas when they reached London, the clan leaders could attract only three volunteers: Edward Hewitt, a butcher, a travelling journeyman blacksmith by the name of Cooke, and James Sparks, a stocking maker.[98] Far the most committed of the trio was Sparks, who is said to have seized his five shillings, hugged it 'as it were a treasure trove' and exclaimed: 'this is the day I have long wished for'. Sparks gave valuable information on likely friends and foes of the Jacobites and guided outparties to the seats of neighbouring gentry in search of horses and money. It was on one of these trips that he met his nemesis, for at Hugo Meynell's at Bradley he was left behind drunk when the Highlanders retreated, was taken prisoner and executed in 1746.[99]

Although one or two of the citizens refused to illuminate their houses and had their windows broken in reprisal, most accepted this order and the burden of billeting, if not with good grace, at least with resignation. One house played host to six officers and forty men plus 'eight flabby horses, some without saddles or bridles, and ropes about their heads and necks and poor saddles stuffed with straw'.[100] After eating their bread, cheese and ale, the ordinary soldiers would bed down on straw before a fire in the hall or in front of the fires in the laundry-room. This party consumed from Wednesday evening to Friday morning a side of beef, eight joints of mutton, four cheeses, six fowl and 'quantities' of white and brown bread, ale, beer, tea and spirits, though their wasting of the household's substance seemed to occasion less outrage than their saying grace before meals 'as if they had been so many pure primitive Christians'.[101]

That evening the Prince dined with his principal officers at Exeter House. While some of them boasted that they would be in Northampton by Friday, Charles Edward debated with others the correct method of his entry into London.[102] Lord George Murray was emphatically not impressed with the proceedings that night: to O'Sullivan, who claimed to be impressed with the bells and illuminations, Murray replied scornfully that such things signified nothing. Lord George retired early (and somewhat ostentatiously) from the merry scene to concentrate on more practical matters. With his host, lawyer Heathcote, he sat up late going through the list of those in Derby who had subscribed to the associations for the defence of king and country so that a similar levy might be imposed on them for the Jacobite army.[103]

While Charles Edward was dining, the Mayor of Derby, Robert Hague, decided to approach him and asked the guards at Exeter House for an interview with 'the Pretender'. The guards responded angrily to this insulting term. Hague was kicked down the stairs and admonished to go to the Court of St. James if he wanted to see a pretender.[104] But apart from Hague's contretemps, none of the citizens of Derby had any reason to complain of their treatment at the Highlanders' hands on their first night in town. Edward Graves was drinking punch with some Jacobite officers at the house of a Mr. Mellers in the course of cursory search for arms. One of the officers opened a drawer and found a gold watch and some bank notes but refused to touch them, saying that the only exactions that would occur would be those at the direct order of the Prince.[105]

The most important military movement in the Jacobite army on the night of Wednesday the 4th was the seizure of Swarkeston Bridge commanding the main road to London, which was held until the 6th by a party of some eighty men.[106] Cumberland, on hearing of the march towards Derby, had ordered the bridge broken down but his orders were sent too late to be implemented — indeed one of his spies just got out of town in time and escaped over Swarkeston Bridge minutes before the Highlanders sealed this exit.[107]

Cumberland, learning the disagreeable news that the Jacobites had marched from Leek to Ashbourne and Derby, asembled all the troops at Stone — both those he had brought up from Stafford and those that Richmond had pulled back from Congleton — and at four on Wednesday morning commenced the march back to Stafford.[108] His own inclination was to march for Derby but his men had scarcely had six hours' rest in ten days, most had been without food for twenty-four hours, and they had been exposed to unusually severe weather: Cumberland described the night of 3rd/4th December as 'one of the coldest nights I ever felt'.[109] Another problem was lack of straw, which made it impossible to bivouack in the open. The impracticability of Joseph Yorke's suggestion (in a letter to his father the Lord Chancellor), that the cavalry and mounted dragoons be despatched to Derby forthwith, was clear.[110]

On return to Stafford Cumberland divided his infantry, leaving half in the town and sending the other half to Lichfield.[111] Meanwhile he made plans to intercept the Highlanders at Northampton. The Duke of Richmond was sent south with the dragoons and ordered to be at Coventry on Thursday night and in Northampton on the 6th.[112] Cumberland also despatched a courier to London, asking that an army be formed on Finchley Common in case the Highlanders still managed to give him the slip.[113] Then he had to deal with a fresh problem that awaited him at Stafford. Although there was good news from Chester, in that this suspectedly 'disaffected' town was sending twenty-three waggons and carts loaded with provisions and ammunition to his army,[114] Cumberland now received disquieting information from Nottingham, which would be within a day's march of the Jacobites when they reached Derby. Apparently the Duke of Newcastle's steward Mr. Clay had amassed a large cache of arms in Nottingham castle, and though he had earlier been ordered to dispose of it, it now appeared that he had not done so. Grumbling to Newcastle that this information came to him very late in the day, Cumberland meanwhile ordered Montagu's regiment, then at Leicester, to move up to Nottingham and, acting in concert with the Derbyshire Blues, to defend the castle.[115] If, on the other hand, Devonshire thought the castle indefensible, he was to seize the arms and take them down to Northampton. As it happened, Clay and Devonshire had already decided to remove the arms and ammunition from the castle.[116]

Further discredit was now incurred by the Derbyshire Blues. Hearing that the Highlanders were on the way to Derby, the Blues put even greater distance between themselves and the Scots by decamping to Mansfield, leaving Nottingham to shift for itself. Not even the arrival of Montagu's horse from Loughborough at midnight on the 4th stiffened their resolve, and Montagu's in turn became demoralised; they departed for Southwell and Newark in haste, though even there they were not welcome as the townspeople feared reprisals from the Highlanders. The contagion of panic germinated by the Derbyshire Blues also manifested itself in the case of Montagu's by their firing on a farmer driving a herd of cows to pasture, mistaking them for an advance Jacobite detachment.[117]

Another headache for both Cumberland and the government in London was the inactivity of Wade, whom Joseph Yorke accused of having stayed four days in Richmond, Yorkshire.[118] Cumberland expressed great dissatisfaction with 'grandmother Wade'; he wrote to Newcastle that 'it is of infinite consequence that someone more able be sent'.[119] Wade was in fact at Wetherby this Wednesday, where he held a Council of War. He had originally intended to march via Leeds and Blackstone Edge to Manchester and had already got together a supply of bread in Leeds for that purpose. When news of the advance to Ashbourne came in, Wade called a Council at which the unanimous decision was taken to proceed to

Doncaster.[120] It no more occurred to Wade this night than it did to Charles Edward that the Jacobites might shortly be retreating the way they had come.

Thursday 5th December

Morale in the Jacobite army can rarely have been higher than in Derby on Thursday 5th December. The Chevalier Johnstone recounts that the soldiers crowded before the cutlers' shops, disputing about who should be the first to sharpen their swords.[121] Although the people of Derby later complained that the Scots had paid whatever price they thought fit in the shops, this was in the main propaganda *ex post*. Insofar as any such incidents did take place, they have to be seen in the context of a town reluctant to subscribe for the Stuarts. For in addition to the collection of the public monies, an equivalent subscription to that raised for the Derbyshire Blues was demanded.[122] There was a systematic attempt to evade this payment: an initial exaction of £100 from the post office was later modified to £50 but was not even paid then. The postmaster made good his escape to avoid reprisals, so the Highlanders took away the post-chaise as compensation.[123] All in all, over £500 was collected in 'subscriptions' in addition to more than £600 of public money (£665-12-8¾).[124]

With good quarters, pay and provisions, the clansmen boasted that they felt able to fight double their own number.[125] All the letters posted in Derby (and later taken by the Whigs) attest to the euphoria and high morale among the Jacobites.[126] Peter Ouchterlony, a Scottish coffee-house keeper, accurately pinpointed the main reasons: 'Even what has happened already must appear to posterity liker a Romance than any thing of truth.'[127] Alex Blair of Elcho's wrote to his wife that as the Scots were now nearer to London than either Wade's or Cumberland's forces, they felt ready to tackle both armies together.[128] There was little to disturb the good spirits of the troops this day, unaware as they were of the momentous decisions being taken by their leaders at the Council meeting in Exeter House. Apart from serving warrants on the leading burghers for sums equivalent to those paid as subscriptions to the associations for the defence of George II (Tullibardine used this means to collect £50 from his reluctant host Thomas Gisborne), and on the mayor and aldermen for forage for the army, there was little for the men to do except take advantage of the food and drink in the town.[129] It is not without significance that the only account of activities outside the Council this day (i.e. dealing with those not in conclave at Exeter House) finds the infamous Samuel Maddock robbing a friendly visitor William Davis — who came into town to see the army 'out of curiosity' but would not take up arms — of five guineas and his pocket book.[130] The only other diversion was that provided by Whig spies — not Vere, who this day passed into the personal custody of Lochiel[131] — but two more government agents who had entered Derby from the south. One of these was Eliezer Birch. Having covered the 137 miles between London and Stafford in twenty-five hours between 6 p.m. on Monday the 2nd and 7 p.m. on Tuesday, he was then despatched by Cumberland to Derby.[132] On entering Derby he was recognised by some members of the Manchester regiment. Taken prisoner, he escaped by jumping out of the window of the guard room at Exeter House and swimming four miles down the Derwent.[133] The other agent, a much more important figure, was Dudley Bradstreet, Newcastle's own spy, who travelled up from London to Lichfield for a conference with Cumberland, arriving at 3 p.m. this Thursday.[134] Cumberland immediately commissioned him to go to Derby and 'to delay them but twelve hours'. At about 6 p.m. Bradstreet arrived in Derby and gave out that he was a leading member of the English gentry, come to see Charles Edward. In this way he secured introductions to both Perth and Kilmarnock, for whose benefit he invented an army allegedly lying south of Northampton, ready to annihilate the clansmen.[135]

Following a service in All Saints Collegiate Church — sometimes curiously described as a Roman Catholic High Mass, though this was clearly impossible[136] — a full meeting of the War Council was held, with all regimental colonels present. Both Charles Edward and Lord George Murray entered the Council chamber with diametrically opposed viewpoints and assumptions. At Manchester Murray had agreed to march the length of Derbyshire to give the English Jacobites a final opportunity to rise. As far as he was concerned, retreat was the only feasible policy now that they had not done so; all that remained to discuss was the conduct of the retreat.[137] To Charles Edward it was just as obvious that, having consistently outwitted Cumberland and got ahead of him in the race for London, the army should press on to the capital. According to one unconfirmed source, this clash of opinion had already taken place between the two men even before the Council began,[138] but if not, it soon did when proceedings got under way at Exeter House.

Lord George Murray spoke first and expressed, at first mildly, the arguments that to his mind dictated retreat. The most important was that there were now three armies in the field against them: Cumberland's, Wade's and the force now reported to be gathering to the north of London.[139] Even if the Highlanders defeated Cumberland, Murray estimated that Scottish casualties would be in the 1000–1500 region, which would make the Jacobite army unfit to face a new force a few days later. If, on the other hand, they were defeated in an encounter with Cumberland, there would be no hope left, since the militia would then descend like vultures on the stricken Scots and, so far from Scotland, there would be no chance of a successful retreat.[140]

Charles Edward responded at first by ignoring the points Murray had raised. After Murray had finished speaking there was a long pause before the Prince began to discuss the order of march next day and who was to have the van.[141] At this Murray cut in brusquely to say that it had not yet been decided whether it was advisable to advance at all. The Prince then turned for support to his other officers, most of whom declared themselves of Murray's mind. Charles Edward was aghast and chided them with seeming to turn their backs on a certain victory and a certain Stuart restoration.[142] Lord George replied that no one was against a restoration and all were prepared to die in the Stuart cause but that this would certainly happen anyway if they advanced. Elcho, who with Murray and Lord Ogilvy formed the triumvirate that most vehemently opposed an advance on London, said that the Prince should realise that if he went forward he would be in Newgate gaol within a fortnight.[143] Ogilvy and Elcho endorsed Murray's argument that unless one presupposed (unrealistically) that all three armies would be panic-stricken at the mere thought of having to face the clansmen, there was no chance of defeating two and possibly three armies in succession. Only the absolute certainty of success could justify the army's proceeding further south; as it was, the likelihood was that the Prince would be killed or taken prisoner and his councillors censured at the bar of international opinion for idiotic quixotry.[144]

Faced with this barrage of pessimistic arguments, the Prince tried again. He pointed out the advantages enjoyed by the Jacobite army that Murray had not mentioned: their position was very sound tactically with Swarkestone Bridge in their possession; the clansmen were deeply feared as a result of Prestonpans; the 'Elector's' army was unreliable while morale among the Jacobites was at its zenith. Most of all, he stressed the results that would accrue from an advance to London: the English Jacobites would finally declare themselves, and the French would meanwhile land in Kent or Essex; whereas to retreat would mean to lose credit, morale and discipline, quite apart from the fact that the war would follow them into Scotland.[145] As a trump card the Prince produced a letter he had just received from Lord Drummond in Scotland, which proved the sincerity of the French. Murray immediately proceeded to turn the French argument back on the Prince. Drummond's arrival in Scotland meant that France was concentrating its invasion efforts there and not in England.[146] Moreover, Drummond's presence prompted two further considerations: if French aid was being sent to Scotland, this would be totally ineffectual if the Prince were meanwhile defeated in England; on the other hand, the combined forces of Drummond and Strathallan at Perth made up an army as large as the Prince's present invading force; it would therefore be best to go back to Scotland to join forces with them. Murray summed up the case for retreat by saying that advance was only feasible given one (or both) of two circumstances: either a rising of the English Jacobites or a French landing, neither of which had happened.[147]

Charles Edward retorted that he was confident the English Jacobites would rise but, on being challenged by the Council, he revealed to general horror that he was not in touch with them and had no specific promises of aid from them.[148] Elcho made an angry intervention at this point, vehemently denouncing the 'Prince's friends in England'. The Jacobite army, he said, had come to join the French and the Duke of York and to link up with the Prince's English supporters. But the reality was that no one of rank had yet joined the army in England, the ordinary people were plainly hostile, the French had not landed, there were two armies between them and London, and Wade was cutting off their retreat. We have come, Elcho declared, to aid our English friends, not to make a king for them while they remain on the sidelines.[149] In sum, he himself was prepared to march on London only if the Prince showed the Council a letter from his supporters expressly requesting him to do so.

The Prince replied that the possession of the capital would itself paralyse the Whig government, create consternation and open the floodgates of popular Jacobitism in London. Murray remarked tartly that this presupposed that the Highlanders could get possession of London.[150] Even if Cumberland was beaten on the way south the vanquished remnants of his army, especially the cavalry, would join the guards and other troops in London. The scattered infantry, meanwhile, by lining the hedges with cannon, could devastate the Highlanders as they marched by. Then there was the continuing problem of Wade in the rear. Even assuming the last two difficulties did not materialise and the Scots won through to London, what kind of figure would the weary and battered clansmen cut on their entry into the capital? Their appearance would surely discourage even those of their supporters prepared to waive the hazard of having two Hanoverian armies still in the field.[151]

At this stage the only allies Charles Edward could discern on the Council were Clanranald, who argued passionately for an advance, O'Sullivan who supported the Prince but was not prepared to speak openly for marching southwards, and the Duke of Perth.[152] Even Perth, who at first took no part in the debate, resting his head on the fireplace as he listened to Lord George Murray, began to wilt under the impact of the latter's arguments. So when Murray of Broughton entered the Council chamber by mistake and was about to beat an embarrassed retreat, Charles Edward asked him to stay on and give his opinion.[153] John Murray, however, disappointed his royal master by siding with the majority who wished to return to Scotland. The final arguments of the morning were marshalled by the trio of Elcho, Ogilvy and Lord George.[154] London, they alleged, was a chimera: the citizens there would put up as much resistance, at least, as those of Carlisle, and it would be impossible to besiege the city with Wade and Cumberland still unbeaten. And with Hanoverian armies still at large, even if London were taken, the Jacobites would then in turn be besieged.[155]

As a compromise Perth now suggested that instead of a retreat to Scotland the army should proceed to Wales.[156] This proposal too was opposed by the majority on the ground that they could be cut off there and prevented from rejoining their other troops in Scotland.[157] Finally it was agreed to adjourn the meeting until the early evening when a final decision would be taken. Meanwhile a flexible set of instructions was issued to the army. The orders to Lord Ogilvy's regiment provided the first indication that a withdrawal was being contemplated. Stating that the baggage must be kept together, the orderbook added significantly 'either at the front or the rear'.[158]

Nevertheless, during this Thursday morning all Jacobite activity was predicated on the certainty of advance. Scots officers conned maps to work out the best routes to Northampton and London. As the Duke of Richmond shrewdly saw, the possession of Swarkestone Bridge was of immense value to the Highlanders as it was the only point at which sizeable numbers of troops could cross en route to Leicester and the south.[159] The best itinerary, therefore, would be to Leicester over Swarkestone Bridge and via Ashby; to go by way of Loughborough would necessitate ferries across the River Trent (the major Cavendish ferry bridge was not built until 1758), and though this was theoretically feasible — indeed Richmond lamented that all ferry boats on the Trent had not been sunk — it would also certainly mean that the Scots would have to make a detour to Nottingham first.[160]

On the morning of the 5th several parties were sent out from Swarkestone Bridge to reconnoitre the routes south. The commander at the bridge sent a detachment to

Melbourne to order billets for 2,000 men that night.[161] Another small party visited Loughborough, and two of this intrepid group pushed on to Leicester where they demanded quarters for the whole army — which they alleged would be there that night — before doubling back to Loughborough and, early on Friday, to Swarkestone Bridge.[162] Little is known of these scouting parties, but one or two of the participants can be identified. An Edinburgh man named Bartholomew wrote to his mother early on Thursday: 'I have only time to write these few lines as we are to part south in a quarter of an hour but hope to write to you from London in less than ten days.'[163]

The most likely neighbouring town to receive a visit from the Highlanders was, however, spared. With the Scots a day's march away and their route said to lie by way of Loughborough and Nottingham, their vanguard was hourly expected in the latter. Nottingham shops were shut all day, many citizens packed their bags and left, and the Mayor and Aldermen allowed 15d. for drink to the lookouts watching for the expected entry of the 'Young Pretender'. One set of contingency orders given out after the first meeting of the Council ordered the vanguard to march on the 6th to Nottingham before proceeding to rejoin the main army at Leicester. The atmosphere in Nottingham on the 5th was well described by Newcastle's steward Clay: 'We have been kept in continued fear and suspense at this town day and night since their coming in to Derby to their going from thence and have been forced to provide all sorts of fresh meat for them in every house as well private as public houses, in hourly expectation of them but thank God they did not come to eat it.'[164]

With the adjournment of the morning Council meeting the Prince spent a strenuous afternoon trying to find a way to get the Council's decision reversed. He began, possibly in company with German Pole, by visiting some of the neighbouring gentry — these may have included Sir Henry Harpur at Calke Abbey, Sir Francis Burdett at Foremarke, Sir Thomas Grerley at Drakelow and John Stanhope at Nether Hall — in the hopes of securing an open commitment from at least some English Jacobites, with which he could confute the arguments of the Council.[165] But though many may have wished the Stuarts restored, none dared declare this support in writing or by overt action. The Prince was therefore reduced to lobbying his principal officers for a change of heart. The only headway he made was with Perth, who agreed to argue in the evening for an advance, as did Tullibardine, who had not been at the morning meeting.[166]

Yet in general the mood among the Jacobite officers overwhelmingly favoured Lord George Murray. Lochiel, who had kept his own counsel in the morning out of deference to the Prince, let it be known in conversation with Lord George Murray and Keppoch that he favoured retreat.[167] His conclave with these two was suddenly interrupted by a drunken Sir John MacDonald who burst in upon them and upbraided them for cowardice: 'It is absurd', exclaimed MacDonald, 'to think of making such a long retreat in the face of regular troops in their own country. If we are to perish, 'tis better to do so with our faces to London, than to Scotland.' With great restraint Lochiel calmly replied: 'If you knew all you would agree with us.'[168]

The problem from the Prince's point of view was that most of those who were in favour of going on, such as David Morgan, were not members of the Council. Sir

William Gordon of Park enthusiastically embraced Perth's idea of going to Wales, as did Moir of Stoneywood, but neither of these was on the Council.[169] But at least these men gave the Prince honest opinions. The ultimate in machiavellianism was achieved by Murray of Broughton, who had argued for a retreat in the morning. When he realised from the strength of feeling that this was inevitable anyway, he informed Charles Edward that he personally favoured an advance to London and had only argued against it at the morning meeting as he thought it was pointless to expect an army to fight if the morale of its officers was so low.[170]

Tullibardine, who had agreed to use his influence on the Prince's behalf, began to realise, as a result of a conversation he had with Lord George Murray's entourage just before the evening Council meeting, how set the chiefs were on a return to Scotland. Apart from Elcho there were present at this colloquy Lord George's great ally Menzies of Shian (who in the absence of Sir Robert Menzies, now a cripple, led out three hundred of his clan to form the third battalion of the Atholl brigade), Murray's battalion major, James Robertson of Blairfettie, and David Stewart of Kynachan, a major in Lord Nairne's battalion.[171] When Atholl sounded the three officers on their opinion, they expressed utter incredulity that the Prince should have come so far into England without positive assurances from the Jacobites in London or in the regular army.

So it was that Charles Edward went to the evening Council meeting with slender hopes of reversing the earlier decision. O'Sullivan still supported him as did Murray of Broughton, for his own reasons, and Clanranald and Perth were still firm, although the addition of Tullibardine to the Prince's allies was counterbalanced by the opposition of Lord Nairne who, like Tullibardine, had been absent from the morning Council meeting.[172] Lord George Murray opened proceedings by assuming that retreat would be agreed and outlining his thoughts on the best way to retire in face of Cumberland. Only retreat, he argued, enabled the Highlanders to retain control of events, since a successful withdrawal depended on skill and a battle only on luck. Murray guaranteed that he could get the army safely back to Carlisle. Even if Cumberland marched faster than anyone expected, he could only conceivably get in front of them at Warrington and, if this happened, the Jacobite army could cross higher up the Mersey and still avoid both the Duke's troops and Wade's.[173] On the whole, though, it was unlikely that any regular troops could keep pace with the clansmen, so that if they set out on the 6th they would have two days' start on Cumberland. As for Wade, his army was still in Yorkshire, beset by sickness and fatigue, and would present no obstacle even if encountered. A retreat would also confer other benefits, Murray argued, such as that when passing through towns they had stayed in on the march into England, the men could all go to their former quarters; in this way there would be no need to pause for rest until Preston. All Murray asked was that he should not be made responsible for the cannon, which should go well ahead of the troops so that it would not impede the march.[174] Lord George offered to stay in the rear of the army, using each regiment in turn as rearguard, with the proviso that if attacked, the main army could provide support without a general halt, unless of course he was assailed by the enemy in overwhelming strength. By the time they reached Carlisle there would certainly be good news from Scotland, and the French would be mightily impressed by such a march in and out of England.[175]

The majority of the Council seemed very pleased with Murray's propositions. Only Perth spoke out openly against him this time, advocating an immediate assault on Cumberland.[176] As for Murray of Broughton, the tables were instantly turned on him. When he and Sheridan attempted to endorse Perth's view, they were asked to record their opinion in writing but declined to do so and were thus effectively silenced.[177] The Prince then spoke, pointing out that there was greater danger in retreat than in an advance because the Highland army in the latter case would be between the two armies of Wade and Cumberland, whereas Wade could not be a factor if it advanced.[178] This answer was taken up by a new triumvirate of Cluny, Keppoch and Lochiel, the most influential of the clan chiefs, who argued that clansmen without baggage could march at least twenty miles a day — a pace Cumberland could not conceivably match — and that they could defeat Wade, if encountered, en route to Scotland.[179]

At this stage the *coup de grace* was dealt to Charles Edward's cause by the introduction to the Council chamber by Perth of Dudley Bradstreet.[180] Bradstreet's story was that Cumberland planned to cut the escape route to Scotland the moment the Jacobites moved south from Derby, and while the Duke of Richmond's cavalry harried their western flank, another army commanded by Hawley or Ligonier and composed of 9,000 men would bar the way to London. At this Charles Edward cried out in rage: 'That fellow will do me more harm than all the Elector's army.' Although Bradstreet was then withdrawn, his work had been well done. Clanranald and Tullibardine immediately changed their minds on receipt of this new 'intelligence', and Lochiel, whose punctilious regard for the Prince had led Bradstreet, wrongly, to imagine that he favoured pushing on to London, now made his most forthright intervention yet in urging immediate retreat.[181]

The Prince was manifestly distraught: 'You ruin, abandon and betray me if you do not march on,' he cried, but in vain. Even those who had hitherto supported him were silent, until in the end, as he later testified, 'he could not prevail upon one single person' to support him.[182] Reluctantly he gave the order for retreat, remarking with acerbity, 'in future I shall summon no more councils, since I am accountable to nobody for my actions but to God and my father and therefore I shall no longer either ask or accept advice'.[183]

Whatever the jubilation of the clan chiefs and Lord George Murray that their views had prevailed, there were not a few who realised, once the decision to retreat was made public, that this was the end of the Stuart cause. 'It is all over, we shall never come back again', was Sheridan's despondent comment.[184] These fears seemed symbolically realised at the reception given by the Prince for sympathetic Derby citizens immediately after the second Council meeting. The press of people thronging to see the Prince upset the table by which the royal standard was located, and the falling table broke the standard.[185] Others were less restrained than Sheridan. Sir John MacDonald told Morgan that he held the trio of Lord George Murray, Elcho and Ogilvy mainly responsible for the decision; these three were 'weary of the affair ... they were for quitting him and betraying him [the

Prince]'.[186] The recriminations that proliferated once the retreat was known about have obscured the truth. Newcastle's agent Vere laid much of the blame on Lochiel, in accordance with camp gossip, but how unreliable this was emerged when John McKenzie of Glengarry's was taken prisoner and testified. According to McKenzie, whose testimony was taken seriously by the Whigs, Lord George Murray had wanted to press on for London, and it was Perth who had advised withdrawal.[187] This led to a guard being placed on Murray, who was suspected of being a traitor.[188] McKenzie's evidence was totally worthless, yet he was close to the heart of events in Derby, illustrating the point that resentment and disappointment coloured the reflections of many of the Jacobites and distorted the record.

Why was the decision taken to retreat from Derby and what were its consequences? No one reason is adequate to explain the debacle, although psychologically and in purely textbook military terms there were compelling enough reasons. Many of the Scottish leaders were ill at ease so far from their home base and, as they saw it, dangerously exposed. They tended to take their cue from Lord George Murray as the most talented military tactician in the army, but Murray was no gambler, rather the reverse and almost a defeatist. Accordingly, if Murray said their position at Derby was hopeless, this was good enough for most of the clan leaders. Other factors weighed with them too. It has been suggested that Lochiel was anxious for his clansmen and dreaded the loss of life attendant on a battle with Cumberland and, particularly when he had heard and been impressed by Bradstreet's fabrications, was keen to retreat.[189] This too had a powerful effect, for if Murray was the mind of the Jacobite army, Lochiel was its heart. Over and above this, the Scottish leaders deeply resented the failure of the English Jacobites to rise. There had always been those who opposed the invasion of England on nationalistic grounds, believing that the Prince should concentrate on a Stuart restoration in Scotland and its detachment from England. They felt bitter that, even after embarking on a venture for which few of them had any enthusiasm, their 'friends' in England should still be awaiting the outcome of their march to London before committing themselves. In a word, the fundamental half-heartedness with which many of the Highland leaders had entered into the invasion of England now manifested itself with devastating effect. Given that the whole operation was a gamble, those who voted for it in Edinburgh should either have declared against it at the time or committed themselves in a do-or-die way.[190]

Murray's military arguments were sound enough on paper, although it is not clear why he should have insisted so much on military orthodoxy at this point in a campaign which had been highly unconventional from the very beginning. With hindsight we can see that the Prince's strategic insight was superior for three main reasons. First, there was no significant barrier between the Jacobite army and London. The arguments about whether the Highlanders at Derby really were ahead of Cumberland at Lichfield in the race for the capital miss the point, which is that the maximum number of troops Cumberland could have got to Northampton in time to oppose the clansmen was 4,000, given the exhaustion of his troops. Man for man there can be no question about the superiority of the Scots, so that a battle fought with roughly even numbers could have had only one result. Beyond

Cumberland there was only a small contingent of guards and a motley assortment of defenders at Finchley.[191] As Bradstreet gloatingly remarked when the Council leaders swallowed his story about a further army under Ligonier or Hawley: 'Observe that there were not nine men at Northampton to oppose them, let alone nine thousand.'[192]

Secondly, there was considerable Jacobite support in London. Apart from the Irish Catholics there, most government ministers feared that the mob would go over en masse to Charles Edward if he once reached the capital. As William Pitt later remarked: 'If the rebels had obtained a victory and made themselves masters of London, I question if the spirit of the population would not have taken a different turn.'[193] Thirdly, the decision to retreat led to significant consequences both in London and Versailles. In Boulogne and Calais a major French expedition was gathering under the Duc de Richelieu for a descent on the English coast. Although news of Derby did not immediately lead Richelieu to abandon the expedition, it did seriously weaken his resolve, so that he was less able to deal with the other obstacles to his enterprise, such as the adverse weather and the Royal Navy. Derby also seemed to endorse the view of those in the French court who had always argued that no French army should be sent to England, since the 'English Jacobite party' was a figment in the minds of Jacobite exiles.[194]

In London the Duke of Newcastle was freed from his abiding anxiety that the Whigs would have to fight on two fronts, against the Jacobite army to the north of London and against the French to the south. More than that, he now realised that there had been no concerted plan between Charles Edward and the French for the invasion of England. Contemporary testimony on Thursday 5th December also shows that the decision to retreat from Derby was the wrong one. There is strong evidence that the North Oxfordshire squires would have joined any southward advance of the clans from Derby.[195] It is also possible that the later claims that Sir Watkin Williams Wynn's men had begun to march towards Derby and that his courier arrived there on Sunday the 8th with this news was not an entire fabrication.[196]

Even more telling evidence is in the correspondence of the Whig military commanders on this day. While Ligonier ordered a detailed reconnaissance of all routes from Lichfield to Northampton and Leicester, in hopes of intercepting Charles Edward, the Duke of Richmond received orders to march to Coventry (27 miles away) and to proceed thence to Northampton (a further 31 miles).[197] But even given that the Highlanders had some 61 miles of 'deep bad way' to traverse between Derby and Northampton, Richmond still remained apprehensive that they might get to London before him. He advised Newcastle to keep all the defenders of London in one encampment and not to canton them since the enemy moved too fast for soldiers to be got together quickly to oppose them.[198] Even greater concern was shown in his next letter to Newcastle: 'Are we all mad? that you don't send for 10,000 more forces be they Hessians, Hanoverians or devils if they will but fight for us . . . The whole kingdom is asleep. Our cavalry can't be here before February and the Pretender may be crowned at Westminster by that time.'[199] In the same missive Richmond turned to the now perennial subject of complaint, Marshal Wade. Wade was in fact still in Wetherby, and so far was he from posing the threat that Lord George Murray had imagined that his main concern at this hour of crisis was to advise Newcastle that the command of the proposed 1746 campaign in Scotland be given to someone else on account of his advanced years.[200]

NOTES

1. Barnes p. 82.
2. Dore pp. 49–50.
3. Williamson p. 65.
4. *British Magazine* 1746 p. 229.
5. Allardyce, ii. p. 379; *Manchester Magazine* 29 July 1746.
6. SP Dom 82 ff. 173–74.
7. SP Dom 76/119–20.
8. SP Dom 83 f. 218.
9. Taylor, *Anon. History* p. 101.
10. Home pp. 321–23; Ray p. 142.
11. Maxwell of Kirkconnell p. 71.
12. Chambers p. 189.
13. HMC, 13 vi. p. 163.
14. SP Dom 76/20; 'Two Yorkshire Diaries' p. 112.
15. Allardyce, ii. p. 444.
16. Elcho p. 34.
17. Davies p. 108.
18. Ibid. p. 111.
19. Renaud pp. 80–82.
20. SP Dom 76/20.
21. Elcho p. 334.
22. Stephens p. 91.
23. Add. MSS. 33050 f. 73.
24. Add. MSS. 33050 f. 39.
25. Burne pp. 94–96.
26. SP Dom 76/20.
27. Elcho p. 334.
28. Ibid. p. 335.
29. SP Dom 80 ff. 96–97.
30. SP Dom 80 ff. 164–65.
31. Add. MSS. 33050 ff. 43, 47.
32. Add. MSS. 33050 f. 93.
33. Richmond to Cumberland, 2 December 1745, SP Dom 76/20.
34. SP Dom 70/22.
35. Ibid.
36. SP Dom 76/19.
37. SP Dom 76/20.
38. Stuart MSS 272/92A.
39. Fitzherbert MSS.
40. Earwaker, *Constables,* iii. pp. 72–73.
41. Talon p. 232.
42. Chambers p. 189.
43. *London Gazette* No. 8490, 3–7 December 1745.
44. *Ogilvy's Orderbook* pp. 300–01.

45. Ray p. 142.
46. *Ogilvy's Orderbook* p. 301.
47. Add. MSS. 33050 ff. 21, 33.
48. Fitzherbert MSS.
49. HMC, 13 vi. p. 164.
50. SP Dom 76/27, 119; Wm. Salt Arch. Soc. vii. p. 112.
51. Vezzozi p. 86; Elcho p. 335.
52. *Gentlemen's Magazine* 1745 p. 621.
53. Sleigh p. 203.
54. Elcho p. 336.
55. Sleigh p. 205.
56. Barnes p. 83.
57. Sleigh p. 203.
58. SP Dom 82 f. 170.
59. Burne p. 58.
60. Elcho p. 335.
61. Whitworth p. 112.
62. Burne p. 61.
63. HMC, Laing, ii. p. 355.
64. Ibid.
65. Herring-Hardwicke loc. cit. p. 733.
66. Cox, *Three Centuries* i. p. 198.
67. Simpson, *Derby and the Forty-Five* pp. 130-40.
68. Beresford pp. 46–47.
69. Ibid.
70. HMC, 15 ii. p. 250.
71. SP Dom 80 ff. 96–97.
72. *Ogilvy's Orderbook* pp. 300–01.
73. Frazer, ii. p. 195.
74. SP Dom 85 f. 261.
75. Staffs CRO 491/34 (T.H. Hulme's Commonplace Book) f. 143.
76. O'Sullivan p. 100.
77. HMC, 13 vi. p. 164; Broughton pp. 30–31.
78. Maxwell of Kirkconnell p. 72; Simpson (1826) p. 246.
79. Simpson (1933) p. 122.
80. Blaikie, 'John Daniel's Progress' pp. 175–76.
81. Allardyce, i. pp. 287–93.
82. Hutton p. 268.
83. Elcho p. 336; Hutton p. 270.
84. Davison pp. 81–90.
85. Hutton p. 270.
86. Chambers p. 190.
87. Hutton pp. 271–72.
88. Ibid. p. 268.
89. Cox, *Three Centuries* i. p. 311.
90. O'Sullivan p. 100; Tomasson p. 107.
91. Simpson (1933) p. 147.
92. Hutton p. 268.
93. Simpson (1933) p. 123.
94. SP Dom 76/38.
95. SP Dom 76/37.
96. Simpson (1933) p. 148.
97. Blaikie, 'John Daniel's Progress' p. 176.
98. Hutton p. 273.

99. Ibid. pp. 273–74.
100. Ibid. p. 275.
101. Simpson (1933) pp. 150–55.
102. HMC, Lothian p. 155.
103. Tomasson p. 107.
104. Simpson (1933) p. 147.
105. SP Dom 76/119; 77/79; 78/15.
106. Simpson (1933) p. 153.
107. SP Dom 76/45 & 52.
108. *Gentlemen's Magazine* 1745 p. 621.
109. SP Dom 76/45.
110. Yorke, *Hardwicke* i. pp. 471–75.
111. Charteris p. 230.
112. Add. MSS. 32705 f. 405.
113. SP Dom 76/45.
114. Jarvis, ii. p. 23.
115. SP Dom 76/45.
116. SP Dom 76/47.
117. McLynn, 'Nottingham and the Jacobite Rising of 1745'.
118. HMC, 14 ix. p. 135.
119. Add. MSS. 32705 f. 403.
120. SP Dom 76/50.
121. Johnstone p. 67.
122. Atholl, *Chronicles* iii. Appendix xxxix.
123. Allardyce, i. pp. 287–93.
124. Ibid.
125. L.P. ii. p. 495.
126. SP Dom 76/57,58,59; 77/58.
127. SP Dom 76/53.
128. SP Dom 76/56.
129. SP Dom 76/116.
130. Stott (1929) p. 8.
131. Add. MSS. 33050 f. 65.
132. Ray pp. 159–61.
133. Potter, loc. cit.
134. SP Dom 76/36.
135. SP Dom 76/40; Jarvis, ii. pp. 94–104.
136. Simpson (1933) pp. 175–88.
137. Chambers, 'Marches' pp. 48–53.
138. Johnstone pp. 68–69.
139. Chambers, 'Marches' pp. 54–55.
140. Maxwell of Kirkconnell p. 73.
141. Tomasson pp. 108–110.
142. SP Dom 76/98.
143. Elcho p. 86; Ewald, i. p. 299.
144. 'Elcho's Journal' in Tayler, *Anon. History* pp. 151–52; Add. MSS. 29913 f. 9.
145. Johnstone pp. 72–73.
146. Simpson (1933) pp. 188–90.
147. Tomasson pp. 108–110.
148. 'Elcho's Journal' p. 152.
149. Ibid. pp. 151–52.
150. Maxwell of Kirkconnell p. 74.
151. Chambers, 'Marches' pp. 54–55.
152. AEMD, Angleterre 79 f. 235; O'Sullivan p. 102; Tomasson p. 110.

153. Murray of Broughton pp. 434–35.
154. Staffs CRO: SMS 49/53/44.
155. Elcho pp. 337–39.
156. Chambers, 'Marches' p. 55.
157. Tayler (1928) p. 278.
158. *Ogilvy's Orderbook* p. 302.
159. SP Dom 76/52.
160. Burne p. 62.
161. Briggs pp. 22–23.
162. HMC, Lothian pp. 152–53; HMC, 5. p. 400.
163. SP Dom 80 ff. 239–40.
164. McLynn, 'Nottingham and the '45', pp. 63–69.
165. Simpson (1933) pp. 190–92.
166. Tomasson p. 114.
167. 'MacDonald's Memoirs', in Tayler, *Anon. Hist.* p. 61.
168. Ibid; Chambers, 'Marches' p. 57.
169. O'Sullivan p. 102.
170. Tomasson pp. 110–14.
171. Ibid. p. 114.
172. Simpson (1933) p. 194.
173. Maxwell of Kirkconnell p. 75; Chambers, 'Marches' p. 56.
174. Johnstone pp. 72–73; Chambers, 'Marches' p. 57.
175. Chambers, 'Marches' p. 56; Elcho p. 339.
176. O'Sullivan p. 102.
177. Maxwell of Kirkconnell p. 75.
178. Simpson (1933) p. 194.
179. SP Dom 80 ff. 96–97.
180. Jarvis, ii. pp. 100–101.
181. SP Dom 80 ff. 163–64.
182. Home p. 324.
183. Tomasson p. 114.
184. Chambers, 'Marches' p. 57; Tomasson p. 114.
185. Blaikie, 'John Daniel's Progress' p. 178.
186. SP Dom 80 ff. 163–64.
187. SP Dom 77/76.
188. SP Dom 77/60; Vezzozi pp. 87–89.
189. Tomasson p. 114 et seq.
190. Cruickshanks p. 100.
191. Simpson (1933) pp. 198–204.
192. Bradstreet pp. 126–27; Smollett, xi. pp. 225–27.
193. Sharpe, iii. pp. 50–56.
194. McLynn, *France and the Jacobite Rising of 1745*, Chapters 6 & 7.
195. Robson pp. 1–9.
196. SP Dom 80 ff. 166; *Quarterly Review* 1899 p. 453.
197. Whitworth p. 113.
198. Add. MSS. 32705 f. 409.
199. Atholl, *Chronicles* iii. p. 100.
200. SP Dom 76/50.

7

The Retreat through Lancashire

Friday 6th December

THIS day, which came to be called 'Black Friday', dawned in London to scenes of panic and consternation as the presence of the Highlanders in Derby became generally known. Literary figures as various as Smollett, Gray and Fielding have left eloquent testimony to the atmosphere in the capital this Friday.[1] Once again, as after Prestonpans, there was a run on the Bank of England; it is alleged that the Bank reverted to the 1720 stratagem of paying its depositors in sixpences to staunch the outflow of funds.[2] As Fielding scathingly commented, most of the propertied people in London demonstrated their public-spiritedness by packing up their money, jewels and plate.[3]

Newcastle, having informed the Mayor of London of the parlous military position and Cumberland's efforts to get between the 'Young Pretender' and the capital at Northampton, gave him detailed instructions on the defence of the city.[4] These involved augmenting the guard in the city of London; taking steps to suppress tumults or insurrections, such as stationing guards in the squares and open places of the city; holding daily meetings of the city magistrates; making an exact count of all horses in the city; instituting a system of signals to warn of any commotion; and most important of all, sending an account of the available manpower within London, its location, and the Mayor's views on how it could be increased and how the able-bodied could be persuaded to take up arms. Within the city trained guards were to take up their quarters in the Royal Exchange, while part of the Bridewell hospital was to serve as a guard room for the night guards appointed by the commission of lieutenancy. The two city marshals were to be instructed to visit the night watches in the several wards to see that the constables did their duty.[5]

Meanwhile an attempt was made to gather as many troops as possible north of London. Five companies of Guards were ordered to march for St. Albans; five companies of Mordaunt's foot were told off to Highgate and Hampstead; Hawley's dragoons were despatched to Barnet.[6] The intention was that all available units should eventually rendezvous at Finchley Common, where thirty pieces of artillery were being sent from the Tower. Most controversially of all, on Tuesday 3rd December seven companies of Lord John Murray's Highlanders — 'the Black Watch' — newly arrived from Flanders, were ordered to march via Maidstone and Dartford to north London and environs. These were the Highlanders whose mutiny in 1743 had led to stern repression and executions. As a consequence they were widely thought to be unreliable at the present juncture. Although Lord Stair said he would vouch for them, George II was not alone in distrusting them and thinking that, faced by their countrymen at Finchley, and with the desire for revenge for 1743 still strong, they would go over to the Stuart prince to a man.[7]

London, then, on 6th December was like a ghost town, with shops and play-houses shut and the general panic faithfully reported by numerous foreign agents and businessmen.[8] British merchants abroad also received verification of the crumbling resolve in the capital from their friends there, and indeed Newcastle did not trouble to deny it: 'the march of the rebels towards London occasioned a good deal of consternation here', he told Lord Irwin a week later when, with the danger passed, he was able to use a somewhat bland tone.[9] Quite apart from the strength of Jacobitism in London, Newcastle had the problem of a recalcitrant corporation to deal with. Alderman Heathcote, a convinced Jacobite, came as close to non-cooperation as he could by telling Newcastle that he could not provide for the security of the city if part of the militia were not set aside for that purpose.[10]

There was little enough to cheer the Whigs this day and they clutched at such straws as they could. One of these was the appearance of the Duke and Duchess of Norfolk, nominal leaders of the English Catholics, and newly arrived from their seat in Nottinghamshire, at the Court of St. James at the very time that the most virulent anti-Catholic and anti-Jesuit proclamations were being uttered.[11] Another was the offer to Newcastle by the guild of weavers to supply one thousand apprentices capable of bearing arms.[12] The lawyers too attempted to form themselves into a fighting band under Chief Justice Willes and offered to serve as bodyguard to George II's family, should the monarch decide to take the field in person as he had done two years earlier at Dettingen.[13]

Given that retreat by the Highlanders was now thought inconceivable, the question on everyone's lips was: what would the clansmen's route to London be? Both Oxfordshire and Buckinghamshire were alarmed that the Scots were coming their way, and several families packed their valuables and decamped. While the towns of Newbury and Welbeck were in confident expectation of seeing Charles Edward soon, on the assumption that he would aim to be in London on the 8th, another school of thought opted for a link-up with the French as his most likely move.[14] This might mean proceeding through Cambridgeshire to a seaport in Suffolk to greet a landing from Dunkirk or a junction somewhere nearer London. The Deputy Lieutenants of Kent called out the entire county militia against a possible French landfall on the south coast.[15] Newcastle did not think that a junction with the French would be made but feared rather a war on two fronts. His own ideas on the Highlanders' likely itinerary were shaped by the ancillary report, also received this Friday, that the Jacobites were in possession of Nottingham. Assuming the news to be true, it meant that all Cumberland's efforts to get his army back to Northampton to bar the way to London were useless, since Charles Edward could bypass him by marching via Stamford, Biggleswade and Welling, or by Stamford, Huntingdon, Royston and Ware. Since the most likely route was through

Stamford and Huntingdon, the first regiment of Guards was despatched to the latter town.[16]

But in Derby the (to the Whigs) unthinkable was happening and the retreat commenced. Charles Edward, who had been accustomed to march on foot at the head of the army, showed symbolically his dissent from the decision to withdraw by mounting his horse and riding at the rear.[17] Lord George Murray had now to make good his pledge that he would carry the army safely back to Scotland if only its leaders would agree to retreat. As he saw it, he had little to fear from Cumberland whom he could outmarch. The real danger came from Wade, and the peril would increase after Preston, especially if the Lancashire militia delayed the Jacobite army by breaking down Ribble Bridge.[18] However, Murray took comfort from the one day's start he had gained. Wade would not learn of the retreat before Friday evening, and even then he would probably wait for Cumberland's orders before making any move. If Wade then marched by Skipton or by Settle across the Pennines, he would effectively lose two days and the Prince's army would get to Lancaster before him.[19] The one daunting possibility that remained was that Wade might march straight to Penrith across good mountain roads. In that case there were two options open: either to fight a way through Wade's army — which would mean being several days' march ahead of Cumberland — or to abandon the cannon and baggage and take to the mountains so as to reach Scotland that way.

Clearly the maximum time had to be gained before the enemy realised that the retreat was in earnest. Accordingly, scouting parties were sent south from Swarkestone Bridge with orders to double back later and rejoin the main army.[20] The guard at the bridge was kept there until the last possible moment. And the main army was marched out of Derby by a circuitous route so that not even the rank and file would know at first that withdrawal had been decided on. The retreat began at 7 a.m. and many of the infantry were well on the road to Ashbourne before dawn broke and they realised they were heading northwards.[21] At this point the Highlanders' morale, at its acme in Derby, began to plummet. It seems there were loud cries from the ordinary soldiers that they had been betrayed. Many declared their intention of returning to their homes once they reached Scotland.[22] Murray of Broughton's wife was said to have cried like a child.[23] About a mile out of Derby a grim-faced Charles Edward was seen by Vere in company with Morgan, who rode a bay horse.[24] Morgan was now seriously worried about his own future but could get little reassurance from the taciturn Prince. The official explanation for the retreat was that the army would re-enter England once it had joined Drummond's forces in Scotland.[25] But in conversation with Morgan both Sir John MacDonald and O'Sullivan had scoffed at that story and declared that in their opinion the whole venture was over. Morgan now decided to leave, both because he considered that the Stuart cause was already doomed and because he thought that such a small number of men would never get back safely to Scotland.[26]

Morgan's alarm was shared by the lesser officers in the army, who at first thought that some bad news must have occasioned the retreat. But when they learned that Charles Edward had marched so far into England without the least invitation from any of the English gentry, they bitterly upbraided their superiors for having brought them so far as Derby; they had all along imagined that such an invasion must have been undertaken in concert with the English Jacobites.[27] Two of the minor officers, Gordon Francis of Kinkardine Mill, and Arthur Gordon, a major in Pitsligo's, went so far as to send a message to Cumberland, offering to desert if he would give them a pardon.[28] The cancer bade fair to spread through the whole army. In John Roy Stewart's regiment Roy Stuart threw down his gun when nearing Ashbourne and said that he would go no further. He was clapped in irons and kept under close guard until he gave his word that he would take up his arms again and act like a soldier.[29]

By 11 a.m. only a few stragglers were left in Derby. The Prince himself left about 9 a.m. He rode across the Market Place, proceeded up Rotten Row and then turned down Sadler Gate towards Ashbourne. At about the same hour Perth and his aide-de-camp entered Samuel Heathcote's house with pistols cocked in search of the spy Birch who had escaped the previous day from Exeter House. Heathcote was suspected of harbouring him on his premises but in reality Birch had swum to the bank of the Derwent at the bottom of Heathcote's garden, where he stripped off his clothes before plunging into the river once more and only appearing on dry land again two miles away.[30]

While Derby absorbed the psychological shock of the Highlanders' sojourn — profound enough to prevent the occurrence of market day on Friday the 6th and church services on Sunday the 8th[31] — the clan leaders, immediately Derby was behind them, issued powder and ball to their men as if an engagement was imminent.[32] The general rumour was that a battle was to be fought with Wade, but to boost their sagging spirits the regimental colonels told their men that reinforcements under Drummond had entered England and would meet them at Lancaster or Preston, where they hoped to crush Wade and then turn back and march on London once more.[33] A party of four Whig sightseers, who rode out of Ashbourne to see the army, encountered it four miles out of Derby.[34] As they watched from a hill, the order of march could be clearly discerned. First came Elcho's Lifeguards and Kilmarnock's horse, followed by the Atholl Brigade with the royal standard. Perth's, Ogilvy's, Roy Stewart's, Glenbucket's and the Manchester regiment preceded Lord George's bugbear, the artillery and baggage carts with their convoy of English cannon, Swedish field pieces and baggage horses. The MacDonald regiments of Glengarry, Keppoch and Clanranald were followed by the other clan regiments, the Camerons, Appin Stewarts and MacPhersons, with Pitsligo's horse and the hussars bringing up the extreme rear.[35] No objection was raised when the four onlookers left their horses at a nearby farm, borrowed walking shoes and fell in with the army for the rest of the march to Ashbourne, where they started to arrive about 3 p.m.[36]

Already on the thirteen and a half miles from Derby to Ashbourne there were signs that the iron discipline and freedom from rapine which had so impressed the English on the march to Derby were breaking down. This was particularly noticeable in the case of the Manchester regiment, whose members clearly had more to fear than the Scots. One of those later executed, John Berwick, stole a horse with saddle and holsters; Jamed Dawson went to Bradshaw Hall to search for arms and brought back a brace of pistols for Townley; Townley himself ransacked (with others of his regiment) a house by the roadside and extracted a sackful of arms which he took with him to Ashbourne.[37] More seriously, two Scots shot dead one Humphrey Brown at Clifton near Ashbourne for refusing to hand over his horse and wounded an innkeeper.[38] Okeover Hall, too, was plundered of horses, bridles, saddles and boots, and four Scots spent the night there to the terror of the steward Jeremaiah Kitching.[39] On the other hand, two laggard Scots were shot dead on the road to Ashbourne by a farmer and his sons.

The hardening attitude of the Jacobites was even more in evidence in Ashbourne, where some forty people were tried by a summary court-martial as spies and left in confinement pending a further hearing.[40] A tense and nervous night was spent in Ashbourne. While Charles Edward lodged at Ashbourne Hall, and those who had formerly spent a night here with Lord George Murray returned to their old billets, others were forced to crowd into limited accommodation. About three hundred were housed at the Talbot inn where the landlord later complained that he had been paid far less than the market rate, having received just £10 for items amounting to £44.[41]

The tension at Ashbourne was reflected in the military dispositions made that night. While two officers and fifty men of Glengarry's mounted a special guard at the end of the street leading to Derby, another detachment guarded the turnpike house with the gate shut; outside were two foot sentries and a cavalry patrol. Perth's were told off to guard the artillery, while fifty of Glenbucket's kept vigil at the market place. A couple of miles out on the Derby road a dozen of Elcho's Lifeguards took it in turns to reconnoitre with the same number of Kilmarnock's, so that an unceasing patrol was kept up all night.[42] Another dozen of Kilmarnock's patrolled the road to Burton-on-Trent, where a branch road of the Buxton–Derby turnpike forked off to the right from Ashbourne. Such was the general nervousness that Townley posted two sentries at his bedroom door in case Cumberland should come upon him suddenly.[43]

The likelihood of this was not great since, as Lord George Murray had hoped, it was late on the 6th before the truth of the Highlanders' position was realised by the enemy. The feint towards Loughborough from Swarkestone Bridge deceived many. The clansmen were expected at Leicester and then successively reported in Loughborough, Rothley and Belgrave.[44] Another report, which caused alarm in Mansfield, placed them in Nottingham, heading for Loughborough and Leicester, though so great was the confusion by this time that the Bishop of London was able to write that he did not know whether their presence in Nottingham indicated a thrust towards London or towards Yorkshire![45] Another report, this time from Stamford, had the Prince's advance guard marching to Mansfield and the main body to Alfreton. Nottinghamshire was a fertile source of invention, for when it was learned that the Highlanders had actually gone to Ashbourne, it was given out that this was because they had found Cumberland's army waiting for them on the road to Loughborough, south of Swarkestone Bridge.[46] By the evening, however, the true information at last started to imprint itself, and all towns north of Ashbourne as far as Doncaster had definite news of the retreat.

Cumberland, who this Friday moved from his headquarters in Lichfield at Michael Rawlinson's mansion to stay with Lord Guernsey at Packington Hall in Warwickshire, planned to assemble the bulk of his forces on Meriden Heath near Coventry.[47] While the Duke of Richmond reached Coventry and another force under Colonel Cuthbert Ellison arrived in its environs, the rest of the Hanoverian forces were cantoned along a line from Wolverhampton to Coventry, some in Coleshill, others in Sutton Coldfield and Abbots Bromley.[48] In such scattered detachments Cumberland still feared the Jacobites might pick them off one by one, so his plan was to assemble everyone except Richmond and his men — who were to intercept the Stuart prince at Northampton — on Meriden Heath, ready for a forced march to London. Cumberland's position was desperate: his men were exhausted, every one according to the Duke having worn out 'one if not two pairs of shoes' on the marches of the last four days; in addition, the weather now turned harsh with snow, frost and rain 'as severe as it is possible to conceive'.[49] The Duke's relief when he heard of the retreat to Ashbourne can be imagined. The Jacobites' destination, he imagined, must be Wales for, as he wrote to Wade: 'they cannot flatter themselves with hopes of passing by you into Scotland.'[50] For this reason he made no attempt to alert the by now considerable body of troops in Chester to the changed circumstances. But when he realised later that night that Wade was still only as far south as Doncaster, he changed his mind and wrote querulously: 'it seems to me much to be feared, that if you can't move westward into Lancashire these villains may escape back unpunished into their highlands to our eternal shame'.[51]

Cumberland's worst fears were to be realised. When Wade, who arrived in Doncaster that night with Wentworth and Oglethorpe accompanied by two regiments of cavalry and one of dragoons, heard of Charles Edward's retreat, he ordered his infantry to halt at Ferrybridge (where they had marched from Pontefract) preparatory to starting north once more.[52] While the dragoons were sent on to Bawtry and Blyth, he remained in Doncaster to get definite intelligence of the clansmen's route. His intention was not to intercept the Highlanders but to strike north again in order to protect Newcastle and Yorkshire.[53] Every single item in Wade's letter to Cumberland on the 6th must have infuriated the Duke, from his assumption that it was Cumberland's seizure of Swarkestone Bridge that compelled the Stuart prince to retreat to the generally whining tone in which he described his situation: 'These marches and countermarches of the rebels reduce us to almost insuperable inconveniences, at this season of the year; for when we have provided bread, wood and straw with great difficulty in one place, we are obliged to march unprepared to another and are often stopped on our march for want of waggons to carry our bread, which we can neither purchase nor hire but at very exorbitant rates, if we can find them at all; and I could have wished that the commissary had been provided before he left London with a number sufficient to have carried eight or ten days' bread or biscuit, for I dread the consequences of the want of both, as there is no flour to be got in any of the towns, above what is necessary for the support of the inhabitants.'[54] It was clear that once again Wade was likely to disappoint Whig hopes and allay Lord George Murray's fears.

Saturday 7th December

The march of the Highlanders from Ashbourne commenced at about 1 a.m. Since Leek was too small to accommodate the entire army, the plan was that the van would go on to Macclesfield.[55] Accordingly, the first to leave Ashbourne headed for Macclesfield were Elcho's, Pitsligo's, Ogilvy's and John Roy Stewart's.[56] The artillery and the rearguard did not clear the town until 7 a.m.: Lord George Murray claimed that the Prince's sullen recalcitrance was jeopardising the entire operation, since the rear could not leave until Charles Edward was ready.[57] A party of horse remained behind in Ashbourne until noon to see if there was any sign of a pursuit from Cumberland.[58]

The ill humour and resentment on both sides — the Jacobite army and the inhabitants of Staffordshire and Derbyshire — was now obvious, and many trivial incidents occurred to illustrate the new pattern. Two inhabitants of Ashbourne received gunshot wounds after an affray with the Scots.[59] On the march to Leek the innkeeper at the Hanging Bridge was also shot.[60] And on arrival in Leek the Highlanders abandoned their previous courtesy and took from the town what they wanted; this was in retaliation for the actions of the townsfolk who on the 3rd had captured two Jacobite stragglers and sent them to Stafford gaol. The particular offender was Mr. Lockett's son who had been the prime mover in this affair. Consequently the most aggressive Whigs, Mr. Lockett, Jnr., Mr. Mills and Mr. Statham, left town rapidly with the constable on the approach of the Highlanders. It was particularly their houses that were pillaged and stripped of clothes and linen; Mr. Lockett, Snr., was meanwhile threatened with shooting if he did not produce his son.[61]

At Okeover Hall, as the previous night's party departed, another arrived, demanded money, and took the little of value that was still available.[62] Many farmers around Leek, whose teams had been pressed, accompanied the Highlanders back as far as the Mersey in hopes of recovering them, but most gave up. The only item of significance that the Jacobites relinquished was the post-chaise taken from the Derby Post Office, which was found abandoned on the road beyond Ashbourne.[63]

Low morale in the Jacobite army, the obvious result of bitterness and disillusionment over Derby, was now everywhere remarked on, and it was at Ashbourne that the disappointed David Morgan finally fled from the army. Morgan enlisted the services of a Mr. Chatterton and planned to hide out in a farm house near Stone until the clansmen ceased to look for him. Chatterton found him a guide, and Morgan slipped away unnoticed at about five on Saturday morning while the pipes were playing for the day's march. Alas, he immediately fell in with the Staffordshire militia and was taken to Stafford gaol on suspicion of high treason. By 9th December Morgan was writing pathetic letters to London for a pardon, denying that he had ever been in the Jacobite army. Unfortunately for him, Vere had plotted his movements closely since Tuesday December 3rd, so he had no chance of escaping the gallows.[64]

Apart from Morgan, desertion continued only on a very small scale during the march to Leek. Michael Brady quit the Manchester regiment, only to be executed later, and his fate indicates why the desertion rate was not higher.[65] The main deterrent was clearly the unlikelihood of reprieve, even if one were to survive the savagery of the locals, who were reported to have flayed alive one Scottish straggler. Anyone straying far from the marching column was likely to be captured, at the very least, as happened near Leek to the former gardener Robert Hamilton, a soldier in Perth's regiment.[66] The most curious development, considering that the army was in retreat, was that there were two recruits for the Prince in Leek. One, James Miller, was later taken prisoner when the Manchester regiment was left behind in Carlisle at the end of the English campaign. The other was John Gould of Brownhills, whose friends rode with him as far as Macclesfield in an attempt to dissuade him.[67]

Once at Leek, four officers were detached from the Manchester regiment and sent to Manchester to try to enlist more men there. Captains Deacon and Brettargh, Lieutenant Holker and Ensign Syddall rode forward rapidly and reached Stockport that evening.[68] They went first to Crossford Bridge, which they found had been pulled down again (this had been done by a party commanded by James Cheetham, a Manchester Whig), so they returned to Stockport.[69] Here they were greeted with hostility by the townspeople, who had had advance intelligence of their visit. The four then had to fight their way through to the ford at Stockport, but not before one of them had his horse shot from under him. Arriving in Manchester on three horses, they were chased by a mob raised by the constables down Market Street and into St. Anne's Square. Here Syddall dismounted and gave his pursuers the slip and then made his way to his house, where he found the windows had all been broken by the mob.[70]

When the vanguard left Leek for Macclesfield, a strong rumour arose that they had taken the road for Bakewell and Chesterfield.[71] Given the reports also current about the build-up of a French invasion force at Dunkirk, this seemed to indicate a march through Lincolnshire to meet the French on the Norfolk or Suffolk coast.[72] There were still some who hoped for this, like the Jacobite lady at Newport Pagnell who is said to have delayed government troops for over an hour by locking up Lathbury Bridge on her property,[73] but most people decided to manifest their 'loyalty' to George II now that the Jacobites were retreating. Sir Richard Wrottesley armed his stewards and tenantry in support of his father-in-law Lord Gower but (conveniently) was just starting out when the news of the retreat came in. According to one story they got no further than the Old Bull inn, a mile from Wrottesley Hall, where the whole contingent got drunk.[74]

By now the more perceptive of the Whigs began to realise that the Jacobites might get back to Scotland after all. The poor state of the roads, the shortage of daylight hours, and the atrocious weather all seemed to favour the clansmen rather than the regular troops.[75] Cumberland indeed made no attempt at pursuit this Saturday. His army rested for twenty-four hours after the four desperate days of forced marches and counter-marches.[76] The crucial element in the military struggle was now horses, since Cumberland's only chance of overtaking the Scots was to use his dragoons and put part of his infantry on horseback to form a pursuing force. Fortunately for him, the gentry of the West Midlands, influenced no doubt by the retreat from Derby, chose this moment to demonstrate their loyalty to the House of Hanover. Whereas the militia in Wolverhampton had had to hire horses at 2/- each to bring Cumberland's baggage back from Stafford, the mounts the Duke needed for his pursuit of the Highlanders were provided free. Sir Lister Holt of Aston Hall near Birmingham, who was MP for Lichfield, supplied 250 out of his own stables. And the town of Birmingham distinguished itself in Cumberland's eyes by providing no less than 600 horses free of charge.[77]

Wade meanwhile was fulfilling all the worst expectations of him in Whig circles. Expresses countermanded the march of the infantry south to Doncaster, and commissaries were sent for forage to Wetherby, but morale in his army was adversely affected by news of the impending march north. The steady improvement in weather conditions on the advance south might well cease and the return to frost and snow have to be faced.[78] Wade now had to act fast if he was to make any impact on the campaign. On paper, to get to Preston in time to intercept the Jacobites he would have to march eighty-one miles to their seventy-eight. The alternative was to try to cut the road at Kendal by proceeding west via Settle and Kirkby Lonsdale. Either one of these manoeuvres required great energy and despatch, but Wade was slothful in his reactions. He did not reach Wakefield until 10th December, a distance of just twenty miles from Doncaster and twelve from Ferrybridge; his cavalry had therefore averaged seven miles a day in three days and his infantry only four.[79] Small wonder that Chesterfield wrote to Newcastle that his Marcellus (Cumberland) was to be preferred to his Fabius (Wade). Newcastle shrugged this off — 'I have a lesser opinion of them since their retreat' — and was already concentrating much more on the imminent threat from France.[80]

Sunday 8th December

The Jacobites began to leave Leek at six this morning amid snow and ice and arctic temperatures.[81] At eight the artillery, bane of the retreat, departed. An eyewitness described the army as 'not above 4,000 fighting men and those much dispirited and tired with marching'.[82] Dispirited they may have been, but physical exhaustion was not at this stage a major factor: whatever the case with the vanguard after travelling the twenty-eight miles from Ashbourne to Macclesfield, the Highlanders in the main column would not have been troubled by the fifteen miles from Ashbourne to Leek, even given the wretched condition of this stretch of road. The major problem this Sunday was punctuality: once again Lord George Murray was vexed by the late start, and one coach, with an escort of seventy horsemen, conveying some of the Jacobite ladies, did not leave Mr. Mill's house until 11 a.m.[83]

Several Jacobite outriders in search of booty on the road to Newcastle-under-Lyme triggered an alarm that spread as far as Shrewsbury.[84] The false rumour that the Scots had entered Newcastle led in turn to panic in Shrewsbury, especially when an express arrived at eleven on Sunday night, stating definitely that Charles Edward and his army were on the way there. The leading Whig families began to leave town while the regiment of foot commanded by Lord Herbert marched off in great fright to Wenlock Edge. The townspeople of Shrewsbury spent the night hiding or removing their effects and dispersing themselves.[85] Shrewsbury seemed a likely target for the Jacobites (as on the southward march), either as a stop on the way to Wales or as a means of dominating the Severn. This in turn raised the possibility that the Jacobites could adopt a new strategy by aiming for command of the west; they could descend the river to Bristol, where a substantial contribution could be levied from the city merchants or the town and shipping could be destroyed.[86] This, presupposing a junction with the Welsh Jacobites, was a possible scenario — indeed on this Sunday some Somerset Catholics toyed with the idea of travelling to Wales to meet their Prince there, on the assumption that this was his destination — but in the circumstances of the retreat an unlikely one, although Cumberland could still not be entirely sure that the objective was Scotland and not Wales.[87]

At about 3 p.m. the army re-entered Macclesfield.[88] As in Leek, the Mayor, officials and leading citizens had fled to their country houses, and those who remained barricaded their homes for fear of plunder. This was a sensible precaution, as the clansmen were this time in no mood for barter or conciliation and seized money, plate, clothes and bedding at will. A contemporary chronicler wrote: 'this calamity fell chiefly on the poorer sort but the better end of people suffered a particular hardship of another kind'.[89] This was the favourite Jacobite device of levying an amount equivalent to that subscribed to the associations for the defence of George II. The money was exacted in a peremptory way: the citizens of Macclesfield were given the choice of paying the required amount by 6 a.m. on Monday or having their houses burned about their ears. The Mayoress, who had remained in town, attempted to stall by saying that she did not have a subscription list, so that the amount payable could not be known. But when the Scots threatened her with death if she did not produce the list, the Town Clerk came up with a copy, so the erstwhile subscribers were doomed to pay.[90]

This severe Jacobite attitude was undoubtedly a reaction to the hostility of the people of England, now manifesting itself more and more as the army retreated. As Elcho remarked: 'whenever any of the men straggled or stayed behind, they either murdered them or sent them to the Duke [Cumberland] and all the way from Derby to Carlisle all men that were left sick on the road were either killed, abused or jailed'.[91] One particularly gruesome instance was related by John Daniel. A young English recruit, marching some miles ahead of the army, lay down under a hedge to sleep. As he slept his throat was cut by a woman and her son. When the army came on the scene the murderers were caught and the chiefs were for executing them forthwith, but once again the clemency of the Prince prevented punishment, as it had done with Vere.[92]

Furthermore, the militia, which had tracked the army since Derby without coming in close, now seemed to be growing bolder. As Elcho and the vanguard neared Stockport at 6 p.m. this Sunday — the same hour as the last of the artillery entered Macclesfield — they were fired upon by the militia and a Highland officer's servant was killed.[93] In retaliation for this and the previous night's assault on the four officers of the Manchester regiment, Elcho's men opened fire on a militia patrol and killed some of them.[94] As a further reprisal a few houses in Stockport were burned. Another Highland party was shot at in a village outside Stockport and the same punishment was meted out.[95] To show the dangers of further defiance, the leading citizens of Stockport were paraded and a handful of hostages taken as surety for the town's good behaviour; these were led into Manchester on Monday with ropes around their necks.[96]

The resistance in Stockport was one of the outer ripples of a turmoil initiated in Manchester. The leading Manchester Whigs, like Justice Bradshaw and Dr. Mainwaring, decided to make a determined attempt to delay the Prince, in the hope that Cumberland's forces could catch up with them.[97] The town's 'loyal' inhabitants were ordered to arm themselves with guns, swords, pickaxes and shovels and to prepare for a two-hour siege. Notices were read out in Oldham, Ashton and Saddleworth, asking for a massive turnout in Manchester on Monday the 9th.[98] These pleas met with considerable success: five hundred men were on their way from Rossendale and Bury alone when they received instructions to turn back. The Magistrates in Manchester had meanwhile reflected and come to the (correct) conclusion that such a course of action could only have catastrophic consequences for their town. Messrs. Cheetham and Booth therefore despatched the bellman to order the country auxiliaries to disperse; the constables set a guard on all roads into Manchester from the north with express instructions to let no one pass.[99] In this way the bubble of would-be resistance was quickly punctured; only the diehards under Mr. Hilton attempted to salvage their pride by heading for Cheadle Ford to break it down, but even this task proved impossible, so about nine this Sunday evening they gave up.[100]

With the Highlanders strung out from Macclesfield to Stockport, some on the Leek–Buxton road, others at Swythamley and Winde, it was clear that Manchester was marked down for another occupation. By midnight this Sunday the Manchester authorities learned also that Cumberland had still not set out from the West Midlands and that Wade was no nearer than Doncaster.[101] Wade indeed must have been fortunate to escape proceedings against him for his actions in the days immediately following the retreat from Derby. At a Council of War held by the Marshal at Ferrybridge this Sunday, it was decided to march by way of Wakefield and Halifax into Lancashire. But because it was impossible to provide the necessary firing, straw and forage before the 10th, the projected march westwards could not take place before then.[102]

One of the reasons Wade did not have the resources he required was simply the uncooperativeness of the civilian population. Volunteers for his army *could* be obtained — there were two hundred from Sheffield for example[103] — but financial aid was another matter. The corporation of Doncaster wrote to Wade to complain about the number of sick soldiers sent to the town, for whom it was unable to provide. Moreover, the inhabitants of Doncaster refused to have Wade's soldiers quartered on them and objected even to admitting them to their houses; Wade's dragoons, who had been quartered in the Wheatley Hills, were received with sullen hostility.[104] The true reasons for Doncaster's non-cooperation were of course financial, but the alleged objection was to the number of foreign mercenaries in Wade's army.

Yorkshire, it seemed, could be stirred only when there was a direct threat from the Highlanders. Some in the city of York thought this could yet happen and that if the Jacobites came their way this time the experience would be a terrible one, as there would now be no incentive for them to behave reasonably. A tougher line was taken in Leeds, where a band of citizens, on hearing of the retreat, proposed to arm themselves and march to meet the Jacobite army. They were swiftly dissuaded when it was pointed out to them that should they be rash enough to encounter the Stuart prince and his host, they would sustain enormous loss of life and the clansmen would certainly come to Leeds to burn it down in retaliation.[105] Much 'valour' not in evidence on the Jacobite march into England now manifested itself on the retreat, and even more remained at the verbal level or was never put into action for one or other 'compelling' reason.

Monday 9th December

About noon this day the main body reached Stockport. The Jacobite soldiers were described as marching in great confusion and hurry with tired horses and infantry so footsore they could not walk properly.[106] Here the Prince learned the details of the previous night's fracas. One Joseph Stockport had been identified as the man who fired the fatal shot; in retaliation his cowhouse and barn had been burned, his cattle killed and his father taken hostage to Manchester.[107] In addition Elcho had left behind exact intelligence of the other hostages he had taken with him in reprisal for Stockport's (the town's) hostile behaviour; these were Messrs. Alcock, Robinson, Osborne, Bone, Lenach, Kemp and Lucas (the last was the town constable, whose particular offence was that he had 'struck a Highlander').[108]

Without pausing in Stockport the main force pressed on and joined Elcho's and the van just outside Manchester after a nineteen-mile march from Macclesfield. Here they learned that the town's population was hostile, actuated by the belief that the Highlanders had been defeated.[109] The first detachment of horse to penetrate the town limits had retired in haste: this corps, some thirty strong, had ridden past the Byroms' house but had been stoned and pelted with clods of earth before riding back to Elcho.[110] Elcho ordered his men to stand at the ready with guns cocked and ready to fire while he awaited the advent of the Prince.[111] The commanders of the clan regiments were in no mood to humour Manchester, having been irritated on the march from Macclesfield by sniper fire: one militia marksman had badly wounded a Jacobite horseman, who is said to have dropped a notebook into a ditch as a result, which when later recovered contained the names of numerous Jacobite sympathisers.[112]

After a short conference it was decided that quartermasters could not be sent into Manchester to order billets while the town was in an uproar and inclined to attack.

First, the bellicose spirit of the Manchester Whigs had to be tamed. Accordingly Charles Edward despatched two battalions of infantry and two squadrons of horse to disperse the mob.[113] Then two proclamations were uttered. In the first of these a virtual curfew was ordained in Manchester that night and a notice posted forbidding any two people to walk together after 9 p.m. on pain of death.[114] The second laid a levy of £5,000 on the town for its insolence. Later, under pressure of pleas from the Manchester Jacobites, the levy was reduced to £2,500 and a copy of the requisition given to the constables and to the collector of land tax in Manchester and Salford, with orders that it be paid by 1 p.m. on Tuesday the 10th.[115] This levy, obviously exacted in the heat of the moment, later puzzled the Whigs, who regarded it as a piece of tactical idiocy, calculated to alienate the inhabitants of Manchester. It was therefore variously conjectured that it was an idea that originated not with the Scots but with the Manchester Jacobites and was directed against their Whig enemies in the town; or that such a sum could never have been obtained by straight extortion and must therefore be a bogus 'levy', designed to mask contributions sent to Charles Edward by the English Jacobites.[116] The latter theory was in line with the belief that Dr. Burton's real purpose in Lancaster had been the conveying of similar monies from Jacobites in York.

The Scottish patrols quickly restored order in the town. A guard was placed around the Jacobite recruit Thomas Syddall's house and a party went in search of the arch-troublemakers, Dr. Mainwaring and Mr. Hilton. Another squadron rode out to Ashton-under-Lyne, some through Longendale, others via the Kenworthy house on the Mottram old road from Stalybridge, where they were said to have killed cattle in a nearby pasture and roasted the joints in skewered-up hides.[117] The reception in Ashton was hostile, so two of the inhabitants were led back haltered to Manchester, barefoot, with their boots strung across their shoulders.[118]

Charles Edward now declared that he wanted to halt two nights in Manchester — O'Sullivan later erroneously alleged that he did[119] — but Lord George Murray pointed out that this might enable Wade to get to Ribble Bridge first. It was therefore resolved to march out next day after the levy had been collected.[120] Meanwhile the most elaborate dispositions for the army were set on foot. Four officers and one hundred men of the Appin Stewarts stood guard at Townhouse; two officers and fifty men of Glenbucket's guarded Salford Bridge; a similar-sized body from Cluny's regiment patrolled Scotland Bridge at Millgate, while a mixed force of four officers and one hundred men from Perth's and Glengarry's watched over the artillery park. Meticulous orders were issued for communication between sentries. The main guard, the Appin Stewarts, were to take prisoners as required, to make certain they did not escape, and were to be relieved in this duty by the Camerons. A dozen Lifeguards patrolled the road to Rochdale unceasingly till daybreak, in close liaison with Cluny MacPherson's men at Scotland Bridge. Pitsligo's horse was given the task of covering all the territory from the town to the artillery park and beyond, on the road leading to Crossford Bridge. A similar body patrolled the road to Stockport.[121]

When calm had been restored in the town, all the Scots returned to their previous billets. The constables were sent for at 7 p.m. and shown the warrant from the

Prince, ordaining the curfew and the levy. Walley was severely rebuked for the behaviour of the mob and warned that anyone causing a nuisance during the passage of the army through Manchester would be shot on sight.[122] He was also asked to give an explanation for the incarceration in the house of correction of a Highland straggler on Monday 2nd December.[123]

Early that Monday morning Cumberland at last commenced pursuit with his cavalry, dragoons and one thousand mounted infantry.[124] He proceeded first to Lichfield from Packington and then began the gruelling ride to Cheadle, a twenty-seven mile journey 'through as difficult country as cavalry ever went through' by way of Abbot's Bromley, Uttoxeter, Stramshall and Tean.[125] Though buoyed up by the reports he everywhere received of a disorderly Jacobite retreat, with tales of weapons discarded wholesale and the ululations of Jacobite ladies,[126] Cumberland's hopes of getting to Manchester before the enemy were soon dashed by the deep snowdrifts through which he had to ride. Earlier that day, in a sober mood, he had partially conceded the impossibility of his cavalry dash. Writing to Newcastle from Lichfield he said: 'I fear it will be fruitless for they march at such a rate that I can't flatter myself with the hopes of overtaking them, though I set out this morning on a march of at least thirty measured miles.'[127] The one clear advantage he possessed was that his men were now in good spirits: Walpole's sentiments expressed in a letter this Monday — 'we dread them no longer' — were those generally held.[128] Lord Nairne's brother James, an officer in Cumberland's army, indited a letter from Coventry full of scurrilous contempt for the Jacobite army, and the opinion he expressed, that the Scots must either go to Wales or to Scotland to be destroyed, was now almost universally accepted.[129]

However, if Cumberland now thought it unlikely that he could catch his quarry, still less did he think that Wade could. After the War Council at Ferrybridge on Sunday the 8th Wade remained inactive on Monday, waiting for his army to be supplied before taking the Halifax–Rochdale–Manchester route.[130] His plan was that an advance contingent be sent on ahead of his main force to travel via Wakefield, Halifax, Rochdale and Blackstone Edge, but there was much scepticism among his own officers about the feasibility of the idea. As General Wentworth remarked: 'to what end I can't say for it is certain that the rebels will have so much the start of us that we shan't be able to come up with them'.[131] Certain it was (as Cumberland's aide-de-camp Colonel Rob Napier declared when the Duke's exhausted cavalry entered Cheadle that night) that what slight hope of overhauling the Highlanders remained rested entirely with George II's favourite son.[132]

Tuesday 10th December

Tuesday morning dawned inauspiciously for the Jacobites. Although Charles Edward had the night before reluctantly agreed to march on to Wigan next day, no orders had been issued on the 9th, and in the end Lord George Murray went to bed in disgust. At about 2 a.m. he was awakened by O'Sullivan to be told that the Prince had now signed the order to proceed to Wigan.[133] (The fact that no march from Manchester was mentioned in the orders for 10th December is undoubtedly why some participants in the rising, consulting their regimental records later in order to write their memoirs, later stated that the army stayed two nights in Manchester on the retreat — O'Sullivan and Daniel, for example.) But having done so, Charles Edward was in no hurry to leave and put off his departure until the last moment, hoping to see something of the Welsh Jacobites who, Vaughan assured him, would surely join him in Manchester if only he stayed there long enough.[134] The consequence was that although the vanguard moved out about 9 a.m. and the artillery between 11 a.m. and noon, the rearguard did not leave Manchester until 4 p.m. when it was already dark.[135] This was a further trial to Lord George Murray, already under strain owing to the problem of stragglers. He had already worked out a system whereby senior officers took it in turns each day to round up stragglers, but this operation foundered on the reef of clan loyalties; the normal rearguard was the logical choice to provide the 'straggler' officer, but such a man would not be obeyed by men from other clans. Murray accordingly had to form a corps of officers, one from each of the clan regiments.[136] Even so, such laggards could not be prevented from going into houses and pillaging. Luckily there was no desertion in Manchester except for Michael Brady, a sergeant in the Manchester regiment, who was later captured and executed at York.[137]

Before they quit the town, the Highlanders succeeded in securing the £2,500 they had levied. James Bailey, one of the principal Whig merchants in Manchester, had been held as surety but was released on his word of honour to Charles Edward and given two hours to find the money by the 1 p.m. deadline. Bailey then went to the principal coffee house to confer with his mercantile colleagues. It was proposed that Messrs. Bailey and Dickenson should issue promissory notes, payable in three months, to such as had money to hand. In this way the £2,500 was raised and paid over, but not without some anxious moments for Manchester and the extension of the deadline to 2 p.m.[138]

But the problems with Manchester were not yet over. When crossing Salford Bridge to collect the money, a large body of Scots was fired on.[139] Pandemonium ensued and one of the leading citizens shouted out that everyone should shut his shop and get inside away from the shooting. With the unwilling aid of the Salford constable and his deputy, the culprit was delivered up, but not before a bribe of five guineas had been paid. There were other sniping incidents during the stay at Manchester and at least one casual murder. A clansman was assassinated, while in another murder attempt a local butcher was killed when mistaken for a Highlander.[140] As O'Sullivan rode out of town a sniper, taking him for Charles Edward, narrowly missed him with a shot, while several volleys were fired at Elcho's and Ogilvy's, who formed the extreme rearguard.[141] However, the mob melted away once the cavalry wheeled round as if to charge. Other incidents took place outside Manchester. In Ashton a skirmish took place with casualties on both sides. In another affray in the same town a shoemaker retaliated for having his horse taken by shooting at a Highlander; he then had his house, corn and hay burnt in retribution.[142]

The eighteen-mile march to Wigan was accomplished over very bad roads, covered in frost and snow.[143] One observer, Richard Hay of Baldingstone near Bury, watched the army passing at Four Lane Ends in Fulton from about 1 p.m. to 5 p.m. 'as wide as the road would take them'.[144] Another observer, this time a spy sent from Warrington, was able to take an accurate count of the Highland foot and baggage as it passed Pendleton Pole, about a mile out of Manchester on the Wigan road.[145] Apart from the intrinsic difficulties of the march to Wigan, the army had to contend with the harassment of the country people and the militia who broke up the roads and laid trees across them to delay progress.[146] Information was sent to the villages and farmhouses in Lancashire, warning the farmers to withdraw and place in safety out of the line of the Jacobite march all horses, carts and other conveyances. The militia meanwhile dogged the heels of the clansmen, waiting to snap up stragglers.[147]

Ogilvy's and John Roy Stewart's, who were to spend the night at Leigh, sat on horseback in Manchester till dusk was coming on and then suffered a 'very painful march' to their night's stopping place.[148] With them was Dudley Bradstreet, who had accompanied the army from Derby and had not yet had the chance to escape or get word to Newcastle. Bradstreet was later to claim that he had prevailed on the Scots not to sack the town when the shot was fired at O'Sullivan about 3.30 p.m. According to him, John Roy Stewart wanted to return and burn Manchester to the ground but the wiser heads were swayed by his (Bradstreet's) eloquence to let matters be.[149] Bradstreet had already done useful service on the march from Derby by persuading Kilmarnock to intercede for Vere with Perth, who wanted him hanged. Whatever the truth of this, Bradstreet's fellow agent continued unharmed, and Vere was able to continue to compile meticulous information about the Highland leaders; in his jottings on Manchester there are detailed accounts of Clanranald and Glenbucket.[150]

At Wigan a billeting bottleneck caused further problems. The giant figure of Andrew Hay was discerned drawing up with Pitsligo's in the main square of Wigan, waiting to be assigned quarters.[151] Since Wigan was too small to accommodate over 5,000 souls, many of the army were dispersed in neighbouring villages. One party sent out from Wigan for this reason on the road to Preston gave rise to a rumour that the Highlanders intended to go to Liverpool.[152] Bradstreet ended up being billeted with the curate at Standish, to whom he divulged his secret and through whose agency a message was sent to Newcastle.[153] Because of the roads and weather the rearguard did not reach Wigan before midnight, and as Lord George Murray explained: 'without the help of lanterns and candles many of them would have straggled all night'.[154] For at least one of Roy Stewart's the day's tribulations did not cease once journey's end was reached. Captain George Hamilton, billeted in a small village outside Wigan, had a small box cut off his portmanteau by a local cutpurse while it was in the charge of his servant and thus lost his official commission as deputy quartermaster to the army which was inside the box.[155]

Cumberland meanwhile endured another gruelling day in the saddle, riding the twenty-three miles from Cheadle through Wetley Rocks, Leek and Rushton to Macclesfield by dreadful roads and in the teeth of the weather.[156] When he arrived at his quarters in John Strafford's house (later Cumberland House),[157] his black mood had already manifested itself. Nearing Macclesfield, he had captured three deserters from the Jacobite army. They had then been taken on a 'Highland trot' by being tied to their horses' tails.[158] It was also reported that a turnpike man had attempted to send the Duke's mounted force on the wrong road and had been summarily hanged for his pains.[159] On learning that after all his efforts the Jacobites were even then entering Wigan and that if they had stayed one day longer in Manchester (as Charles Edward had wanted to), he would have been able to come on them, Cumberland flew into a rage and for the time being abandoned the chase.[160] He spent three nights, until the morning of the 13th, in Macclesfield — a decision he was later to regret and for which he was severely censured in a private letter by the Duke of Richmond.[161] Cumberland expressed his rage in a letter to the citizens of Manchester, demanding that they seize all Jacobite sympathisers, 'and herein you are in no wise to fail as you will answer at your own great peril'.[162] He was, however, well enough satisfied with the attitude of the people of Macclesfield. When the Duke's quartermaster entered that town to seek quarters for 5,000 men he was inundated by both town and country dwellers with provisions, straw and all other military requirements and 'at the approach of the king's forces into that town I never saw such cheerfulness in people'.[163] The contrast with the sullen and hostile reception of Charles Edward's men two nights before was striking. The local farmers dug up barrels of beer they had buried and treated Cumberland's soldiers to it most liberally.[164]

When Wade arrived in Wakefield on Tuesday night en route to Halifax, he heard that the Highlanders were on their way to Wigan, three to four days' march ahead of him.[165] At a hastily convened Council of War it was decided that Wade should return to protect Newcastle, in case the Jacobite army intended to cut across Yorkshire and enter Scotland by the north-east.[166] General Oglethorpe would meanwhile start from Doncaster across the Pennines with Montagu's horse, St. George's dragoons and the Yorkshire Rangers in hopes of getting to Preston before the Stuart prince.[167] There was a general scepticism that the clansmen could now be prevented from re-entering Scotland: as Captain Richmond Webb of Wade's army commented: 'For my part I have given over any thoughts of seeing the rebels but I'll continue to dance over the ice and march through the dirt because other people do.'[168] But most agreed with Wade that Tyneside should be protected, and both Newcastle and George II endorsed his decision to march north-east. Wade aimed to be in Newcastle, 114 miles from Doncaster, after an eight-day trek; he was ordered by the Duke of Newcastle to send Brigadier Wolfe ahead to Hull to take command of the forces there and march them to Tyneside.[169]

The only contingent of Wade's army actually to get under way this Tuesday was Oglethorpe's cavalry. Oglethorpe's arrival at Barnsley late that night meant that no fewer than three military forces arrived at their quarters this day, exhausted after a battle with the elements.[170] With both Oglethorpe and Cumberland now within two days' march of the retreating Highlanders, the campaign in England was about to enter its most critical week.

Wednesday 11th December

This day the Jacobite army's marching orders were to achieve the seventeen miles from Wigan to Preston by nightfall. The main force cleared early from Wigan except for a few stragglers who were taken prisoner by the militia to await Cumberland's pleasure.[171] The rearguard, too, made good time in its assignment to move up from Leigh to Chorley; it was seen passing Standish at 2 p.m.[172] The march to Preston was uneventful. On the high road called Walton Cop near the town of Walton, Charles Douglas, Lord Mordington, a native of Fishwick, was seen in the ranks of the Jacobite army, thus later creating a *prima facie* case for investigation.[173] But in Walton itself the demoralised Douglas, who had joined the Prince in Manchester on 29th November, decided to take his chances with the mercy of his neighbours and quit the army.[174]

On arrival in Preston, where Ribble Bridge was found to be intact, Charles Edward was reported by observers to be looking particularly dejected and his army out of humour.[175] Particular attention was drawn to two coaches and six: in one was the Prince and Sheridan and in another was John Murray of Broughton's wife and Lady Ogilvy; the quartet was described as 'looking like hunted hares and particularly put out by mention of Cumberland and Oglethorpe'.[176] This was of course good Whig propaganda, but it is true that Charles Edward was piqued at the impression gaining ground that he was in full flight from Cumberland.[177] It was this more than anything that made him determined to spend another day in Preston, though he could justifiably cite Lord George Murray's words as vindication, since Murray had claimed at Derby that the maximum peril would be past once they reached Preston.

Lord George himself, though dubious of the wisdom of spending an extra day in Preston, consoled himself with the thought that he could now exchange the unwieldy four-wheel carts currently carrying the ammunition for the two-wheeled vehicles left in Preston on the advance.[178] In addition, there were a dozen box carts in Preston, capable of carrying all the baggage and artillery. As it turned out, Murray was to be grievously disappointed. Although there was ample time for these two operations during Thursday the 12th when the army remained in Preston, to Murray's disgust no action was taken.[179]

Once in Preston, the clan leaders sent out foraging parties to the environs to collect all hay, straw and oats that could be useful to Cumberland's pursuing cavalry — this was later expanded by Whig propaganda to a report that all forage on the line of march was burnt to prevent Cumberland's laying hands on it.[180] At Preston, too, Bradstreet's dream of becoming a double agent came true when Murray of Broughton sent him south with instructions to locate the armies of Cumberland, Ligonier, Hawley and Wade. Needless to say, Bradstreet was never seen by the Highlanders again.[181]

At Macclesfield Cumberland was preparing for the next phase of the campaign. In a letter to Wade, in which his bitterness and pique at the aged Field-Marshal were barely disguised, the Duke explained that his stay in Macclesfield was in accordance with the brief from the Duke of Newcastle, who had ordered him to pursue the rebels no further north than Manchester.[182] Cumberland ordered Wade to move up to Hexham, which would enable him both to cover Newcastle and also possibly to intercept the Highlanders once they left Carlisle. To the Secretary of

State himself Cumberland wrote a somewhat self-congratulatory letter concerning his march from Lichfield to Macclesfield on Monday and Tuesday, grumbling that his heroic feat had not paid off: 'By the reports I had heard upon the march, I flattered myself the rebels would have waited for us at Manchester and if they had halted there all yesterday, I should have been in reach of them with my whole cavalry.'[183]

If Cumberland's self-pitying side was displayed to Newcastle in the first half of the letter, the cruel and ruthless aspect of his personality was expressed in his account of the instructions to the Manchester magistrates, in which he enjoined them to seize 'rebel' stragglers: 'There are I believe to the number of about fifteen or sixteen of their stragglers picked up, who are sent to different jails . . . they have so many of our prisoners in their hands, I did not care to put them to death . . . but I have encouraged the country people to do it, as they may fall in their way.'[184] Cumberland ended by gloating over the execution of one straggler who had turned out to be a deserter from Cope's army at Prestonpans and therefore subject to military discipline.

As far as military dispositions were concerned, Cumberland sent Major Henry Wheatley of Bland's on from Macclesfield with two hundred dragoons to prepare for the next phase of the pursuit.[185] The rest of his force — Bland's, Ker's, Ligonier's, Cobham's, Kingston's and Montagu's light horse — remained with him. Wheatley was originally ordered to link with Bligh's from Chester but the latter regiment was ordered to return to Chester by Newcastle, much to Cumberland's disgust.[186] Accordingly, Wheatley was instructed to meet the Liverpool Blues at Warrington and to find as many recruits and horses as possible, then to rejoin Cumberland at Wigan on the 13th. Cumberland's recruiting agents were not greeted with any enthusiasm and sometimes, as in Hale, met with downright hostility. Whereas the Jacobite army had wanted volunteers only, Wheatley's men began to press 'recruits', which disrupted the Lancashire farmers' labour force; some farm labourers indeed went into hiding to escape pressing.[187]

While Wade's main force proceeded from Wakefield to Leeds, his flying column under Oglethorpe was encountering the most appalling conditions on Blackstone Edge, in the course of its route from Barnsley to Huddersfield.[188] This crossing was notoriously difficult, involving as it did the negotiation of a series of hills, all of them precipitous on both sides. Oglethorpe's cavalry was scarcely totally refreshed even at the start of the journey at Barnsley, since there were already troops billeted there — as at Huddersfield — and only cramped quarters had been available. Then there were the perils of Blackstone Edge to endure: very bad roads, steep hills, villages not large enough to supply the detachment with food, and above all the weather. On Blackstone Edge no sooner had Oglethorpe's men overcome the problem of getting their horses up over the flawed and muddy hill bottoms than they ran into the ice and snow at the top, which caused the horses to slide back down.[189] In addition, both Oglethorpe and Wade had been betrayed by profiteering contractors: shoes that should have lasted a fortnight lasted only a day, and the only reliable goods sent from London were the flannels donated by the Quakers. Although Oglethorpe's men reached Huddersfield that night in an exhausted condition, there was clearly a question mark now against their ultimate utility if they did encounter the Highlanders.

Thursday 12th December

While Ogilvy's regiment and the rearguard moved up from Chorley into Preston, the remainder of the army refreshed itself and prepared for the grim Pennine roads ahead. A couple of recruits trickled in, Roger Fulthorpe, an apprentice of Syddall's, and Thomas Craig, both of whom later pleaded compulsion.[190] Charles Edward was by now perplexed that he had heard nothing from Drummond, not realising that the latter had ignored his orders to follow him into England. It was therefore decided to send on the Duke of Perth with a small force of about 120 hussars to bring them back;[191] the Prince still insisted that he would then turn round and march again into the heartland of England. Lord George Murray was against the plan, arguing that Wade could still get to Lancaster and so be placed between the Prince's army and the reinforcements Perth would bring.[192] Moreover, Murray argued, if Perth did not take a much stronger escort than the one proposed he might well be opposed by the militia and the Cumbrian citizenry, who could bar his way to Scotland. With this in mind, Murray sent no messages to Scotland with Perth, lest they be intercepted — a wise precaution as it turned out.[193] Lord George was swiftly overruled and Perth spent the day assembling his party. Unfortunately his mounted men were kept waiting in the street an unconscionable time while preparations were made, with the result that instead of clearing from the town in the morning, it was evening before Perth's force got under way; by that time Cumberland's spies had sent word of what was afoot to the Cumberland and Westmorland militia.[194]

One of the reasons Perth was late setting out from Preston was that he and the Marquis d'Eguilles had spent long hours working on a document that argued for making a stand at Preston. The memorandum which they produced contained some compelling arguments for not retreating further than Preston.[195] It was argued that at Preston there were plentiful supplies for the men and horses, which were unavailable in Carlisle and still less in Scotland, given that the Jacobites did not now control Edinburgh and the Lowlands, which had been reoccupied by Hanoverian forces landed by sea immediately Charles Edward crossed the border south. Taxes and public monies could be collected from a wide area of England with Preston as a base, and recruits could only be encouraged if the retreat were called off. Above all, there was the possibility of a French landing to be considered. No landing would take place if the French learned that the Highlanders had returned to Scotland; on the other hand the options were still left open to march to meet a French force either on the west coast or near London, if the army dug itself in at Preston. On the other hand, what would be the consequences of returning to Scotland? Two-thirds of the army would immediately desert, and even if they returned for a spring campaign into England, all credibility would by then have been lost. The French, Spanish and English allies of the Stuarts would be even less likely to intervene if all they could see after the 1745 campaign in England was the Highlanders back in

Scotland in a worse state than the previous September because of the loss of Edinburgh. The rapid retreat of the clansmen, without having been defeated or even attacked, would argue lack of courage, intelligence, uncertainty of aim or even treachery within the army; these conclusions would diminish the zeal of Jacobite partisans, attenuate the fear that was the Highlanders' principal psychological weapon and at once lose old friends and discourage new ones. Moreover, once in Scotland, plans to re-enter England were unrealistic: given that Berwick was not in Jacobite hands, only Carlisle could serve as the gateway into England and it would not be so easy to take it a second time. And even if the army did not disperse once it reached Scotland, the loss of Edinburgh had already cut it off from its principal source of revenue; the army could then only be paid by the imposition of extraordinary exactions which, even if practicable, would make the Jacobites intensely unpopular.

It is clear that once the Highlanders reached Preston and the worst fears about being cut off and having to fight two armies had been assuaged, some of their leaders questioned anew the wisdom of the decision taken at Derby.[196] The Perth/d'Eguilles paper and Perth's departure were two obvious signs of this. The dispute that now went on between the Prince, O'Sullivan and the Irish, Perth and d'Eguilles on one side, and most of the clan leaders led by Lochiel and Lord George Murray on the other, was reduced to a handful of fiercely debated propositions. The clan leaders argued that the Scots had entered England to fight a battle, not to go into winter quarters. Their opponents claimed that the corollary of this argument was that once in Scotland the clansmen would desert — which was an excellent reason for keeping them in England.[197]

Lord George and Lochiel contended that the army needed to return to Scotland to gather recruits, to rest in preparation for a spring campaign, and to guard the lines of communication with the north of Scotland, the solid base of operations. Perth and d'Eguilles countered that recruits could be obtained in England, that if the second army under Drummond and Strathallan joined them the issue of communications with the Highlands was irrelevant, and that Scottish interests were best served by not drawing a pursuing army into Scotland and by living off the public money of England, not Scotland. Murray's abiding fear was of course interception by Wade, particularly if he joined forces with Cumberland and got behind the Jacobite army, which would prevent either escape to or reinforcement from Scotland. Perth and d'Eguilles dealt with this argument in various ways. In the first place they dismissed Wade's army as of no account: it had endured a Flanders campaign, a sea crossing, had gone south from Newcastle to Doncaster and was now crossing west to Preston (so they thought). How could such an exhausted force, full of militiamen, the sick and the intractable Dutch, overcome the Highlanders in the depth of winter? On the other hand, if Wade joined forces with Cumberland, the position of their combined army could be made untenable if Charles Edward pursued a 'scorched earth' policy. If all food and forage between Preston and Carlisle was garnered and all surpluses burnt, the Hanoverian armies could no longer be sustained. To Murray's argument that Carlisle was untenable as a 'fail-safe' retreat if Cumberland tried to turn the flank at Preston, the Perth faction retorted that without food supplies and heavy cannon Cumberland could make no impression on the town.

If Lord George Murray's arguments had been weak overall at Derby, they acquired a new cogency once the decision to retreat had been taken, and there is no doubt that if the Perth/d'Eguilles plan had been implemented, it would have ended in disaster. But these arguments about calling off the withdrawal undoubtedly appealed to Charles Edward and certainly influenced his thinking at Lancaster, when he finally decided to face his pursuers.

The mood at Preston shows how wide of the mark were Cumberland's analyses this day.[198] From Macclesfield he reported to Newcastle that the Highlanders were in total retreat, throwing their arms away and beginning to disperse.[199] On one point he agreed with d'Eguilles and Perth: the uselessness of the Dutch for either an English or Scottish campaign; accordingly he recommended that they be shipped home once Wade reached Newcastle.[200] The only significant movement of Cumberland's forces this Thursday was the arrival in Manchester of a large body of dragoons and four troops of the Duke of Kingston's horse. Kingston himself lodged at the house of Mr. Houghton at Baguley Hall near Northenden.[201] Oglethorpe's flying squadron meanwhile had reached Rochdale after another battle against nature and the elements on the ride from Huddersfield.[202] With Hanoverian forces widespread in the Manchester area, the authorities considered it important to prevent Jacobite sympathisers from sending word to Charles Edward of the troops on his tail, for even after the retreat northwards a good deal of support (albeit tacit) for the Stuart prince remained, and in Jacobite hearts there was great bitterness towards those who had raised the mob against the Prince's army on the way through Manchester.[203] Watchmen were therefore set on Salford Bridge and all other exits from the town while detailed reports on the Highlanders' progress were transmitted to Cumberland at Macclesfield.[204] But in London developments were taking place that would alter the entire face of the campaign. As reports of a French build-up in Dunkirk intensified, Newcastle decided that London was virtually defenceless against a French invasion.[205] He therefore sent out detailed orders, which amounted to a rescinding of the pursuit of Charles Edward. Ligonier at Coventry was instructed to return to London with all speed, together with all battalions in the Midlands except Sempill's and Campbell's, which were to join Wade.[206] Cumberland too was to return to London with the rest of the cavalry and the mounted foot plus all the forces stationed in Manchester.[207] George II particularly wanted his favourite son with him in London at this juncture since, as Newcastle wrote to Ligonier: 'we are under the greatest alarm of an immediate embarkation from Dunkirk and perhaps some other ports . . . we shall be but very ill-prepared to receive them till you come to our assistance, not having . . . 6,000 men in all'.[208] In any case opinion in London was opposed to a war on two fronts; Chancellor Hardwicke said that the pursuit of the Highlanders was in vain and anyway some people feared what might happen if Cumberland did catch them.[209] So, not for the last time in the campaign, the Duc de Richelieu, who was destined never to land a single French soldier on English soil, had nonetheless made a vital contribution to Charles Edward's 1745 campaign.

Friday 13th December

As day broke this Friday, Perth was entering Lancaster. Immediately he learned of Bracken's treachery and how he had tried to have the Jacobite prisoners incarcerated in a sloop off the Lancashire coast but that the town magistrates had been afraid to take such a step.[210] Perth promptly freed the prisoners in Lancaster castle, incorporated them in his own force and as a reprisal thoroughly plundered Bracken's house in Church Street. Mrs. Bracken was asked to produce 600 guineas as compensation for her husband's behaviour but she managed to escape through a cellar window, whereat the Highlanders systematically destroyed all furniture and manuscripts in the house.[211] Another target for their wrath, as a collaborator with Bracken in his treachery, was Dr. Fenton, vicar of Lancaster. A gift of £21 from Fenton's neighbour Mr. Gillison did not deter the Scots from ransacking Fenton's house but they desisted when his wife gave them another £20, not, however, before they had threatened to shoot Fenton if they laid hands on him.[212] The irony of all this was that Bracken himself was later accused by the Whigs of high treason.[213] Perth then moved on to Burton, which was reached in the afternoon. The Duke's cavalry sat some time on horseback in the main street to gauge the feeling of the townspeople before dispersing to their lodgings.[214]

In Preston Charles Edward's army began to move out towards Lancaster even before daybreak. At 4 a.m. the artillery was despatched by flambeau and torch light under escort by John Roy Stewart's (in front) and Ogilvy's (at the rear).[215] At dawn came the main army with Glenbucket's in the van of the foot with the prisoners — among them Vere, who spent this day compiling detailed notes on Alexander MacDonald, chief of Keppoch's — Cluny MacPherson's men in the rear and Clanranald's with the royal standard.[216] Pitsligo's horse rode ahead of Glenbucket's while Elcho's cavalry brought up the extreme rear and Kilmarnock's formed the outriders on the wings of the army. A detachment of twenty-five of Elcho's Lifeguards patrolled both the Wigan side of Ribble Bridge and the land between the bridge and Preston, having identified a piece of land where the rearguard could form up in battle order if the enemy came in sight. The orders of the day reflected a certain tension: 'if any one stays after the rearguard it is at their own peril, as they are not to be waited on'.[217]

The tension may have been exacerbated by the Highlanders' reception in Preston; the townspeople evidently now considered that they were dealing with the losing side and there were even some disgruntled clan chiefs who proposed to Charles Edward that the town be burnt. According to one report, the division of opinion between those advocating 'soft' and 'hard' lines led to the unsheathing of swords in one Preston inn.[218] The Highland 'hawks' certainly had a point, for when the Scots were clear of Lancashire a strong backlash was in evidence. 'No popery' mobs destroyed many Catholic chapels; St. Mary's Friargate in Preston was demolished and the house and chapel of Rev. John Harrison, parish priest at Cotton, burned to the ground.[219]

At 1 p.m., barely an hour after the last of Elcho's patrols had quit the town, the first of their pursuers arrived.[220] First came a company of Oglethorpe's Georgia

Rangers, followed by Oglethorpe himself with the Royal Hunters and detachments from St. George's regiment of dragoons, Montagu's horse and 120 of the Duke of Kingston's light horse, making 500 men in all.[221] Despite the exhaustion of his troops, who had accomplished an epic journey of over a hundred miles through ice and snow in seventy-two hours, Oglethorpe immediately despatched a mixed party to pursue the rear, reasoning that with eighteen long miles to travel (on what was destined to be the longest single day's trek on the Jacobite retreat), the Highlanders could be overhauled.[222] Oglethorpe's raiding party caught up with Elcho and the rearguard at Kilmoor (sometimes called Elall moor) between Garstang and Lancaster. A brief skirmish ensued in which Elcho's had the best of it, helped by covering fire from behind the roadside hedges by Cluny MacPherson's men. Oglethorpe's men retired to Garstang, having lost three men dead in Kingston's horse, one Yorkshire ranger killed and another captured when his horse was shot from under him.[223] There were also some wounded, since an attorney from Newcastle-under-Lyme named Mills was later found mortally wounded on the road.[224] Without supporting artillery or infantry there was little more Oglethorpe's men could do at this point, especially since his men 'are severely fatigued by their last marches over snow and ice so that they cannot act with that vigour that they would otherwise do'.[225]

In Preston Oglethorpe found that the citizens had picked up about twenty stragglers from the Jacobite army, and he decided to question them. What he elicited from the prisoners was, however, pure fantasy. Captain John Mackenzie of Glengarry's regiment, a young man of twenty-one, swore that he had heard from Lochiel, Keppoch and Lochgarry that at Derby Lord George Murray had wanted to press on to London and that Perth had been in favour of retreat. Since Murray was then suspected of wanting to lead the Prince into a trap by advancing, he was placed under open arrest, having his sword taken from him and two men set to watch him at all times.[226] Even more ludicrous was the intelligence received from a prisoner in Ogilvy's regiment: under questioning he claimed that Charles Edward was so panic-stricken that he had already left the army in disguise.[227] These wild rumours were conflated with absurdly exaggerated reports of the skirmish near Garstang to produce a preposterous story, widely disseminated in England, of the Highlanders' annihilation. After retreating pell-mell, the story ran, jettisoning guns, swords and targes in their terror, the Highlanders were overtaken by Cumberland at Lancaster, surrounded and routed; only a few remnants managed to escape north under the Duke of Perth.[228]

In reality the Jacobite army made its way through Scotsforth and along the heights by the Greaves farm overlooking Morecambe bay into Lancaster in good order.[229] Their morale was reasonably good: indeed a further recruit joined them on the retreat through Lancashire, Edward Barrow of Eversley Hall, who was seen by a large crowd of onlookers as he rode down to Lancaster Town Hall with the army.[230] While Chadwick from the Manchester regiment defiantly played 'The King shall have his own again' on the church organ, the Prince at supper declared indignantly that he was sick of retreating so fast in face of 'the son of a usurper'.[231] Now that they had reached Lancaster, surely even that defeatist Lord George Murray could not put up a convincing argument for declining battle.[232] So when Murray got into Lancaster very late that night with the rearguard and reported to headquarters as was his wont, he was amazed and disappointed to learn that a day was to be spent in the town and possibly even a battle fought. Murray argued that to halt was imprudent, since Wade could join Cumberland to produce an unbeatable army, but the Prince was adamant that he wanted to show the 'elector of Hanover' that, contrary to the canards, he was not in flight but merely carrying out a strategic withdrawal.[233] Consoling himself with the thought that at least now Wade could not get between the Jacobite army and Scotland — his worst nightmare — Murray reluctantly acquiesced.[234]

Despite the stir caused by the skirmish with Oglethorpe's outriders, the truth was that Cumberland was not yet within striking distance. Only on the morning of the 13th, having spent three nights in Macclesfield, did the Duke move up to Wigan.[235] His 2,000-strong force marched in two columns, one going through Stockport, Wilmslow and Holling Ferry, and Cumberland with the other group proceeding via Warrington; there, many of the influential gentry joined him on the last stretch into Wigan, where he arrived at night.[236] The citizens of Manchester, who had been summoned by the constables to attend Cumberland on his progress through the town, were therefore disappointed (or relieved).[237]

At Wigan Cumberland learned with annoyance that no attempt had been made until that day to break up the roads in Cumberland and Westmorland. The Lord-Lieutenant, Lord Lonsdale, informed the Duke's secretary, Sir Everard Fawkener, that he had only just ventured to give such an order, not having received any instructions whatever from either Wade or Cumberland.[238] The only truly hopeful development for the Duke this Friday was the departure of the future hero of Falkirk, General Huske, north-west from Ferrybridge in a bid to head off the Jacobite army at Penrith.[239] Conditions seemed favourable for Huske: there was a good turnpike to Greta Bridge and another good one from there to Penrith.

But in London the pursuit of the Highlanders was now beginning to seem an unimportant matter compared with the looming threat from France. Horace Walpole expressed the common opinion that Cumberland was in any case too far behind the Jacobites now to succeed in pursuit, since he could not catch up with them without ruining his cavalry altogether.[240] A memorandum giving the business of the day for George II's attention does not even mention Cumberland's pursuit. Pressing items on the king's agenda included: an answer to Wade's latest letter, recruitment for the army, a decision on who was to command in Scotland, the disposition of the army in England, the hiring and transport of Hessians, the dispatch to London of all prisoners at Newcastle, Irish business with Lord Chesterfield, and Scottish affairs involving the Duke of Argyll and Lord Loudoun.[241] The only issue remotely touching Charles Edward and Cumberland was the case of David Morgan, whom Ligonier was ordered to fetch from Stafford to London with an escort of thirty men.[242] For Newcastle, the principal item of business in the north of England was the incorporation of the associated regiments under Lord Malton into Wade's army.[243]

Above all else, though, on this second 'black Friday' was the seemingly lengthening shadow of France, with Richelieu poised in Picardy to strike across the Channel. The consternation in London on this Friday was by all accounts little inferior to that on Friday the 6th.[244] Another run on the banks took place. Great attention was paid to the alarm posts — a relay system of warning beacons ringing the capital — and proper signals for warning the Guards of any rising in London. This was in accordance with the signalling system ordained by Newcastle this Friday to verify the actual landing of the French.[245] Seven cannons were to be fired, one every half-minute at the Tower, to be answered by the same signal from St. James's Park and vice versa.[246] Contemporary chroniclers recorded that the population of London was about equally divided between those who anticipated the firing of the Tower guns with growing apprehension and those who looked forward to it with joy, as heralding the moment of Stuart restoration.[247] It was the continuing uncertainty about the French plus the certainty in Newcastle's mind at least that they would eventually make landfall that finally doomed Cumberland's chase through Lancashire and Cumbria and was to result in no less than two sets of countermanded orders.

NOTES

1. Jarvis, ii. p. 209; SP Dom 76/96.
2. Sharpe, iii. p. 54.
3. Ilchester, i. p. 127.
4. Add. MSS. 34712 ff. 386–89.
5. SP Dom 76/85.
6. Jarvis, ii. pp. 212–32.
7. Stuart MSS 272/92 B; Marchant p. 237.
8. Stuart MSS 272/46 A.
9. SP Dom 77/11.
10. SP Dom 77/89.
11. *Gentlemen's Magazine* 1745 p. 621.
12. Sharpe, iii. p. 53.
13. Ibid.
14. Climenson, i. p. 226.
15. Bonhote pp. 77–78; Ritchie p. 111.
16. McLynn, 'Nottingham'.
17. Allardyce, i. pp. 287–93.
18. Maxwell of Kirkconnell p. 82.
19. Ibid. p. 81.
20. *Birmingham Gazette*, 9 December 1745; *London Magazine* 1745 p. 611; Thompson p. 70.
21. Johnstone p. 73.
22. SP Dom 77/60.
23. SP Dom 76/118.
24. Howell, *State Trials* 18 p. 382; Yorke, i. p. 425.
25. Johnstone p. 83.
26. SP Dom 80 ff. 165–66; *Gentlemen's Magazine* 1746 p. 399.
27. Elcho p. 342.
28. Tayler, *Jacobites of Banff* pp. 205, 221.

29. *Gentlemen's Magazine* 1746, p. 525.
30. SP Dom 76/117.
31. *Derby Mercury,* 12 December 1745.
32. Maxwell of Kirkconnell p. 78.
33. Ibid. p. 79.
34. HMC, Various Colls, viii. p. 140.
35. *Ogilvy's Orderbook* p. 303; Atholl, *Chronicles* iii. p. 99.
36. SP Dom 76/77.
37. Stott (1929) p. 9; Howell, *State Trials* 18, p. 338.
38. *Derby Mercury,* 20 December 1745.
39. Wm. Salt Arch. Soc. viii. p. 126.
40. HMC, Various Colls, viii. p. 139.
41. Tayler, *Anon. Hist.* p. 104; Barnes, p. 85.
42. *Ogilvy's Orderbook* p. 304.
43. *Manchester Magazine,* 5 August 1746; Harland p. 230.
44. Stuart MSS 272/92 B.
45. HMC, 5 p. 400; 13 vi. p. 165; Mounsey p. 120.
46. Fitzherbert MSS.
47. Pitt p. 103; Yorke, i. pp. 476–77.
48. Hughes, i. pp. 87–88.
49. SP Dom 76/69.
50. Ibid.
51. Ibid.
52. HMC, Various Colls, viii. pp. 138–39; 13 vi. p. 165; Fitzherbert MSS.
53. SP Dom 76/72.
54. Ibid.
55. Maxwell of Kirkconnell p. 79.
56. Elcho p. 343; *Ogilvy's Orderbook* p. 305.
57. Chambers, 'Marches' p. 58.
58. HMC, 13 vi. p. 167.
59. *General Evening Post* No. 1906, 12–14 December 1745.
60. Simpson (1826) p. 261.
61. Sleigh p. 208 et seq; Fitzherbert MSS.
62. Wm. Salt Arch. Soc. vii. p. 112.
63. *London Magazine* 1745 p. 611; *Gentlemen's Magazine* 1745, p. 622.
64. Add. MSS. 29913 ff. 5–9; Howell, *State Trials* 18 p. 384.
65. Gordon & Arnot, ii. pp. 46–47.
66. Ibid. ii. pp. 274–75.
67. Simpson (1933) p. 225.
68. Stott (1929) p. 9.
69. Earwaker, *Constables* iii. p. 23.
70. HMC, Various Colls, viii. p. 140.
71. HMC, 13 vi. p. 165; Fitzherbert MSS.
72. Staffs CRO: D/798/3/1/1.
73. *Verney Letters,* ii. p. 200.
74. Wm. Salt Arch. Soc. vi (2) pp. 347–48.
75. Hughes, ii. pp. 87–88.
76. Whitworth p. 113.
77. McLynn, 'West Midlands and the '45', pp. 27–31.
78. HMC, Laing, ii. p. 355.
79. Ibid.
80. Chesterfield-Newcastle Correspondence pp. 93–95.
81. HMC, 13 vi. p. 167.
82. Ibid. p. 165.

83. HMC, Various Colls, viii. p. 139.
84. SP Dom, 76/112.
85. *Shrops. Arch. & Nat. Hist. Soc.* p. 67.
86. SP Dom 76/95.
87. SP Dom 76/148.
88. HMC, Various Colls, viii. p. 141.
89. Davies p. 110.
90. Ibid. p. 111.
91. Elcho p. 343.
92. Blaikie, 'John Daniel's Progress' p. 180.
93. Elcho p. 343.
94. Maxwell of Kirkconnell pp. 79–80.
95. Barnes p. 88.
96. Stott (1929) p. 9.
97. Talon p. 233.
98. Bowman p. 272.
99. *Palatine Notebook* iv. p. 21; Earwaker, *Constables* iii. p. 24.
100. Earwaker (1889) pp. 155–56.
101. SP Dom 76/115; Marchant p. 211; Ray p. 190.
102. SP Dom 76/121.
103. *Birmingham Gazette,* 23 December 1745.
104. Tomlinson p. 230.
105. *Birmingham Gazette,* 16 December 1745.
106. Fitzherbert MSS.
107. HMC, 13 vi. p. 168.
108. HMC, Various Colls, viii. p. 142; Fitzherbert MSS.
109. Maxwell of Kirkconnell p. 79.
110. Talon p. 233.
111. Elcho p. 344.
112. Bowman p. 272.
113. Maxwell of Kirkconnell p. 80; Elcho p. 344.
114. Earwaker (1889) pp. 156–57; HMC, Various Colls, ii. p. 288.
115. Add. MSS. 32709 f. 231.
116. Add. MSS. 33050 ff. 3–4.
117. Bowman p. 272.
118. 'Two Yorkshire Diaries' p. 115.
119. O'Sullivan p. 103.
120. Blaikie, 'John Daniel's Progress' p. 180.
121. *Ogilvy's Orderbook* pp. 305–06.
122. Talon p. 233.
123. Jarvis (1961) pp. 86–87
124. SP Dom 76/94.
125. Yorke, i. p. 478.
126. Ibid. p. 480.
127. SP Dom 76/93.
128. Walpole to Mann, 9 December 1745, Walpole, ii. pp. 159–60.
129. Atholl, *Chronicles* iii. pp. 100–02.
130. HMC, Laing ii. p. 355.
131. HMC, Various Colls, viii. p. 141.
132. Burne pp. 86–87; *VCH,* i. p. 267.
133. Chambers, 'Marches' p. 59.
134. *Quarterly Review* 1899 p. 452.
135. HMC, 13 vi. p. 168.
136. Chambers, 'Marches' p. 58.

137. *London Magazine* 1746 p. 488.
138. Talon p. 245.
139. Ibid.
140. *Manchester Magazine,* 24 December 1745.
141. O'Sullivan pp. 103–04; Elcho p. 345; Blaikie, 'John Daniel's Progress' p. 180.
142. Bowman p. 272.
143. Add. MSS. 35598 ff. 189–90.
144. *Palatine Notebook,* iv. p. 21.
145. *London Magazine* 1745 p. 612.
146. HMC, 13 vi. p. 166.
147. Jarvis, ii. pp. 29, 58.
148. *Ogilvy's Orderbook* p. 306.
149. SP Dom 81 ff. 60–61.
150. Add. MSS. 33050 ff. 45, 55.
151. Add. MSS. 35886 f. 100.
152. *Birmingham Gazette,* 16 December 1745.
153. Jarvis, ii. pp. 101–02.
154. Chambers, 'Marches' p. 59.
155. *Gentlemen's Magazine* 1746 p. 524.
156. Elcho p. 345.
157. Davies p. 112.
158. *Dublin Journal* No. 1961, 24–28 December 1745.
159. *Birmingham Gazette,* 23 December 1745.
160. Ray p. 189.
161. Richmond to Newcastle, 24 December 1745, Add. MSS. 32705 f. 458.
162. SP Dom 76/21.
163. HMC, Various Colls, viii. p. 141.
164. Coward p. 366.
165. SP Dom 76/115.
166. SP Dom 76/147.
167. Ray p. 190; Marchant p. 211.
168. HMC, Laing, ii. p. 356; cf. Staffs CRO: D. 143/1.
169. SP Dom 76/108.
170. W.O. 71/19 ff. 212, 228.
171. Catton MSS 5/57; HMC, 13 vi. p. 169.
172. SP Dom 73/87; *Ogilvy's Orderbook* p. 306.
173. SP Dom 80 ff. 86–90.
174. SP Dom 78/34.
175. Barnes pp. 90–91.
176. *Manchester Magazine,* 24 December 1745.
177. Elcho p. 345.
178. Chambers, 'Marches' p. 60.
179. Ibid. p. 63.
180. HMC, 10 iv. p. 296.
181. Jarvis, ii. p. 102.
182. SP Dom 76/121.
183. Ibid.
184. Ibid.
185. W.O. 71/19 f. 222.
186. Fitzherbert MSS.
187. Dore p. 50.
188. W.O. 71/19 f. 228.
189. W.O. 71/19 ff. 212–13.
190. Stott (1929) p. 10.

191. Blaikie, 'John Daniel's Progress' p. 184.
192. Maxwell of Kirkconnell p. 80.
193. Tomasson p. 118.
194. Marchant p. 212.
195. Tayler, *Jacobite Letters to Lord Pitsligo.*
196. Tomasson p. 118.
197. Tayler, *Pitsligo.*
198. Charteris p. 236.
199. SP Dom 76/147.
200. Ibid.
201. Fitzherbert MSS; Earwaker, *Constables* iii. p. 25.
202. W.O. 71/19 f. 228.
203. *Palatine Notebook* iv. p. 23.
204. Earwaker, *Constables* iii. p. 24.
205. Yorke, i. pp. 481–82.
206. SP Dom 76/146.
207. SP Dom 76/145.
208. SP Dom 76/146.
209. Yorke, i. pp. 481–82.
210. Gordon & Arnot, i. pp. 75–76.
211. HMC 10 iv. p. 296.
212. Roper pp. 91–92.
213. Ibid. pp. 98–99.
214. SP Dom 77/63.
215. *Ogilvy's Orderbook* pp. 306–07.
216. Add. MSS. 33050 f. 59.
217. *Ogilvy's Orderbook* p. 307.
218. *Birmingham Gazette,* 23 December 1745.
219. Blundell, ii. p. 228.
220. Elcho p. 345.
221. HMC, 14 ix. p. 138; *Manchester Magazine,* 17 December 1745; Marchant p. 214; Ray p. 191.
222. SP Dom 77/4,43.
223. HMC, 13 vi. pp. 169–70; *Birmingham Gazette* 23 December 1745.
224. *Morning Advertiser* No. 414, 20–23 December 1745.
225. SP Dom 77/4.
226. Atholl, *Chronicles* iii. pp. 102–03.
227. Add. MSS. 35889 f. 66.
228. *Trans. Gaelic Soc.* (1896–97) pp. 165–66; 'Two Yorkshire Diaries p. 117; Jarvis (1954) pp. 375–76.
229. Roper p. 91.
230. SP Dom 81 ff. 306–07.
231. Hibbert-Ware, ii. p. 108.
232. Elcho p. 346.
233. Maxwell of Kirkconnell pp. 82–83; Chambers, 'Marches' p. 60.
234. Tomasson p. 119.
235. *Manchester Magazine,* 24 December 1745; Fitzherbert MSS.
236. SP Dom 77/39.
237. Earwaker, iii. p. 25.
238. SP Dom 77/40.
239. HMC, 13 vi. p. 167.
240. HMC, 14 ix. p. 137.
241. SP Dom 77/15.
242. SP Dom 76/107; 77/18.

243. SP Dom 77/10.
244. Add. MSS. 34712 ff. 40–42; Marchant pp. 232, 247–49.
245. SP Dom 77/12.
246. SP Dom 76/101; 77/82,132.
247. SP Dom 76/30,34,62.

8

Alarums and Excursions in Cumbria

Saturday 14th December

EARLY this Saturday Perth's small party entered Kendal — it was market day in the town — to be greeted by the kind of reception that was to turn the next two days into a nightmare for the Duke. Westmorland was now rousing itself under Cumberland's commands and the promptings of the Deputy Lieutenants. Already a party had been sent to demolish Wasdale Bridge, three and a half miles south of Shap, on the main Kendal–Shap road.[1] Another had been sent to break up the Kendal–Appleby road — the most likely route for the Jacobite artillery and baggage waggons — at Grayrigg Hawse.[2] In Kendal, Perth faced the furious hostility of an armed and truculent citizenry, emboldened by the reports now widespread that Charles Edward's army had been surrounded and annihilated at Lancaster and that this detachment of horse under Perth was all that survived.[3]

The nine or ten dozen hussars, with Perth riding in a carriage because of illness, rode up to Finkle Street where the mob suddenly fell on them with a fusillade of clubs and stones. Perth's men made a stand just below the fishmarket, where the Duke ordered them to fire over the heads of the mob to frighten them, it being useless in his opinion to attempt to stop an angry crowd by firing into them when reloading had to be considered.[4] However, in their panic and haste Perth's cavalry ignored the order and four people fell dead from their first volley. But in the scramble to get into a better defensive position, four of the Highlanders were taken prisoner and a fifth, Perth's cook, was knocked off his horse. This animal was a highly prized steed, said to have been surrendered at the siege of Carlisle by a Captain Wilson, and strapped to the saddle was a portmanteau containing a considerable sum of money. Nobody saw which of the townsfolk leaped onto the horse, but it was ridden off at full tilt in the heat of the encounter, and neither horse nor rider was ever heard of again. Perth's servant later died from his injuries and was buried in Kendal churchyard.[5]

The Highlanders turned round again at Stramongate to face the howling mob. They formed up in order and seemed about to charge back through Kendal with the intention, some cried, of gutting it, but were disconcerted by the wounding of the cavalry leader by sniper fire from under the bridge and by Perth's shouting to them from his carriage that stocks of powder were now low.[6] A decision was taken to retire to Shap; from there Perth's men rode up to Eamont Bridge but saw that the

167

Penrith beacon had been fired.[7] Since this was the signal for the countryside to rise in arms and since further enquiry revealed that the hedges from Clifton to Penrith were heavily lined with snipers — to say nothing of a further report that 120 of Wade's soldiers were in Penrith itself — Perth ordered retreat to Shap, where a tense and vigilant night was spent.[8]

In Lancaster, Charles Edward's army prepared for the encounter with Cumberland that everybody considered imminent. The night of 13th/14th December had seen the army once again at maximum readiness with patrols thrown out at all danger points. The road to Preston was guarded by detachments from Roy Stewart's, Keppoch's and Ogilvy's, all lodged at the extreme end of the town in houses and barns grouped around the building known as the White Cross. Pitsligo's horse patrolled the Preston road from a base at a windmill about half a mile out, on the left-hand side of the road from Lancaster, keeping this station all night until 8 a.m.[9] Till the same hour another cavalry detail patrolled the road to Hornby. At daybreak, while Lancaster's tailors and shoemakers were set to producing large quantities of their wares for the army and foraging parties scoured the villages to the north like Baulk, the burning question of the hour — battle with Cumberland — was debated.[10] To Lord George Murray the definite decision to offer battle to the Hanoverians was unknown until O'Sullivan awoke him with the Prince's orders that the two of them (Murray and O'Sullivan) should reconnoitre a battlefield. Despite Murray's misgivings, he made no objection when reporting to Charles Edward's HQ and so frustrated the expectations of those who had encouraged the Prince to take this step and now awaited a fiery refusal from Lord George, in hopes of seeing him discredited once and for all.[11] Without proffering an opinion on the desirability of joining battle, Murray merely proposed that as ground suitable for regular troops might not be right for the Highlanders, one of the clan chiefs should go with him. As Lochiel was present, he was asked to attend and readily agreed.[12]

With an escort of horse and foot Lochiel, Murray and O'Sullivan rode back down the road to Preston, and about half a mile out of Lancaster O'Sullivan chose a stretch of flat ground just by the roadside.[13] Lochiel and Murray did not agree that this was the most favourable site for the clansmen. Two miles from Lancaster was a field set on rising ground which the two Scots reckoned could contain the whole army and so situated that they could ensure that, whatever quarter the enemy came from, their own van would be under cover from enemy fire until Cumberland's troops were close upon them.[14] To the left of the chosen field was a hill which Murray thought should be investigated to prevent a recurrence of enemy tactics at Prestonpans. The three leaders climbed to the top while their men rode around the bottom. Lochiel and Murray expressed themselves delighted with their choice of terrain but O'Sullivan was sceptical. He agreed that the Scots' ground was more suitable for the clansmen than regular troops, always providing 'Cumberland was obliging enough to come there'.[15] But he pointed out that it was against all the rules of war for an army to fight so far from its base: the field was two miles from Lancaster and a long way from the road, which left Cumberland the option of taking Lancaster and so cutting off all communications and possibilities of retreat.[16]

Murray countered by pointing out that this consideration was outweighed by the overwhelming superiority of his terrain to O'Sullivan's as the latter would permit Cumberland to use cavalry.[17] O'Sullivan then asked how the clansmen could break through to Scotland in case of defeat, especially if Cumberland sent on a force to occupy Kendal before offering battle. It was discovered that there was a ford at a mill almost exactly where the moor on which Lochiel and Murray proposed to fight joined the Preston road. This could provide the means for a breakout by a defeated Jacobite army, avoiding Lancaster and allowing a gateway to Scotland.[18] O'Sullivan then pointed out that the party sent to defend the ford against Cumberland's seizure would have to operate at too great a distance from the main army, and with exiguous forces — no more than 5,000 — at their disposal, the risk involved in splitting forces was unacceptable.

Murray saw an opportunity to turn O'Sullivan's objections to his own advantage and incorporated them in the report he wrote for the Prince. He added that he had found a favourable battlefield for the clans to fight on, provided they were not overwhelmed by the combined numbers of Wade's and Cumberland's armies.[19] Murray of course was overrating the potential threat from Wade because of faulty intelligence. While he was on the summit of the hill with Lochiel and O'Sullivan, a party of some twenty-five or thirty horsemen, clothed in green with leather caps, had been descried. Henry Ker of Graden, who commanded the escort, was sent in pursuit.[20] Two of the green-clad Georgia Rangers — for such they proved to be — were captured along with a quantity of horses, mounts of other rangers who jumped off and hid in the hedges and enclosures to avoid being taken. One man was shot dead when he refused quarter.[21] Ker then rode to the next piece of rising ground on the Preston road and made sure no other enemy troops were in sight before returning to Lancaster with his prize.[22] From the prisoners Lord George learned that the Georgia Rangers were in Garstang and that a large body of Wade's dragoons had entered Preston a few hours after the Jacobites had left on the 13th.[23] Hearing that the cavalry arms of the two armies had linked up, Murray inferred that Wade's and Cumberland's infantry must also be united and close behind.

Charles Edward himself questioned the prisoners and then pondered Murray's qualified statement of confidence. The Prince inclined to reject Murray and Lochiel's choice of field in favour of O'Sullivan's, whose textbook advice seemed sounder to him, but he feared the impact on morale if the Scottish leaders were overruled.[24] This was a potent consideration in Lancaster: the despondency of the chiefs led to one rumour that they intended to ship out directly for France from Morecambe Bay.[25] Another rumour had it that a duel had been fought between Lord Elcho and Lord Ogilvy 'which ended much to the disadvantage of the latter'.[26] Then there was the worrying junction of Wade's and Cumberland's armies, as reported by the prisoners. Perhaps Murray was right and the *élan* of the Highlanders would be no match for the sheer weight of enemy numbers. All in all, it seemed most prudent to continue the retreat until the military position became clearer. The Prince accordingly abandoned the idea of a battle.[27]

Charles Edward's sojourn in Lancaster, which he opted for out of bravado and for reasons of prestige, was interpreted, even by those whose intelligence was good and who did not accept the fantasy of his annihilation there by Cumberland, as a symptom of desperation. It was argued that the Stuart prince could not be contemplating making a stand, since the town of Lancaster was open on all sides and hence there could be no escape for the clansmen. Another theory was that Wade and his five regiments of foot had got to Kendal before them and barred the passage to Scotland. This no doubt accounted for the propaganda story, admittedly later retracted, that the Highlanders had hanged large numbers of people in Lancaster.[28]

The reality was that Whig fortunes, so far from having reached such an apogee, were not even progressing according to reasonable expectations. Cumberland's cavalry force was preparing to move out of Wigan towards Preston at midnight when Newcastle's orders of the 12th were received, ordering the Duke to turn round and march with all speed via Manchester to London. Cumberland's men were just setting out this Saturday morning when Newcastle's later letter, expounding his second thoughts and countermanding the earlier orders, arrived.[29] The Secretary of State explained that in the light of Cumberland's letter, which he had received in the interim, he was now ordering an advance on Preston. The two factors that had weighed with him were: the precipitate flight of the Jacobites, and the arrival of Oglethorpe from Yorkshire.[30]

This delay was not particularly serious in terms of time lost, since Cumberland quit Wigan for Preston by 7 a.m., but it did seriously impede Oglethorpe's operations by introducing a strong element of uncertainty.[31] At first all troops in north Lancashire had been ordered back to Wigan, and this impaired the eventual implementation of Oglethorpe's orders. These were to advance within three miles of Lancaster with both regulars and irregulars in the hope of picking off Jacobite patrols. If the Highlanders retreated from Lancaster, Major Wheatley was to move up from Garstang and all available forces were to track them as closely as possible.[32] A number of factors prevented the carrying out of this clear-cut plan. In the first place there was the recall to Wigan and its subsequent cancellation. Then there was the check administered to the Rangers by Ker of Graden. Finally there was the uncertainty on the night of 14th/15th December about whether Charles Edward really was withdrawing from Lancaster. By nightfall some of Oglethorpe's men had got as far as Scotsforth and Galgar, just to the south of Lancaster, without being able to ascertain the truth.[33] The truth was simply that the Highlanders were staging an ingenious phased withdrawal. The artillery left at eight on Saturday night, but the rearguard was still in town at eight on Sunday morning. The consequence was that the luckless men under Oglethorpe's command spent the night in open fields to the north of Garstang.[34]

By now Wade had reached Boroughbridge, just forty-eight miles from Doncaster, in a dispirited and miserable withdrawal to Newcastle. His troops were constantly camped out in the rain and cold weather, and a large number of sick had to be left behind in the towns and villages through which the army passed.[35] Wade explained to London that he had been unable to follow the advice of his generals and put his men under cover each night, since this would work against the requirements of mobility and preparedness to fight at a moment's notice. Finally, this Saturday he gave up all pretence that his army was now a credible fighting force and ordered them billeted in larger towns until they were near Newcastle. Wolfe had been sent ahead as temporary commander in Tyneside, while all the troops who could be considered fighting fit — about 4,000 in all — had been sent on with Huske in the forlorn attempt to intercept the Highlanders at Penrith.[36]

In London meanwhile there was taking place what has been described as a 'confusion of confusions' following increasingly alarming reports about the French. A royal proclamation ordained that all people living on the coast should drive all horses, oxen and cattle twenty miles inland to prevent their being used by French invaders.[37] Three thousand foot and 1,000 horse were told off to the Essex and Suffolk coast and 4,000 foot with 1,500 cavalry to the coasts of Kent and Sussex. All forts and castles were to be double garrisoned, if necessary by raising new regiments, and a magazine of arms was to be set up in each fortress, so that there would be no need to rely on the Tower of London in emergency. To his generals Newcastle sent a series of instructions. Wade was praised for his dispatch of Oglethorpe, Huske was notified of his appointment to command in Scotland (later rescinded), while Ligonier was ordered to march for London, whatever the developments on Cumberland's front, because of the threat from the French.[38] Ligonier was in fact in no position to move quickly to London's assistance, partly because of his own illness, but mainly because of acute transport problems; even the advance party sent from Coventry under General Anstruther was seriously retarded owing to supply inelasticities in provisions, straw and waggons.[39] While not able to help Ligonier, Newcastle suggested easing Wade's problems by incorporating the volunteer regiments in Yorkshire into his army. Technically, since they had been recruited on the understanding that they would not serve outside Yorkshire, they had to be disbanded and re-recruited for Wade. But this proposal, even with the backing of Malton, met with such strong opposition on grounds of dislike of a standing army that it had to be shelved. In any case, Lord Irwin in the East Riding opposed the suggestion on the grounds that there was still a threat to the county from a possible French landing on the east coast.[40]

The next dramatic development in London was the receipt of news that the French had actually landed in Pevensey Bay, a false report made more credible by the constant asseverations by the Admiral of the Fleet on the Downs, Vernon, that in certain weather conditions he would be powerless to stop Richelieu. Once again orders were sent to Cumberland to break off the pursuit of Charles Edward and come south with all speed.[41] This second intermission in the pursuit of the Scots seemed so unlikely to have been dictated by objective circumstances that Cumberland and others later attributed it to a ruse by the English Jacobites, who were alleged to have spread false intelligence about a French landing in order to ensure that their Prince got away safely to Scotland.[42] It came at a bad moment psychologically for Cumberland, since he now had adequate supplies of food and forage from Liverpool and Manchester, some of which were not recovered until seven weeks later, and at Carlisle too.[43] If Richelieu did nothing else in late 1745 than stymie the pursuit of the Scots, he can still be said to have performed a valuable service to Charles Edward.

Sunday 15th December

From Shap the Duke of Perth began a hazardous attempt to reach Scotland, in the teeth of an armed countryside flushed with the continuing unfounded reports of a Jacobite defeat. By now armed parties were afoot not only from Penrith but from the villages of Dalston, Sebergham and Brough. Many of the Cumbrian bridges, such as those at Armethwaite and Sebegham, were already guarded by well-armed bands.[44] Perth decided to break out by the route along the eastern bank of the River Eden. The route of his hussars took them through Cliburn and Temple Sowerby, where they crossed to the other side of the Eden and from Culgaith to Langwathby moor. The Penrith posse had meanwhile crossed the Eden lower down at Langwathby Bridge and, coming on to the moor at Appleside Hill, virtually collided with the Highlanders.[45] After the exchange of a few volleys, the startled Scots retreated, and what came to be known as the 'Sunday hunting' was on in earnest. Perth's party was chased through Culgaith, Newbiggen moor and Kirkby Thore.[46] By this time the Highlanders were hopelessly lost, and only after pressing Jack Boucher into service as a guide did they retrace their steps perilously to Shap, via Bolton (on the Eden), Moorland, Newby-Mill Flat and Reagill. The Cumberland and Westmorland irregulars still dogged them relentlessly and were only shaken off when Perth moved further on, to Orton.[47] After a short rest there, Perth's party returned to Kendal on the Sunday night and rejoined the main army.[48]

By 8 a.m. the last of the Highlanders were quitting Lancaster. The clan regiments proper were in the van of the march to Kendal, first the Atholl brigade, then the MacDonalds — Clanranald, Glengarry and Keppoch (with the royal standard) — followed by the Camerons, Appin Stewarts and MacPhersons. John Roy Stewart's and Ogilvy's were the last infantry to leave Lancaster this Sunday, and bringing up the extreme rear were Elcho's Lifeguards.[49] Many of Roy Stewart's and Ogilvy's had been up all night assisting Kilmarnock's horse to patrol the Preston road. Until daybreak, each time Kilmarnock's set off to reconnoitre the road to Preston an officer and twenty men of the infantry regiments went back with them as far as the windmill, in case of enemy incursion. Kilmarnock's horse then had to gallop on ahead to the front of the army to take up their official place just ahead of the Atholl brigade. The patrols on the Preston road had picked up many signs of the activity of Oglethorpe's men and were aware of their proximity. Lord George Murray still thought that the bulk of Wade's army was not far behind. As the Prince emerged from his headquarters to ride with Balmerino's horse, Murray could not resist a taunt: 'As your royal highness is always for battles, be the circumstances what they may, I now offer you one in three hours from this time with the army of Wade, which is only about three miles from us.'[50]

As the Highlanders left Lancaster at one end, Oglethorpe's men entered it at the other.[51] A party of 'Royal Hunters' then tracked the Prince's rear for about four miles out of Lancaster, keeping about a mile between themselves and Elcho's Lifeguards. At one stage, after the Hanoverian cavalry had ascended a hill to view the Jacobite army, a flank attack seemed likely, so the rear of the clan army halted and faced the enemy for about a quarter of an hour before proceeding.[52] The same manoeuvre was later repeated when passing another hill. For Oglethorpe's men to approach closer was hazardous, since once Charles Edward heard that his rear was being dogged by the Rangers, he ordered Lord Nairne's detachment from the Atholl brigade to line the hedges and cover the retreat.[53]

About four miles from Lancaster Oglethorpe's cavalry was suddenly seen to wheel round and gallop back in the direction of Lancaster. What had happened was that Cumberland had received news of the 'French landing' and ordered Oglethorpe to pull back to Garstang.[54] The consequence was that some of Oglethorpe's men spent Sunday marching from Garstang to Lancaster and back again. By nightfall they were no further advanced than twenty-four hours before. Most of Oglethorpe's troops were reduced to standing in the streets of Garstang all night, and some who had arrived two hours after dark preferred to take their chances once more in encampments on Elkhill moor.[55]

At Preston, Cumberland was furious that his pursuit had been called off. He wrote sardonically to Newcastle later: 'I am very sorry that Mr. Vernon's fright should have saved the rebel army.'[56] The despondency among his soldiers was palpable as units were sent back to Wigan in preparation for a morning march to London on the 16th.[57]

Meanwhile Kendal awaited the approach of the Highlanders with trepidation. The Scots were in a grim mood as they entered the town. Though they had formed up cheerfully enough to face Oglethorpe's raiders, the men had had much to endure. The going between Lancaster and Kendal was so bad that one newspaper reported that 2,000 clansmen had been drowned in flooded rivers on the day's march.[58] Dissension continued within the army about the correct stance towards the hostile populace, almost, according to Joseph Yorke in Preston, to the point of the chiefs fighting with one another.[59] To the treachery offered Perth on Saturday was now added the insolence of the Kendal people in stealing Lord George Murray's horses. Four of Murray's servants entered the town on Sunday evening, slightly ahead of the main army and without adequate protection, and promptly had their horses stolen.[60] The hardliners among the chiefs wanted to exact draconian contributions from Kendal in compensation and then burn the town to the ground. In consequence there was little attempt to enforce the Spartan discipline that Kendal had so marvelled at on the southward progress: homes were plundered and the well-clad stripped of their clothing.[61] The town magistrates pleaded that the events on Saturday had not been fomented by them but had been the spontaneous actions of an ill-advised mob. Lochiel for one accepted their version of the clash with Perth and was instrumental in assuaging the wrath of the other clan chiefs and even in diminishing the financial exaction laid on the town.[62]

But now there developed another major confrontation between the Prince and Lord George Murray, this time over the issue of the artillery. Basically, Murray wanted to abandon it and put the men's safety first, while Charles Edward, who was convinced that it was pointless for Cumberland to pursue him beyond Kendal, was adamant that not a single piece of cannon nor a single carriage be left behind.[63] He felt that his prestige required a withdrawal in good order with his equipment intact and was prepared to fight the combined armies of Wade and Cumberland rather than provide the enemy with any opportunity for imputing fear and weakness to him. Murray, on the other hand, continued anxious that the combined enemy cavalry might come up with them before Carlisle and that the infantry might not be far behind.[64] On the latter subject Murray's worst fears were soon laid to rest. He took out a detachment of Lifeguards in the dark to the south of Kendal and returned after two hours with some militiamen prisoners, who gave him the vital information that Wade's infantry was on the other side of the Pennines.[65] There still remained, nevertheless, the danger from the combined cavalry and the fundamental obstacle of the baggage and artillery.

The difference between the two men came to a head when Murray visited the Prince's headquarters in Stricklandgate. Lord George demanded that the two-wheeled waggons be substituted for the four-wheelers in readiness for the dreadful journey to Shap. Two-wheeled waggons were available in Kendal, 'and though some people should sit up all night at so necessary a work, it would be doing good service.'[66] He also requested that the men be given an extra day's ration of bread and cheese since there was nothing to be had at Shap. O'Sullivan seemingly ignored Murray's arguments but offered him a glass of 'some mountain Malaga which he seemed very fond of'. Murray repeated his conviction that men should be kept working all night at the transfer of baggage and ammunition from heavy waggons to light carts like those that had carried it to Preston on the southward journey. He stressed that heavy waggons could not traverse the steep road over Shap Fell, since the country people had been digging holes and throwing down large stones from the walls onto the main road. O'Sullivan finally agreed to issue the necessary orders but he sat at table until almost 11 p.m. after Murray had gone, drinking with the Prince, before he issued them. By the time he had written the orders most officers had retired to bed and did not receive them until the next morning.[67]

One favourable development for the Highlanders was notified to Cumberland by Lord Lonsdale. He pointed out two main drawbacks to the plans to impede and overtake the Stuart prince.[68] In the first place, it was extremely difficult to obstruct the progress of the Scots north of Kendal since the country was both mountainous and 'very thinly populated and generally so open that there are many different roads to the same place by going very little about'. The upshot was that breaking up the roads in Cumberland would have very little effect. Secondly, Lonsdale pointed out to Cumberland the considerable problem involved in feeding his army between Kendal and Carlisle — significantly the very point Lord George Murray had raised with Charles Edward and O'Sullivan — 'the country produces very little and what there is will be either consumed or destroyed by the rebels if they are before you.'[69] Lonsdale recommended ordering supplies of bread from Yorkshire via Stainmoor.

In London, the reports of a French landing having proved false, Newcastle told Cumberland that he could resume his pursuit. But it was not yet time for complacency, since a French landfall could still materialise at any time. Newcastle emphasised to Ligonier that nothing must stand in the way of his return.[70] Orders were sent to the mayor and magistrates at Daventry, Towcester, Fenny Stratford, Dunstable, Northampton, Newport Pagnell, St. Albans and Barnet to supply at their own expense all necessary horses and waggons that Ligonier might requisition.[71] As for Wade, Newcastle took an amazingly emollient line. Despite the constant criticisms of Wade, the Secretary of State told Devonshire: 'I really think him, upon the whole, a very honest and a very able man; and I do not know where we shall be able to replace him.'[72]

Little of Wade's actions seemed to justify such a confident endorsement. He was still only at Ripon and the bulk of his army was at Boroughbridge.[73] Wade had not only decided to canton his army and march in three divisions to Newcastle via Northallerton, Darlington and Durham, but had resolved to recall Huske from his trek across the Pennines via Greta Bridge, in order that he might command the first detachment of 1,000 men bound for Northallerton.[74] The principal element determining Wade to put his 'much reduced' army under permanent cover was the weather, and it was this factor more than any other which was to dominate the last four days of the 1745 campaign in England.

Monday 16th December

At 6 a.m. the Jacobite army left Kendal, intending to reach Penrith that night. Balmerino's and Elcho's Lifeguards were in the van, followed by the Atholl brigade, Clanranald's and the Camerons with the royal standard. Perth's, Ogilvy's, Glenbucket's, John Roy Stewart's and the Manchester regiment had set off an hour earlier to take the road to Orton with the intention of rejoining the rearguard with the artillery at Shap.[75] The main problem this Monday was clearly going to be the artillery, which Clanranald's had guarded overnight, and a heavy responsibility would devolve on Lord George Murray and the men of Glengarry who formed the extreme rear this day. Glengarry's and Pitsligo's assembled at 7 a.m. between the Cock and Dolphin inn and the bridge that led onto the Lancaster road and waited until the rest of the army and the baggage were out of town. Neither of these detachments had been rested: Glengarry's had been occupied in guarding the bridge to the north of town on the Penrith road (it was the Appin Stewarts who surveilled the Cock and Dolphin road during the night); Pitsligo's had patrolled in alternate parties the road between the southern bridge and the Cock and Dolphin and the road beyond the bridge as far as the second great barn on the left-hand side of the highway to Lancaster.[76]

Before Lord George could get under way with the rearguard, the consequences of O'Sullivan's tardy orders manifested themselves. Many men returned to Kendal to provide themselves with bread and cheese, having received the orders when actually on the march, but by this time the people of Kendal had shut their doors for fear of depredations from stragglers.[77] Murray had to take charge of provisioning these men while minimising plunder, and it was a full two hours before they could be sent on their way.

The violent rains this Monday, combined no doubt with the peculiar strain on the Lieutenant-General, exacerbated an incipient cold in Murray. Since he had to stand several hours in the rain in Kendal while provisions were obtained, Murray was soon racked by a violent cough, made worse in his own view by not having undressed for several nights, and this illness was with him all the way to Carlisle, though he confessed that the day's march on the 16th made him feel better.[78] Another headache for Murray was that for the first time he did not have the assistance of Lord Ogilvy's regiment, which in the early stages of the retreat had been detailed to remain with Murray in addition to the regiment taking rearguard duty by rotation. Often, too, other regimental commanders, knowing the problem of the artillery, had lent Murray assistance, but today all were consulting their regimental interests primarily, and Lord George had only the Glengarry men with him, with the exception of a few volunteers from the Manchester regiment.[79]

All the bad omens were fulfilled, for the rearguard managed to proceed no more than four miles on Monday the 16th. The main army itself was hard put to it to get as far as Shap. Pioneers had to mend the road four miles north of Kendal; the accommodation in Shap was totally inadequate for the army, which spent a miserable night there; and even the Prince was overcharged at the main inn in the village.[80] This was even after fresh orders had been issued to relieve some of the strain on Shap, which involved part of the main column in a detour to Orton and another part being deployed in the villages around Shap like Thrumby and Strickling.[81] But apart from a pillaging expedition to Levens Hall, seat of the Earl of Berkshire, this intensely rainy Monday was notable in the case of the main army only for the slow progress made.[82]

Things were otherwise with the rearguard, where Lord George Murray endured the first day of a forty-eight hour nightmare.[83] Even the exit from Kendal was not free from incident, since as the rearguard filed along the road they caught sight of some men — a parson and five friends — hiding behind a wall and counting their numbers. The Glengarry men fired upon the party and pursued them into a 'very dirty pigeon cote' where they left them.[84] This diversion was a mere bagatelle compared with the problems encountered later. Three miles out of Kendal the rearguard was stopped by a stream impassable to the four-wheeled carriages, since the water ran across a narrow turn in the road which was followed immediately by a steep uphill gradient.[85] Horses were unhitched from the waggons and all yoked to one carriage which was then pushed by all men (including officers) who could get a hand to it — about forty in all. Both Murray and the three volunteer officers from the Manchester regiment went into the water up to their middle for an hour in an attempt to push the wheels. Eventually, in this laborious way and in continual driving rain, the obstacle was passed and all the waggons safely carried over the stream, but by now it was nightfall and they were far from Shap.

There was nothing for it but to spend the night on the road. A quarter of a mile off the road was a farm where Murray got most of the Glengarry men (whose praises he sang extravagantly) under cover in barns and stables. A guard of fifty men was placed in a small house near the stream whence the last loaded waggon had just emerged.[86] All the men were drenched with rain, and the general wetness made it extremely difficult to start fires in the barns. Protocol was waived and Murray brought many of the clansmen into the farmhouse, officially the officers' quarters, to dry themselves. All the milk, cheese and bread in the house was bought and, despite the weather, the people of the farm were persuaded to go half a mile away to another farm to buy more cheese, once Murray had promised to pay an extra penny a pound. By midnight the men were well fed and morale was high once more.[87]

In Preston, in the final episode in the series of orders and counter-orders, Cumberland received permission to resume his hot pursuit and was said to have 'jumped for joy' when he heard that the report of the French invasion was a false alarm.[88] Much residual ill-feeling remained about the orders from London which had prevented Cumberland's overhauling the Highlanders. Ligonier, now en route to London with nine battalions, allowed himself an implicit criticism of Newcastle by stating his conviction that no orders should now impede, nor ever should have impeded, the pursuit of the Highlanders to the Scottish border.[89] Cumberland's secretary Sir Everard Fawkener concurred: 'the twenty-four hours lost at Preston will have been decisive'.[90]

While Cumberland moved rapidly up to Lancaster, Oglethorpe's advance force rode from Garstang to Burton, so as to leave Lancaster free for the Duke's troops.[91] In Burton on Monday night Oglethorpe received an express from the Mayor of Kendal in which he claimed that the Highlanders, unable to penetrate to Penrith, were about to return to burn Kendal to the ground.[92] Fresh horses were immediately found and an advance party under Lieutenant Campbell was sent to take possession of Kendal.[93] Arriving in the town at midnight, Campbell learned that only four miles to the north was a party of some 200–300 clansmen guarding the gun carriages.[94] Meanwhile, at a Council of War held in Lancaster, Cumberland decided to send Oglethorpe to search out and destroy Lord George Murray and the rearguard. In preparation for the expected major clash to follow, Bligh's and Sempill's were to be at Preston by Wednesday the 18th.[95] Oglethorpe was now to be caught up in a web of events that would lead to his (unsuccessful) court-martial in 1746.

Tuesday 17th December

After the road two miles north of Shap was patched up by the pioneers, Charles Edward's main force was able to move up to Penrith by nightfall.[96] Penrith awaited the Prince's return with trepidation on two counts: first, because of the town's part in the 'Sunday hunting' of Perth's hussars; secondly, for its role in the raid on Lowther Hall on 27th November.[97] Revenge was taken for the latter slight by the plunder of Lowther Hall by members of the Manchester regiment; on the former count, the clan leaders were once again dissuaded with difficulty from visiting hostile Cumbrians with fire and burning Penrith down.[98] All the Whig leaders fled together with the hundred or so of Wade's troops to Gamelsby. On arrival in Penrith, a squadron of cavalry was sent up to secure Carlisle and make preparations for the reception of the army, while the Prince waited for the rearguard to come up. As a token gesture Charles Edward left 200 men of John Roy Stewart's in Shap to assist Lord George Murray.[99]

Murray and the Glengarry men were this morning still six miles south of Shap. At daybreak Lord George Murray distributed all the oatmeal and cheese he had been able to buy and attempted to find some solution for the problem of the waggons. All small carts with timber wheels or wheels made from one piece of wood were collected from within a two-mile radius and the ammunition unloaded from the waggons and transferred to the small carts.[100] The Glengarry men were surprised at how little the unwieldy waggons contained — the largest carried no more than could be fitted into two small carts — and it was realised that it was the heaviness and lack of manoeuvrability of the waggons and not their contents that had led to the fiasco of the day before. Murray was particularly bitter when he reflected that twelve fine box carts had been left in Preston, despite his pleas, which could easily have carried everything. One of the conveyances with which Murray and his men had struggled in the rain the day before contained only four barrels, and on breaking open the tops the Highlanders discovered that only two of them had gunpowder inside.[101] The other two were filled with biscuits which had travelled all the way from Edinburgh to Derby and back again. Originally destined to feed the men at the siege of Carlisle, through commissariat incompetence they had been carried through England in place of powder.

Once under way with the new carts, the rearguard managed to travel three miles before encountering a fresh obstacle. The next stream to be crossed was swollen with the heavy rains, and the tiny bridge over it was too narrow even for the new carts. Here too was dramatic evidence of the difficulty the main army had encountered the day before. Immediately after the bridge was the steepest hill on the entire road from Kendal to Penrith, and now it was strewn with carts containing cannon balls which Cluny Macphersons's regiment, penultimate in the rear, had abandoned shortly before, having spent a dreadful night in the open just by the bridge.[102] In the stream could be seen one of the cannon that Cluny's men had lost the night before through trying to force it over the bridge.

Murray grasped at once that it would be impossible to carry all the carts laden with cannon balls up the hill, especially given the weakened condition of the horses. While he was pondering his next step, an aide-de-camp arrived from the Prince bearing the explicit message that not a single cannon ball was to be left behind or he would feel compelled to return in person.[103] Murray replied that he had undertaken at Derby always to be in the rear *provided* that he was not responsible for baggage and impedimenta. Nevertheless, he returned the message that he would do all he could but that the Prince should realise that he (Murray) expected the rearguard to be attacked either that night or next day and in consequence requested some cavalry to patrol behind him and advise of the approach of the enemy. Murray then appealed to the Glengarry men to carry a cannon ball each to Shap, for which he would pay 6d. a head. In this way about 200 cannon balls were carried, tied up in the corner of the men's plaids.[104] Murray told Lochgarry, the regimental commander, that he could not imagine better men to have with him in a crisis, especially since 'the Glengarry men are usually reckoned not the most patient', and he was to be unstinting in his praise for them later, after they had remained unrelieved in the rear for three days and performed all manner of duties uncomplainingly which were usually considered beneath the dignity of a Highlander.[105]

Two miles further on, while crossing a bridge without ledgelets, two carts and four horses toppled into the stream below. The horses were saved but were now useless for further service; the contents of the carts were with difficulty retrieved.[106] The powder was then thrown into a pool to make it unfit for use by the enemy, since it could not be conveyed further.[107] It was an hour after nightfall when the rearguard finally got into Shap, where it was found that all the food in town had been eaten by the Prince's army the night before. The serendipity of having discovered the two barrels of biscuit was now plain: these were distributed and, together with a reserve store of cheese that Murray had purchased the night before, an acceptable meal of toasted cheese (held to the fire by the point of a claymore) and biscuit was consumed.[108]

At Shap the harshness of Charles Edward's orders to leave no arms or ammunition behind was further revealed when several cannon were discovered lying in the streets. Moreover, instead of the cavalry he had requested, Lord George found only John Roy Stewart's foot, who could not in safety undertake patrolling and scouting duties.[109] Stewart himself, being a 'Prince's man' and thus hostile to Murray, was singularly unhelpful. He merely commented that a bonfire should be made of all the impedimenta. The only sympathetic insight into Murray's plight was shown by Perth, who had had the cannon and baggage problem all the way from Carlisle to Derby; some volunteers from his regiment were also sent back to Shap to help.[110]

Lord George's fears that Cumberland's vanguard would be upon him that night were well founded, for shortly after the Highlanders got into Shap, Oglethorpe and his men arrived outside the village. Cumberland's orders of the day had been to pursue Murray and the rear and to attack on sight. When Oglethorpe arrived in Kendal he learned that Murray and his party had spent Monday night on the road four miles to the north and estimated that they would not get beyond Shap that night.[111] A rider was despatched to Cumberland to request further orders. Cumberland replied that if there was only a small party 'not above 400' at Shap, he was to attack it. If the Highlanders quit Shap that night, Oglethorpe was to take possession of it. If, on the other hand, the whole Jacobite army was there, he was to await Cumberland's coming on the 18th.[112] The Duke's intention was to march to Kendal on the 17th, 'to beat boots and saddles at 4 a.m.' and to march at 5 a.m. for Shap.[113]

Oglethorpe's march this Tuesday was in its way as gruelling an experience as that of Lord George Murray and the Glengarry regiment. After an easy journey from Burton to Kendal — an eight-mile stretch of road, 'a narrow, strong lane all the way'[114] — which was reached at midday, Oglethorpe reckoned conditions were propitious for a sustained pursuit of the Highlanders, especially with a full moon that night. Accordingly, his men did not stay long enough in Kendal even to take refreshment. But when they reached the fells outside Kendal, they soon discovered why the Scots had made such slow progress. Not only was the road 'strong, mountainous and bad' so that only a few could march abreast, but the weather changed abruptly, with a cold north wind and sleet and snow.[115] There were heavy showers of both rain and snow, 'the whole day wet and mizzling', and their effect was made worse since Oglethorpe's men marched uncloaked, in expectation of imminent combat.[116] The distress of the Highlanders was evident, as soon after leaving Kendal Oglethorpe's squadron noticed the numbers of carts and spoiled ammunition left behind.[117]

Oglethorpe arrived outside Shap at about 6 p.m.[118] From his resting place, about three-quarters of a mile out on the east side of the village, he pondered the question of an attack. Various factors had to be weighed up: the number of clansmen in Shap, Cumberland's orders, the condition of his own men and horses, the terrain and the weather and darkness.[119] Oglethorpe's intelligence was inconclusive. One count taken from a hill earlier that day estimated the Highlanders' numbers at between three and four hundred.[120] But the same spy, William Strickland, took another count a mile and a half further on and this time he found more like five to six hundred; another report put them as high as 1,000.[121] In addition, Oglethorpe was informed that, whatever their original numbers, the clansmen in Shap had been reinforced by others sent back from Penrith. With only six hundred men of his own, Oglethorpe considered the odds unfavourable. In any case the ground outside Shap was so bad, 'full of pits and holes covered with snow', that his men could not be drawn up in a line but had to be deployed one behind another.[122] Major Wheatley proposed that the column retire half a mile down the road behind a bridge and take up defensive stations pending the arrival of the main force. Oglethorpe objected that both men and horses needed rest or they would be totally *hors de combat* the next day.[123] In addition, it was pitch-black, raining heavily, the soldiers' powder was wet and their weapons needed cleaning. The obvious thing to do was to bivouac on the moor outside Shap, but without forage for the horses this too was impracticable.[124] Some settlement would have to be found that could supply this forage. On enquiring of the villages round about, Oglethorpe was told that the only places that could answer to his requirements were Orton and Banton.[125] Banton was two miles north of Shap on the road to Penrith, and its location appealed to Oglethorpe and his officers. However, no guide could be found to take them to Banton, allegedly because the road there was very bad and it was possible to get lost. Furthermore, two shepherd brothers volunteered the information that there were two rivulets on the way which would be swollen by the rains and the one small bridge per rivulet was impassable to a large body of men. There was also the likelihood of a collision with the Highlanders.[126]

Reluctantly Oglethorpe considered Orton, but as a final measure sent his spies to attempt entry into Shap. Thomas Masterman accompanied the guide to the first house in the village, about a hundred yards further out from the main cluster of houses. Masterman saw a man at the door of the house and threatened to shoot him if he did not come forward. The man replied in Gaelic, calling for his horse and shooting at them. When other Scots voices were heard, Masterman retreated hastily.[127] A final attempt was made to avert the seemingly inevitable march to Orton. Oglethorpe's officers urged him to remain outside Shap and meanwhile to send for forage from Orton. This proved impossible on a number of grounds. According to local information, there was not enough oats in Orton, there were no carriages to convey it thence, and it was too dark for anyone to be willing to attempt the task.[128] Moreover, because the Highlanders had pressed for horses and supplies there on Monday, the country people had driven their horses and corn onto the moors, whence they could not quickly be retrieved.

There was nothing for it but to march to Orton and the order was given about 7 p.m. A disconsolate Oglethorpe was encouraged by reports that the country between Orton and Penrith was fine and open and eminently suited for cavalry.[129] But even the march to Orton turned into a nightmare. To begin with, the guide deliberated for a quarter of an hour before agreeing to take them there.[130] Once on the road, it was so dark that if the guide went so much as four yards ahead, he could no longer be seen.[131] A detachment from the St. George's regiment actually lost its way and did not arrive in Orton till morning. The road was as bad as the one from Kendal to Shap, and a horse falling down a crevice caused a general halt.[132] Orton itself proved to be much further away from Shap than Oglethorpe had realised.[133] On arrival in the village, Oglethorpe was described as 'looking in danger of dying', having now been ill with a fever and thus without proper sleep since the 10th.[134]

The final episode in this nightmare experience — and one which led Oglethorpe to court-martial — was a contretemps with Cumberland. The Duke arrived in Kendal at about 5 p.m. after 'long marches over rocks and mountains frequently among the clouds'.[135] There he received definite intelligence that there was only a rearguard at Shap and issued orders for an immediate attack by Oglethorpe.[136] These orders did not leave Kendal until 9 p.m., by which time Oglethorpe was floundering across the moor to Orton, so he did not receive them until the next day.

NOTES

1. Fergusson, 'Retreat' pp. 193–94.
2. *London Magazine*, 1746 p. 614.
3. SP Dom 77/73; Tomasson p. 118; HMC, Lothian p. 155.
4. Chambers p. 199.
5. HMC, 10 iv. p. 297.
6. Chambers p. 199; HMC, 10 iv. p. 297.
7. HMC, Various Colls, viii. p. 148; SP Dom 77/53.
8. SP Dom 77/63.
9. *Ogilvy's Orderbook* p. 307.
10. HMC, VII. p. 704; Roper p. 93; SP Dom 81 ff. 136–38.
11. Tomasson pp. 118–19.
12. Chambers, 'Marches' p. 60.
13. Maxwell of Kirkconnell p. 83.
14. Chambers, 'Marches' pp. 60–61.
15. O'Sullivan pp. 104–05.
16. SP Dom 77/63.
17. Tomasson p. 120.
18. L.P. ii. pp. 459–60.
19. Tomasson p. 120.
20. L.P. ii. pp. 459–60.
21. Maxwell of Kirkconnell p. 83.
22. L.P. ii. pp. 459–60.
23. Elcho p. 346.
24. Tomasson p. 120.
25. *Birmingham Gazette*, 23 December 1745.
26. *Derby Mercury*, 20 December 1745.
27. Maxwell of Kirkconnell p. 83.
28. HMC, 13 vi. p. 170; *Trans. Gaelic Soc.* (1896–97) p. 166; Fitzherbert MSS.

29. SP Dom 77/76; Add. MSS. 29913 f. 12.
30. SP Dom 77/107.
31. SP Dom 77/61.
32. SP Dom 77/26.
33. SP Dom 77/45; W.O. 71/19 f. 228.
34. W.O. 71/19 f. 213.
35. SP Dom 77/43.
36. Fitzherbert MSS.
37. Marchant p. 247.
38. SP Dom 77/34,36.
39. SP Dom 77/38.
40. Collyer, 'The Rockinghams' loc. cit. p. 357.
41. Whitworth p. 114.
42. Vezzozi p. 96.
43. Earwaker, iii, p. 25.
44. Fergusson, 'Retreat' pp. 224–25.
45. SP Dom 77/63,64.
46. Fergusson, *John Fergusson* p. 195.
47. HMC, Various Colls, viii. pp. 147–48.
48. Elcho p. 347.
49. *Ogilvy's Orderbook* pp. 308–09.
50. Johnstone p. 84.
51. Blaikie, 'John Daniel's Progress' p. 185.
52. L.P. ii. p. 460; Maxwell of Kirkconnell p. 84; Elcho p. 347.
53. W.O. 71/19 ff. 258–59; Add. MSS. 33050 f. 53.
54. W.O. 71/19 ff. 240–41; HMC, 13 vi. pp. 175–76.
55. W.O. 71/19 ff. 213, 241.
56. SP Dom 77/46.
57. Yorke, i. p. 483.
58. *Dublin Journal* No. 1959, 17–21 December 1745.
59. Harris, ii. p. 205.
60. L.P. ii. p. 460.
61. Tayler, *Anon. Hist.* p. 106.
62. Henderson p. 64.
63. Maxwell of Kirkconnell p. 84; Graham p. 37.
64. Maxwell of Kirkconnell p. 84.
65. Johnstone p. 84.
66. Tomasson pp. 121–22.
67. Ibid.
68. SP Dom 77/40.
69. Ibid.
70. SP Dom 77/47.
71. SP Dom 77/48, 73.
72. SP Dom 77/44.
73. SP Dom 77/43; *Manchester Magazine*, 24 December 1745.
74. HMC, Laing ii. p. 356; SP Dom 77/68.
75. *Ogilvy's Orderbook* pp. 309–10.
76. Ibid.
77. Chambers, 'Marches' p. 62.
78. Ibid. p. 61.
79. Tomasson p. 122.
80. Fergusson, 'Retreat' p. 197.
81. HMC, Various Colls, viii. p. 147.
82. Climenson, i. p. 224.
83. Johnstone p. 86.

84. Tomasson p. 122.
85. Chambers, 'Marches' p. 62.
86. Tomasson p. 123.
87. Chambers, 'Marches' p. 63; Tomasson p. 123.
88. Fitzherbert MSS.
89. Whitworth p. 114.
90. SP Dom 77/73.
91. W.O. 71/19 f. 213.
92. W.O. 71/19 f. 241.
93. W.O. 71/19 f. 229.
94. W.O. 71/19 ff. 196–98.
95. HMC, 13 vi. p. 176; Williamson p. 70; *Manchester Magazine*, 24 December 1745.
96. Allardyce, ii. p. 444.
97. SP Dom 77/63; Fergusson, 'Retreat' p. 196.
98. Maxwell of Kirkconnell p. 85.
99. Blaikie, 'John Daniel's Progress' p. 185.
100. Chambers, 'Marches' p. 63.
101. Tomasson p. 123.
102. Ibid. pp. 123–24.
103. Chambers, 'Marches' p. 64.
104. Tomasson p. 124.
105. Blaikie, 'Lochgarry's Narrative' pp. 116–17.
106. Chambers, 'Marches' p. 64.
107. Blaikie, 'Lochgarry's Narrative' p. 118.
108. Tomasson p. 125.
109. Chambers, 'Marches' p. 65.
110. Tomasson p. 125.
111. W.O. 71/19 f. 213.
112. W.O. 71/19 f. 248.
113. W.O. 71/19 f. 198.
114. W.O. 71/19 f. 213.
115. W.O. 71/19 ff. 207, 214.
116. Williamson pp. 71–73.
117. W.O. 71/19 f. 242.
118. W.O. 71/19 f. 205.
119. W.O. 71/19 f. 208.
120. W.O. 71/19 f. 216.
121. W.O. 71/19 f. 267.
122. W.O. 71/19 ff. 216, 233.
123. W.O. 71/19 f. 223.
124. W.O. 71/19 ff. 222–23.
125. W.O. 71/19 f. 217.
126. W.O. 71/19 f. 271.
127. W.O. 71/19 f. 279.
128. W.O. 71/19 f. 211.
129. W.O. 71/19 f. 244.
130. W.O. 71/19 ff. 271–72.
131. W.O. 71/19 f. 272.
132. W.O. 71/19 f. 208.
133. W.O. 71/19 f. 223.
134. SP Dom 77/77 & 78; W.O. 71/19 f. 215.
135. Fergusson, *John Fergusson* p. 125.
136. W.O. 71/19 ff. 197–98.

9

The Reckoning

BEFORE break of day Lord George Murray and the rearguard were on the move. Once again the carts were a problem: many of them were overloaded and in danger of collapsing, and with great difficulty Murray obtained more small waggons from the villages around Shap so as to spread the load.[1] By the time he had travelled four miles beyond Shap, Lord George was seriously concerned. Small bodies of mounted militia were visible on the heights to the right and left of the road, and occasionally enemy scouts were even seen in front of the Jacobite rearguard.[2] Murray took two immediate steps to deal with the attack he considered imminent. He chose forty of the 'cleverest' of Glengarry's and Roy Stewart's, gave them extra money and divided them into two parties for surveillance on the right and left of the road about a quarter of a mile behind the main force. In this way Murray could be sure that no enemy force could approach closer than a mile without his knowledge. His chosen corps performed their job admirably: they sent their swiftest runners 'almost as swift as a horse' to give news of any developments in the rear.[3] Secondly, a messenger was sent to Penrith to tell the Prince that the rearguard was badly encumbered with the cannon and baggage and delayed by the dreadful state of the roads, and to request cavalry support. It is the bitterest of ironies that Charles Edward's increasing anxiety about the dilatoriness of the rearguard derived from a fear of treachery by Lord George. The Prince had never entirely trusted Murray since Derby and suspected that the non-appearance of the rear might mean that his Lieutenant-General had delivered himself and his troops to Cumberland.[4]

At noon came the first skirmish of this historic day. About five miles from Shap (and half-way to Penrith) the Highlanders began to ascend Thrimby Hill. Suddenly a party of some 200 horse appeared at the summit.[5] At first Murray thought they were cavalry sent back by the Prince from Penrith but a trumpet blast soon revealed them as the enemy. In reality they were an advance column of Bland's regiment of light horse sent ahead by Cumberland in hopes of cutting off the baggage and artillery.[6] In the van of the Highland rearguard were the two companies of Perth's regiment which he had sent back to assist Murray, commanded by Lieutenant Brown (the Irish officer from Lally's regiment of the Irish Brigade in France). Murray was at the extreme rear with the Glengarry men, separated from the van by the carts and unable to reach them immediately since the road was at this point a narrow lane flanked by hedges. Seeing that Murray was unable to give immediate orders, Brown took it upon himself to order a charge. Perth's and Roy Stewart's thereupon rushed up the hill with claymores drawn.[7] Seeing this, Murray ordered the Glengarry men to leave the road, cut through the hedges and ascend the hill through the enclosures next to the road. With their famed fleetness of foot the Glengarry MacDonalds, even after this circuitous route, reached the top of the hill at the same time as Perth's, but Bland's men had not stayed to sample the ferocity of a Highland charge. One unfortunate hussar who slipped from his horse was cut to pieces in an instant.[8] From the number of trumpets and kettledrums left behind in the precipitate flight, it was concluded that Bland's had been trying to make Murray think that the entire Hanoverian army awaited him on the hilltop and so to decoy him onto side roads.[9]

Though Lord George was well pleased with the outcome of this clash, he was furious with Brown for having ordered the charge. As luck had it, the enemy had lacked both the courage to face the clansmen and the initiative to bar the Highlanders' passage, for the stone walls on either side of the road at the village of Strickland (at the top of the hill) could have been thrown down, making the road impassable for the baggage.[10] Little progress had been made, two more carts having broken down, when at 2 p.m. the rearguard was attacked once more. As the Highlanders passed the left turn-off to Lowther Hall at 1 p.m., having negotiated Thrimby Hill, Sergeant Dickson (he of the Manchester exploits) pointed out to Chevalier de Johnstone (both of Perth's) what seemed to be a column of horse advancing along the road past Lowther Hall to cut the main Clifton road.[11] This was a mixed company of Bland's (who had fled at Thrimby Hill), Kingston's light horse and the Yorkshire Hunters, trying once more to get between the Highland rearguard and Penrith. At about 2 p.m., a mile from Clifton town-end, this force charged the Glengarry regiment in the extreme rear.[12] A running fight developed for the next mile, until about 2.30 p.m., right up to Clifton moor. As the narrow lanes were lined by hedges and ditches, the Hanoverian cavalry could not surround the Highlanders and was reduced to ineffectual charges, a few men abreast. The Glengarry tactic was to withstand and repel the charges while the waggons continued up the road, then to run back and rejoin them and face round again to meet the next onslaught.

The seriousness of the situation had already been conveyed to Penrith. Part of Lochiel's regiment was sent to Lowther Bridge where John Roy Stewart posted himself as liaison officer between Lord George Murray and Penrith, but, more importantly, Murray at long last got the use of a cavalry detachment at Clifton.[13] The artillery was then sent on with Perth's company to clear Clifton for an engagement with Cumberland.

Cumberland was at this time three miles behind the cavalry force that had assailed Glengarry's at the junction of the Penrith and Lowther Hall roads.[14] His plans had gone seriously awry, since he had hoped to cut off the Jacobite rearguard and artillery either by Bland's western detachment or by Oglethorpe's forces from the east.[15] Bland's column had come within an ace of achieving this objective but Oglethorpe's fortunes reached their nadir this day. The problems were twofold: Cumberland still assumed late on Tuesday night that Oglethorpe had remained outside Shap; Oglethorpe meanwhile had asked the Duke for final orders in view of the situation inside Shap but had marched off to Orton before receiving a reply. About an hour after midnight on the night of 17th/18th December Cumberland received Oglethorpe's last message and replied that if there were no more than five hundred Scots in Shap, Oglethorpe should dismount his dragoons and attack.[16] The Duke did not see how there could be more than five hundred there, since all his intelligence indicated that the main Jacobite army had reached Penrith at noon on Tuesday. In the unlikely event of there being a larger force in Shap, Oglethorpe was at the very least to push in constant patrols during the night.[17] Cumberland rose at 4 a.m. and marched from Kendal at 5.30 a.m., arriving in Shap at noon on Wednesday.[18] Just before he quit Kendal he sent a second message to Oglethorpe to get round Shap and attack 'anything that endeavours to get by you'.

Oglethorpe meanwhile worked at his headquarters at Orton vicarage until six on the morning of the 18th, trying to direct operations while fighting off a fever.[19] It was 2 a.m. before all his men reached Orton, and with patrols posted all night out of the village, many of his soldiers slept at their horses' heads.[20] Shortly after 5 a.m. Oglethorpe ordered his rangers to rejoin the small body he had left on Shap moor. This party, on hearing that the Highlanders had now quit Shap, entered the village just before sunrise.[21] The inhabitants told them that the clansmen had been there in large numbers (one report said 2,000 strong) and pointed out the defences they had laid down which would have cost Oglethorpe dear in casualties if he had attacked. They had lined the walls to ambush the Hanoverians, and the churchyard perched on a hill had been turned into a redoubt with 300 clansmen entrenched there.[22] On proceeding out of Shap a mile and a half, the Rangers saw the Highland rearguard 'marching over Lowther Hill in three columns'. It was at this point that this party of Rangers decided to link up with Bland's horse.[23]

At 8 a.m. the letter written by Cumberland at 12.30 that morning arrived in Orton, but by now Oglethorpe had finally succumbed to the fever and was fast asleep.[24] Fearing to wake him, his officers drew up the remaining troops at about 9 a.m. on the south-east side of the village. There they remained, mounting and dismounting, until 11 a.m. when Oglethorpe was seen hurriedly emerging from his quarters.[25] It was given out that the troops had not moved out at daybreak, as normally happened, because the horses needed to be shod, but the plain truth was that Oglethorpe had overslept. In the general confusion and consternation it was approaching midday before he set out to retrace his steps to Shap.[26]

When Cumberland passed through Shap at noon and there was no word from Oglethorpe, he assumed that he had long since gone round it.[27] But about two miles beyond Shap he was astonished to see a corps of cavalry on his right flank about a mile in the rear. When he discovered that this detachment was Oglethorpe's, his amazement turned to anger.[28] Oglethorpe was bitterly rebuked in front of his troops: 'Had you done what I ordered you to do, none of these people would have escaped,' said Cumberland, to which Oglethorpe made no reply but a low bow.[29]

By 3 p.m., when Cumberland was nearing Clifton, the struggle between Jacobite and Hanoverian soldiery was concentrating in two places: at Clifton town-end and around Lowther Hall.[30] In Clifton village the Highland cavalry attempted to ambush the mixed force of Bland's dragoons, Oglethorpe's Rangers and Kingston's light horse. These, however, were forewarned of this by one of the villagers, and a sharp and furious exchange took place, as a result of which Pitsligo's horse broke and fled ignominiously to Penrith, to Lord George Murray's disgust.[31] Two prisoners were taken, among them Captain Hamilton (or Hambleden) who was captured after single combat with one of Cumberland's hussars.[32]

Meanwhile Murray had sent cavalry into Lowther Hall in the hope of falling on the Duke's army in the narrow lanes before Clifton, since 'if but twenty of their horse could be killed, it would make such an embarrass in the lane, that it would put them to confusion, and choke up the only road they had to retreat except the Appleby road, and that might also be secured, which would give us an advantage that perhaps we should not meet the like again'.[33] Unfortunately for Murray, Cumberland's force emerged from the narrow lanes before this stratagem could be implemented. The three hundred Jacobite cavalrymen could do little more than exchange shots with the enemy horse. Nevertheless, two consequences flowed from the skirmish in Lowther Park. Lord Lonsdale's steward informed Cumberland that he had seen a large body of Highlanders in the wood a little distance from Lowther Hall.[34] The Duke ordered an attack on them but the manoeuvres necessary to assail this phantom force served only to retard his movements by an hour, so that it was dark by the time he emerged onto Clifton moor. Secondly, from two prisoners taken by the Highlanders at Lowther Hall, one a Yorkshire Ranger in green and the other Cumberland's footman, it was learned that Cumberland was just a mile away with 4,000 horse.[35] Murray suspected that this was an exaggeration but seized his opportunity to convince the Prince in Penrith, who still thought the rearguard was being pursued by nothing more than militiamen.[36] John Roy Stewart was sent to Penrith with the prisoners, where he pleaded Murray's case with eloquence, telling the Prince that the entire rearguard would be destroyed if reinforcements were not sent to Murray.

The Prince's adamant insistence that he could spare no one as he was going to hold a review before departing for Carlisle infuriated most of those who had heard Stewart's story. As Elcho bitterly remarked: 'As there was formerly a contradiction to make the army halt when it was necessary to march, so now there was one to march and shun fighting when there could never be a better opportunity for it.'[37] A compromise was reached: forces were sent down to Clifton with the object of saving Murray and the rearguard from annihilation, but strict orders were given to retreat to Penrith and not to engage the enemy. As a consequence, Perth stationed himself on the far side of Lowther Bridge with the Atholl Brigade (though Perth himself was scarcely able to stand, let alone fight), Ardshiel crossed the bridge with the Appin Stewarts and Cluny MacPherson's regiment 'raced off to Clifton like hounds'.[38] Murray had time for no more than a few quick words with Perth: he told him he needed another 1,000 men to be sure of holding his position against Cumberland and meanwhile ordered his men in Clifton to simulate the presence of this extra thousand.[39]

Cumberland meanwhile dismounted his dragoons and laid his dispositions in two lines on the high end of the common. Bland's, Ker's and Cobham's were in the first line and Montagu's and Kingston's in the second.[40] A detachment faced the Appleby road and the Duke's baggage was in the rear of all. Murray, who had the advantage that his men could, from their position and with the distinctive Hanoverian uniforms, see what the enemy was doing while not being seen themselves, countered with an ingenious lay-out of his troops. The Glengarry men were in the enclosures surrounding Clifton town on the west side of the road (Lord George's right).[41] They formed a defensive line that stretched back nearly to the bridge where it joined up with Cluny MacPherson's regiment on the eastern side of the road (Murray's left). Cluny's men and the Stewarts of Appin were in the enclosure on the eastern side which swung away east from the Penrith road. Near this lane on the opposite side of the road from Clifton village and in front of Cluny's and the Appin Stewarts were John Roy Stewart's men. Desultory firing began at 4 p.m.[42] As the sun set, a dark and cloudy night followed, broken occasionally by the moon which 'gave good light but did not continue above two minutes at a time'.[43]

The subtlety of Murray's dispositions was that the most vulnerable part of his army, on his left, could be protected by flanking fire from Glengarry's if the enemy attacked it.[44] As the 'popping shots' between the army continued, Murray was greeted by John Roy Stewart, just returned from Penrith. Stewart gave the Prince's orders for a retreat to Penrith but Murray demurred. He explained his position to Stewart, which was indeed apparent from the 'popping shots', and the consequences if he was forced to retreat.[45] As the Highlanders were within musket shot of the enemy, who would assuredly follow them up the lane, casualties would be heavy and morale would be seriously affected. Beyond Clifton, moreover, the road was very narrow and hemmed in by high walls; it would therefore be impossible to cover the retreat to Penrith in the usual way by lining hedges. Besides, the Highlanders would probably become confused in the dark and, if any prisoners were taken, the Jacobite numbers would be divulged. On the other hand, Cumberland had not dismounted more than five hundred men and Murray said he was confident that he could dislodge them. After a quick conference with Cluny, John Roy Stewart agreed that Murray's plan was the only prudent one in the circumstances and that the Prince's orders had better not be mentioned to the men.[46]

At 5 p.m. Cumberland sent forward his men in two detachments: Ker's and Cobham's against the Highland right and Bland's against the left. Murray just had time to visit Glengarry's on the right to caution them not to fire until the enemy were close and not to shoot across the road; when the enemy retired, they could give them flank fire but were not to follow them up the moor. He then returned to the left of his line where the heaviest attack was concentrated.[47]

Bland's men started to enter the enclosures on the east of the road, towards the extreme end of Murray's left held by the MacPhersons. They took up positions in the last ditch between the enclosures and the moor. Cluny's men fired first but their salvo was apparently not as accurate as the volley in riposte from Bland's, for Cluny was alarmed enough to cry out: 'What the devil is this?' Murray, who was with Cluny, told him that the only way to settle the issue was with a Highland charge; he then drew his sword and gave the dread command 'Claymore'.[48] Cluny shouted the clan slogan and the MacPhersons raced the one hundred and fifty yards to the ditch and fell on Bland's. The dragoons broke under the impact and, having suffered heavy casualties in a hand-to-hand encounter lasting no more than two minutes, retreated onto the road to receive flanking fire from the Glengarry men.[49]

The fighting on the Highland right did not compare in intensity, though Lochgarry, the Glengarry commander, was wounded in the knee.[50] Ker's went straight up the road to encounter Roy Stewart's while Cobham's attempted to get through the western enclosures onto the rear of the Glengarry men.[51] Before significant action could take place, Murray, well satisfied with his repulse of Bland's on the left, ordered a general retreat. First Roy Stewart's withdrew over the bridge, then the Appin Stewarts, next the MacPhersons and lastly Glengarry's.[52] The fighting had lasted barely half an hour and the retreat over the bridge another half-hour, so that Cumberland was left in possession of Clifton by 6 p.m.[53]

Casualties on the Hanoverian side amounted to forty dead and wounded, while the Highlanders lost a dozen.[54] Among the government officers wounded was Colonel Honeywood, recently wounded at Dettingen, who sustained three sword cuts in the head but lived on to 1785 as a long-serving MP for Appleby.[55] Both sides could legitimately claim a victory: Cumberland through remaining in possession of the field, Murray through having inflicted greater casualties, having routed Bland's and forced the Duke to break off his pursuit. The prize for generalship must surely be accorded to Murray, both for his tactics and for his ability to improvise in the heat of battle; it is significant that, left to himself and without interference from Charles Edward, he could always out-think Cumberland.

Cumberland was left to ponder the consequences of this encounter with the Highlanders. In his heart the Duke considered it a defeat, which he attributed to 'great heavy boots [on his men] and it being among ditches and soft watery ground'.[56] He confessed that the combination of darkness, cold weather and tired troops did not tempt him to a perilous pursuit towards Penrith. This was prudent enough: his troops had marched twenty-four miles in ten hours, and the country between Clifton and Penrith was hazardous to negotiate at night, especially when both the Lowther and Eamont Bridges had to be crossed on pontoons. And even if Lord George Murray could not, as he declared to John Roy Stewart, line the walls along the road to Penrith, that town itself could have been turned into an impregnable fortress with the entire Jacobite army defending it by night.[57]

Although Cumberland eulogised his men, especially Ker's and Cobham's who were technically undefeated, there was little cheer for them this night. While the Duke was able to lodge comfortably at the Quaker Thomas Savage's house, and a few of his men found sanctuary in Clifton, most of them had to spend the night on Clifton moor without any cover, under pelting rain, not daring to proceed to Penrith in case an ambush backed with artillery was being prepared.[58] They contented themselves with the wildest rumour-mongering. It was claimed that 'one of the Jacobites' great officers was wounded but we cannot say who'.[59] Another report spread that Lord Elcho had been the joint author with Lord George Murray of the stand at Clifton.[60] This was eventually conflated into the story that Elcho was captured after being cut in the throat by the hussars, from which wound it was doubted that he would recover.[61]

In Penrith meanwhile morale was high and the Prince was 'well pleased with what had happened'. So elated was John Roy Stewart that when he got into Penrith he advocated that the whole army march back and take Cumberland by surprise that night or the following morning.[62] Even Murray opposed this, not wishing to lose more men and looking forward to the junction with Drummond in Scotland. Besides, there were still those who feared an eleventh-hour link-up between Cumberland's dragoons and Wade. The most Charles Edward would do was despatch Clanranald's and Keppoch's to the nearside of Lowther Bridge to make the people of Clifton believe he meant to attack Cumberland.[63]

Then an immediate night march to Carlisle was ordered. Some units had indeed left Penrith for the north even while the engagement at Clifton was being fought, but the bulk of the army moved out around 8 p.m., and all were gone by midnight.[64] Even though the day's orders had originally stipulated a departure for Carlisle at six on the morning of the 19th, the march was no hardship for most of the men whose duties had not risen above guarding the artillery park and patrolling the road to Newcastle. But for the heroes of the hour who had fought in the last battle on English soil, and especially the men of Glengarry who had just spent three of the most gruelling days imaginable among the hills of Westmorland and Cumberland, the orders were a grave disappointment. Murray, whose cough and cold still continued, though almost unnoticed in the midst of his continual exertions, saw to it that the fighting men of Clifton stayed a little time in Penrith for rest and refreshment — 'for some of them had occasion for it' — before leading them out on the eighteen-mile trek to Carlisle.[65] For all that Wednesday the 18th had been ordained by the Whig authorities as a public fast day for the defeat of the rebellion, the honours had largely gone to the 'rebels'.

Thursday 19th December

After an uneventful march from Penrith, the Jacobite army re-entered Carlisle about noon.[66] Charles Edward himself rode near the front of his troops with Elcho's Lifeguards.[67] It was on this leg of the retreat to Scotland that the largest number of desertions took place, mainly from the Manchester regiment, for whom crossing the border held no appeal. No fewer than sixty men and ten women were transferred from Penrith to York castle on 29th December, all of them taken on the Carlisle road, but Cumberland and the Whig propagandists disingenuously passed them off as prisoners captured in the engagement at Clifton.[68]

At Carlisle letters awaited the Prince from Lords Drummond and Strathallan with information about the affairs of Scotland and developments in France.[69] It was decided to call a Council meeting to see whether a stand should be made at Carlisle or whether the army should press on forthwith to Scotland. The idea of remaining in Carlisle was rejected, but the fateful decision was hit on that it would be useful to leave a garrison in the town. Charles Edward's argument for this was that the garrison's presence would be a signal to friend and foe alike that he intended to re-enter England. It would also prevent the need for a second Jacobite siege of Carlisle. O'Sullivan tried to buttress this line of reasoning with some 'military' arguments, designed to show that Cumberland's pursuit would not be feasible with a Jacobite force in the town.[70] If the rivers at the border were not fordable, he argued, Cumberland would have to proceed to Scotland via Brampton, which would give the Prince's army two days' march on him. This was because the Eden at Carlisle was too deep and broad to be crossed except at Carlisle Bridge, and Cumberland could not cross there without coming under fire from the castle, which could decimate his army. Moreover, Cumberland could not take Carlisle with the artillery he now possessed, and even if he could, was it not better to jeopardise a garrison than the whole army? Another argument for leaving men behind that particularly appealed to the Prince was that he would then be able to leave the baggage, artillery and ammunition in Carlisle too and so march into Scotland unimpeded.

Lord George Murray spoke out against the proposal. Although it was true that Cumberland had no heavy cannon with him for reducing the castle, he could easily requisition it from neighbouring Whitehaven, and once this was brought up there could be only one ending to the subsequent siege.[71] As for the baggage and artillery, Murray favoured destroying the lot and throwing it into the Eden. At this point the atmosphere in the Council meeting became distinctly acrimonious. Although Perth did not favour the idea of remaining in Carlisle, he was irritated by Lord George's forthrightness and asked him provocatively why the Atholl brigade was not prepared to defend the castle.[72] Murray stuck to his guns and ended his exposition by pointing out that it was madness to be sidetracked at this eleventh hour, since once in Scotland the whole army would be safe. Carlisle was unimportant anyway: if and when the Highlanders re-entered England, they could come into open country by Brampton and avoid the Eden altogether. And if it was desired to avoid a second siege of Carlisle, why not simply blow up the castle and the gates of the town, so that it would be defenceless when the second invasion took place?

Charles Edward, however, dug in his heels: a garrison would be left behind and the only remaining issue was who would comprise it. Approaches were made to the Manchester regiment, and Townley agreed to accept the assignment.[73] Townley accepted Brown (of Lally's) assessment that Cumberland could not take Carlisle castle, so that if it eventually came to a surrender, reasonable terms of capitulation could be had. Moreover, other members of the Manchester regiment, like Syddall, were enthusiastic for the task of defending the castle.[74] Brown agreed to stay behind with Townley, lending the services of the Irishmen in the pay of the king of France, so that the garrison Charles Edward left in Carlisle comprised about 250 men of the Manchester regiment and one hundred 'French' troops. The sequel was exactly as Lord George had predicted. When Cumberland arrived outside the town after Charles Edward had crossed into Scotland, he ordered up heavy cannon from Whitehaven, demolished the castle and took the entire garrison prisoner on terms of unconditional surrender.[75] Townley and the men of the Manchester regiment were led away to trial and execution (Brown escaped over the wall of the castle, rejoined the Prince in Scotland and was sent back to France as his envoy).[76] In view of this obvious consequence, widely foreseen, of leaving a garrison behind, the Prince's action has seemed inexplicable, to such an extent that the Chevalier de Johnstone actually attributed it to cold-blooded cruelty; the Prince, he argued, left the Manchester regiment to its inevitable doom as an act of revenge against the English for failing to rise to his standard.[77] Such views can safely be discounted: it has to be remembered that the Prince was still convinced that it would only be a matter of weeks before he returned to England with a much larger army.[78]

Meanwhile at eleven that morning Cumberland's troops were entering Penrith. After a brief halt, a mixed column of Rangers, Hunters and Light Horse was sent to patrol the Carlisle road, but the majority of the men were so exhausted that they remained in town.[79] There had been a constant downpour of rain on Clifton moor that morning, and all the men who spent the night there had been totally without food and shelter.[80] In any case, Cumberland was in no hurry to advance on Carlisle before his infantry arrived, since he was uncertain whether or not he would have to fight a battle there. As the first of his foot did not arrive in Penrith before nightfall this Thursday, he was content to rest there that night and lay contingency plans against the possibility of a Jacobite stand at Carlisle.[81] If this happened, Cumberland resolved that he would not attack before Wade's forces had crossed from Newcastle to join him.[82]

Wade's lacklustre campaign was now drawing to an ignominious close, but for his best officer, General Huske, there was bitter disappointment in the news from London. Owing to pressure from Cumberland, it was decided that after all Huske would not command in Scotland: Cumberland's favourite, 'Hangman' Hawley, was given the command with Huske as his deputy.[83] When it is appreciated how each of them bore himself at the battle of Falkirk in January, this decision can be seen to have been disastrous for the Whigs.

Friday 20th December

It was quite late in the morning before the Jacobite army departed from Carlisle. The Prince tarried for some time, concerned with last-minute arrangements with the Carlisle garrison and with the last orders to be issued on English soil.[84] There were to be as few obstacles as possible on the day's march: the sick were to be left behind in Carlisle while six pieces of Swedish cannon and the barest minimum of baggage were to cross the Eden at Warwick Bridge (where, as it turned out, one of the waggons was stuck fast in the mud and abandoned), to be taken across the Esk itself at Canonbie and Langholm.[85] The main force planned to cross the border at Longton where the Esk was swollen with heavy rains and there was no bridge. The prospect of traversing the Esk in midwinter was too much for two of the junior officers, who sent a message to Cumberland that they were prepared to desert immediately if he granted a pardon.[86] Thus the Jacobite army prepared to spend its last minutes on English soil. Maddock in the Manchester regiment, who later turned king's evidence and betrayed his comrades, testified that the last he saw of the army in which he had served with such utter lack of distinction was the sight of Lord Ogilvy at the head of his regiment, armed with a broadsword and a brace of pistols.[87]

The only barrier now to the Highlanders before they could embrace their beloved Scotland once more was the Esk, usually shallow but now a raging torrent, swollen by incessant rain to a depth of at least four feet.[88] The river had to be crossed as soon as possible lest further rain made it an impenetrable obstacle. The triumphant crossing at Longton was a fitting end to this extraordinary campaign in England. Some horses were sent into the stream first to see how they would fare, and when they got across to the other side, though with great difficulty, the clansmen cried out that they too would force a passage.[89] Charles Edward and the cavalry entered the river to form a human barrier against the swift current. Twenty-five yards below the barrier the infantry began to cross ten or twelve abreast, with arms linked or holding one another by the collar.[90] So successful was this manoeuvre that eyewitnesses spoke of the Highlanders 'in good order as if they were marching in a field';[91] the passage so provided by the cavalry was 'like a paved street through the river, the heads of the Highlanders being generally all that was seen above water'.[92] Whether there was any loss of life during the crossing is uncertain, despite frequent assertions by Whig propagandists that the clansmen left their female camp followers to drown in the raging waters; some reports did speak of two women having been drowned.[93] John Daniel states in his memoirs that he himself was nearly lost in this way, and it is certain that the Prince in person prevented a young lad in Keppoch's from being drowned, seizing him by the hair and calling for help in Gaelic before rescue came.[94] Perth particularly distinguished himself in this operation, having a top-class horse with which to negotiate the stream, and he made several forays into the water to bring to the shore individuals who seemed in danger of being swept away.[95]

D'Eguilles was amazed at the sight of 2,000 men fording the Esk at one time and declared that to men of this calibre nothing was impossible.[96] For Lord George Murray the whole exercise was a demonstration lesson of the peculiar qualities of the Highlanders. These were men, he claimed, who could cross a river that was impassable to horses, and this was why all the broken bridges in England had not impeded their march to Derby.[97]

When all emerged on the other side near nightfall, fires were lit to dry off the men and pipes played to celebrate the safe return to Scottish soil.[98] At last Lord George Murray felt able to relax, for until he had crossed the Esk the Lieutenant-General still feared that Cumberland could have bypassed Carlisle and the Eden and gone directly from Penrith to Brampton.[99] In reality, Cumberland had already decided, even before Clifton, that it would be impossible for him to pursue the Highlanders beyond Carlisle because of inadequate provisioning for his men and horses, even though he entertained some slight hopes that the enemy might be stopped at the Esk.[100]

To discover whether he was destined to fight Charles Edward at Carlisle or if Hawley and Huske would have to deal with him in Scotland, Cumberland set out at 4 a.m. from Penrith, advancing slowly in three columns up the road to Carlisle.[101] The Duke proceeded cautiously up the main road with his infantry, with cavalry on both flanks, until emerging onto the open moor at Carlton, where he heard of the withdrawal to Scotland. As Murray had predicted, Cumberland soon saw what had to be done to reduce the garrison in the castle. Declaring it to be no more than an 'old hen-coop', he took the advice of Walter Lutridge, sheriff of Whitehaven, and had heavy cannon brought up from that port.[102] By the end of December he had forced total and unconditional surrender on the luckless Manchester regiment.[103] Cumberland thus had no need of help from Wade's army, the advance guard of which arrived this Friday in Newcastle under Huske, after another grim march, taking four days from Boroughbridge over very bad roads and in dreadful weather.[104] By the time Brigadier Mordaunt arrived at Carlisle via Hexham the fighting was over and the last vestiges of the 1745 campaign in England wiped out. By the end of December, with Wade back in Newcastle, Ligonier in London and Charles Edward in Glasgow, the principals involved at the beginning of the invasion were once again dispersed in diverse corners of the island.[105] In this way ended the final campaign fought on English soil.

NOTES

1. Tomasson p. 126.
2. Chambers, 'Marches' p. 65.
3. Tomasson p. 126.
4. Ibid.
5. Johnstone p. 86.
6. Fergusson, 'Retreat' pp. 197–228.
7. Johnstone pp. 86–87.
8. Chambers, 'Marches' p. 65.
9. Maxwell of Kirkconnell pp. 85–86.
10. Blaikie, 'Lochgarry's Narrative' p. 117.
11. Johnstone pp. 88–89.
12. Fergusson, 'Retreat'.
13. Tomasson p. 127.
14. HMC, 13 vi. p. 171.
15. SP Dom 77/93; 78/17.
16. W.O. 71/19 f. 199.
17. Ibid.
18. W.O. 71/19 ff. 200–01.
19. W.O. 71/19 f. 215.
20. W.O. 71/19 ff. 245–46.
21. W.O. 71/19 f. 269.
22. W.O. 71/19 f. 282.
23. W.O. 71/19 f. 269.
24. W.O. 71/19 f. 237.
25. W.O. 71/19 ff. 206, 224.
26. W.O. 71/19 f. 202.
27. W.O. 71/19 f. 201.
28. Ibid.
29. HMC, Egmont iii. pp. 312–313; W.O. 71/19 f. 204. Cf. also Warrend, *More Culloden Papers*, iii. p. 234; Yorke, i. pp. 485–86.
30. Fergusson, 'Retreat'.
31. Ibid.
32. *Gentlemen's Magazine* 1746, p. 525.
33. Chambers, 'Marches' p. 65.
34. HMC, Various Colls, viii. p. 150.
35. L.M. ii. p. 86 et seq.

36. Chambers, 'Marches' p. 65.
37. Elcho pp. 348–49.
38. L.P. ii. p. 496.
39. Tomasson pp. 128–32.
40. Duff, *Culloden Papers* p. 263.
41. Blaikie, 'Lochgarry's Narrative' pp. 117–18.
42. *Scots Magazine,* 1745 p. 577; Henderson p. 188; Ray p. 201.
43. HMC, 13 vi. p. 170.
44. Fergusson, 'Retreat' p. 219.
45. Chambers, 'Marches' p. 65; Tomasson p. 132.
46. *Trans. Gaelic Soc.* pp. 409–10; Maxwell of Kirkconnell p. 85.
47. *Gentlemen's Magazine* 1745 p. 625; Marchant pp. 219–25.
48. *Trans. Gaelic Soc.* pp. 409–410.
49. Fergusson, 'Retreat' p. 219.
50. Blaikie, 'Lochgarry's Account' p. 118.
51. Mounsey pp. 136–45.
52. Stuart MSS 272/87; Add. MSS. 20668 ff. 400–01.
53. Stuart MSS. 272/129A.
54. HMC, Various Colls viii. pp. 150–53.
55. HMC, Egmont iii. p. 312.
56. Fitzherbert MSS.
57. SP Dom 77/108.
58. HMC, Various Colls viii. p. 150.
59. Ibid.
60. Graham p. 38.
61. *Derby Mercury* 27 December 1745.
62. Coxe, *Pelham,* i. p. 271; Henderson p. 66.
63. Browne, iii. p. 165.
64. *Ogilvy's Orderbook* p. 310.
65. Tomasson p. 132.
66. Maxwell of Kirkconnell p. 87.
67. Howell, *State Trials* 18 p. 472.
68. HMC, 12 vii. p. 356; Jarvis, i. pp. 376–81.
69. Maxwell of Kirkconnell p. 87.
70. O'Sullivan p. 110.
71. Chambers, 'Marches' pp. 73–74.
72. Ibid.
73. Maxwell of Kirkconnell p. 87.
74. Hibbert-Ware, ii. p. 108.
75. Jarvis, i. pp. 207–08.
76. Mounsey p. 146 et seq.
77. Johnstone pp. 95–97.
78. Vezzozi p. 103.
79. HMC, Various Colls, viii. p. 150.
80. HMC, 13 vi. p. 172.
81. *Historical Memoirs of the Duke of Cumberland* p. 317.
82. SP Dom 77/73.
83. SP Dom 77/107,111.
84. *Ogilvy's Orderbook* p. 311.
85. Mounsey p. 145.
86. SP Dom 77/109.
87. Add. MSS. 35886 f. 82.
88. Johnstone p. 99.
89. O'Sullivan p. 111.

90. Johnstone p. 99; O'Sullivan p. 111.
91. O'Sullivan p. 111.
92. Johnstone p. 100.
93. HMC, Du Cane p. 84; Tayler, *Anon. Hist.* p. 109.
94. Blaikie, 'John Daniel's Progress' p. 188; Henderson p. 67.
95. Henderson p. 67.
96. O'Sullivan p. 111.
97. Chambers, 'Marches' p. 75.
98. Johnstone p. 100.
99. Chambers, 'Marches' p. 75.
100. SP Dom 77/73; 78/56.
101. Douglas pp. 73–74.
102. Hughes, ii. pp. 62–63; Jarvis (1954) pp. 324–25.
103. SP Dom 78/87–90,105; HMC, Various Colls, viii. pp. 154–58.
104. HMC, Laing ii. p. 356.
105. SP Dom 77/115; Add. MSS. 32417 f. 440.

Conclusion

ON any analysis the campaign of the Jacobites in England in November and December 1745 remains an outstanding military exploit. History records only a handful of occasions when a small army, substantially outnumbered by an enemy, has penetrated deep into hostile territory and emerged again virtually unscathed. There have been greater triumphs of sustained marching (the 'Long March' of the Chinese Red Army in 1934 is an obvious example) and of mobility within enemy terrain (the great campaign of the Mongol general Sübedei in 1221–22, for instance), but geographical, logistical and infrastructural factors were usually more favourable on those occasions. The most illuminating comparison of the feats of Charles Edward's men is with the withdrawal of the 10,000 in Xenophon's *Anabasis*.

Most of the reasons for the success of the Jacobite army have been mentioned either explicitly or implicitly in the text; in the latter category clearly the vital element was the extraordinarily lacklustre performance of Marshal Wade. In retrospect it seems almost incredible that Wade should have failed to bar the Highlanders' return to Scotland, and even more so that he escaped official censure for his actions. When one considers that General Oglethorpe, Sir John Cope and Colonel Durand all faced courts-martial for their actions in the '45 — and with the exception of Cope none was as culpable as Wade — it seems odd, to say the least, that no one pointed the finger of accusation at the elderly Marshal. On the positive side, the single greatest cause of the successful Jacobite retreat was the generalship of Lord George Murray. Throughout the campaign he consistently out-thought Cumberland and revealed a tactical genius of a high order. Had Murray ever held command in the British army as a general, he might have been the one man to stretch Marshal Saxe to the fullest.

But to concede this is not to favour Murray over the Prince when it came to strategic decision-making. It has been made sufficiently clear above that Sir Alexander MacDonald of Sleat's assessment of the Prince — that he was the best officer in his army — is confidently endorsed in strategic (though not tactical) matters. This of course takes us to the central issue of Derby. The correctness of the decision taken there on 5th December 1745 has been a subject of contention ever since the history of the '45 was first written. The authorities have always split fairly evenly over whether Charles Edward's insight was superior to Lord George Murray's or whether Murray's arguments were the only feasible ones. From the

197

nineteenth century to today one can cite one set of historians (Mackie, Hughes, Jarvis and Lenman) as supporters of the Murray view and another (Lord Mahon, Eardley Simpson and Eveline Cruickshanks) as advocates of the viewpoint advanced here. My reasons for thinking that Charles Edward was right are given in the text. I would merely add that a thorough study of the French side of the '45* has strengthened me in my view. I cannot do better here than quote an esteemed colleague: 'By forcing the retreat Lord George Murray and the others threw away the best chance there had been of a restoration of the Stuarts, threw away all that the bravery of the Highlanders and their own military skill had achieved. The '45 was a gamble from the beginning, but they threw in their hand when they held most of the trump cards' (Eveline Cruickshanks, *Political Untouchables* (London 1979) p. 100). To be fair to Lord George Murray (whom I greatly admire), it has to be conceded that the pluses for a decision to advance on London only just cancelled out the minuses, and few people can ever have had to take such a decision at once momentous and marginal, where the arguments on either side were so finely balanced.

The '45 was the swansong of the Jacobite movement. This was the last occasion when an armed uprising attempted to replace the Hanoverian kings with the exiled Stuarts. Although the military potential of the Jacobites was only finally destroyed with Hawke's victory at Quiberon Bay in 1759, most of his biographers feel that, by the time of the Seven Years' War, Charles Edward himself had already started on his downward path of self-destruction and was no longer a credible leader. The extinction of Jacobite hopes did not of course prevent Charles Edward from continuing to hanker after the throne of his ancestors for the rest of his life, since, as he once remarked, 'all the rest is brown bread'.

---

*F.J. McLynn, *France and the Jacobite Rising of 1745* (1981)

Bibliography

1. Manuscript sources.

Stuart MSS. Royal Archives, Windsor Castle.
State Papers, Domestic, George II, Series 36. Nos. 67–100. Public Record Office, London.
State Papers, Ireland, Series 63, Nos. 408–10.
Archives Etrangères, Mémoires et Documents, Angleterre. Ministry of Foreign Affairs, Paris.
Additional MSS. British Library, London.
Stowe MSS, British Library.
War Office Papers, Public Record Office, London.
Jacobite Papers, Staffordshire County Record Office.
Fitzherbert MSS, Derbyshire County Record Office.
Catton MSS, Derby Public Library.

2. Newspapers.

London Evening Post 1745
Morning Advertiser 1745
General Evening Post 1745
Manchester Magazine 1745–46
Birmingham Gazette 1745
Derby Mercury 1745
Dublin Journal 1745
London Magazine 1745–46
Gentlemen's Magazine 1745–46
British Magazine 1745–46
Scots Magazine 1745–46

3. Books and articles cited.

Allardyce. J., *Historical Papers relating to the Jacobite Period* 2 vols (New Spalding Club 1895)
Atholl, 7th Duke of, *Chronicles of the Families of Atholl and Tullibardine* 5 vols (1908)
Bailey, F.A., 'The Minutes of the Trustees of the Turnpike Roads from Liverpool to Prescot, St. Helens, Warrington and Ashton 1726–1789', *Lancashire and Cheshire Historical Society Transactions* 88 (1936)
——, 'Pre-turnpike Roads', *LCHS* 89 (1937)
Baker, T.C. & Harris, J.R., *St. Helens 1750–1900* (1959)
Barnes, F.S., 'Some occurrences during the Jacobite Rising of 1745', *LCHS* 21. N.S. (1905)
Beamont, W., 'Some Occurrences in Warrington during the Jacobite Rising of 1745', *LCHS* (O.S.) 7 (1855)

Beresford, J.B., *Storm and Peace* (1936)

Blaikie, W.B., *The Origins of the '45* (containing 'John Daniel's Progress') (1916)

——, *The Itinerary of Prince Charles Edward Stuart* (containing 'Lochgarry's narrative') (1897)

Blundell, F.O., *Old Catholic Lancashire*, 2 vols (1925)

Bonhote, J., *Historical Records of the West Kent Militia* (1909)

Bowman, W., *England in Ashton-under-Lyne* (1970)

Boyse, S., *An Impartial History of the Late Rebellion in 1745* (1748)

Bradstreet, D., *The Adventures of Captain Dudley Bradstreet* (1755)

Brand, J., *The History and Antiquities of Newcastle*, 2 vols (1789)

Briggs, J.J., *A History of Melbourne* (1852)

Brockbank, E.M., *Honorary Medical Staff of Manchester Infirmary 1752-1830* (1904)

Broughton, C.F., *A History of Ashbourne* (1839)

Browne, J., *A History of the Highlands* 4 vols (1853)

Burne, S.A.H., 'The Staffordshire Campaign of 1745', *North Staffordshire Field Club Transactions* 60 (1924–25)

Chambers, R. (ed.), *Jacobite Memoirs of the Rising of 1745* (containing Lord George Murray's 'Marches of the Highland Army') (1834)

Charles, G., *Transactions in Scotland* (1817)

Charteris, E., *William Augustus, Duke of Cumberland* (1925)

Chinney, G.A., *Records of the Borough of Leicester* (1965)

Clemesha, H.W., *A History of Preston* (1912)

Chimenson, E., *Elizabeth Montagu, Queen of the Bluestockings 1720-61* 2 vols (1906)

Colin, J., *Louis XV et les Jacobites. Le projet de débarquement en 1743-44* (1901)

Collyer, C., 'Yorkshire and the '45', *Yorkshire Archaeological Journal* 38 (1952–55)

Coward, T.A., *Picturesque Cheshire* (1903)

Cox, J.C., *Three Centuries of Derbyshire Annals* 2 vols (1890)

——, *Memorials of Old Derbyshire* (1907)

Coxe, R.J. & Hope W.H., *Chronicles of the Collegiate Church of All Saints, Derby* (1881)

Coxe, W., *Memoirs of the Administration of the Right Hon. Henry Pelham* 2 vols (1829)

Cruickshanks, E., *Political Untouchables. The Tories and the '45* (1979)

Cumberland, Duke of, *Historical Memoirs of the Duke of Cumberland* (1767)

Davies, C.S., *A History of Macclesfield* (1971)

Davison, A.W., *Derby: Its Rise and Progress* (1906)

Defoe, D., *A Tour through the Whole Island of Britain* 2 vols (1962)

Doran, J., *London in the Jacobite Times* (1877)

Dore, R.N., *A History of Hale* (1972)

Douglas, F., *History of the Rebellion* (1755)

Dugald, G., *An Impartial History* (1779)

Duff, H.R., *Culloden Papers* (1815)

Earwaker, J.P., 'Manchester and the Rebellion of 1745', *LCAS* 7 (1889)

——, *'Constables' Accounts of the Manor of Manchester* 3 vols (1892)

Elcho, Lord, *A Short Account of the Affairs of Scotland in 1744, 1745 & 1746* (ed. E. Charteris) (1907)

'Elcho's Journal' — see Tayler, *Anonymous History*

Ettinger, A.C., *General Oglethorpe* (1936)

Ewald, A.C., *The Life and Times of Charles Edward Stuart* 2 vols (1875)

Fergusson, C., 'The Retreat of the Highlanders through Westmorland in 1745', *Transactions of the Cumberland and Westmorland Archaeological and Antiquarian Society* 10 (1889) pp. 186–228

Fergusson, J., *John Fergusson* (1948)

Fiennes, C., *The Journeys of Celia Fiennes* (1949)

Fishwick, H., *A History of Garstang* (Chetham Soc. O.S.104) (1878)

——, *History of the Parish of Rochdale* (1889)

Fortescue, J.W., *History of the British Army* (1899)

Frazer, Sir. W., *The Chiefs of Grant* 3 vols (1883)

Gibbon, E., *Memoirs of My Own Life* (ed. G.A. Bonnard) (1966)

Glover, J., *Memoirs* (1774)

Gordon, Sir B. Seton.& Arnot, J.G., *The Prisoners of the '45* (Scottish History Society, 3rd Series 13–15), 3 vols (1928–29)

Graham, D., *An Imperial History* (1774)

Green, H., *Knutsford, its traditions and history* (1969)

Hardwick, C., *History of the Borough of Preston* (1857)

Hardwicke: 'Correspondence between Archbishop Herring and Lord Chancellor Hardwicke during the '45', *English Historical Review* 19 (1904)

Harland, J., *Collectanea relating to Manchester* (Chetham Soc. O.S.68) (1866)

Harris, G. *Life of Lord Chancellor Hardwicke* 2 vols (1847)

Harrison, W., 'Preturnpike Highways in Lancashire and Cheshire', *Transactions of the Lancashire and Cheshire Antiquarian Society* 9 (1891)

Hartley, S. & Bateson, H., *A Centenary History of Oldham* (1949)

Henderson, A., *The History of the Rebellion 1745-46* (1748)

Hibbert-Ware, S., *History of the Foundations in Manchester* 3 vols (1834)

Historical Manuscripts Commission: Lothian, Egmont, Laing, Du Cane, Portland MSS.

——: Fifth, Third, Seventh, Tenth, Twelfth, Thirteenth, Fourteenth, Fifteenth Reports.

——: Various Collections; Hastings MSS.

Home, J., *History of the Rebellion* (1802)

Howell, T.B., *A Complete Collection of State Trials* 34 vols (1816–28)

Hughes, E., *North Country Life in the Eighteenth Century* 2 vols (1952)

Hughes M., *A Plain Narrative* (1746)

Hutton, W., *The History of Derby to the Year 1791* (1791)

Ilchester, Lord, *Henry Fox, First Lord Holland* 2 vols (1920)

Ingham, A., *Altrincham and Bowdon* (1897)

Jarvis, R.C., 'The Rebellion of 1745' *LCAS* 56–57 (1941–44)

——, *The Jacobite Risings of 1715 and 1745* (1954)

——, 'The Manchester Constables in 1745' *LCAS* 71 (1961)

——, *Collected Papers on the Jacobite Risings* 2 vols (1972)

Johnstone, Chevalier de, *A Memoir of the '45* (1820)

Lenman, Bruce, *The Jacobite Risings in Britain* (1980)

Leighton, R., *The Correspondence of Charlotte Grenville, Lady Williams Wynn* (1920)

Lloyd, J.M., *The Township of Chorlton-cum-Hardy* (1972)

Lockhart, G., *The Lockhart Papers* (1817)

Lunn, J., *A History of Atherton* (1971)

—*A History of Leigh* (1972)

The Lyon in Mourning, ed. Henry Paton (Scottish History Society) 3 vols (1895)

MacDonald, A., *A Short History of Repton* (1929)

MacDonald, C.S., *Hopwood Hall* (1963)

McLynn F.J., 'Ireland and the Jacobite Rising of 1745', *Irish Sword* Vol. 13 No. 2 (1979) pp. 339-352

—'Nottingham and the Jacobite Rising of 1745', *Transactions of the Thoroton Society* 1979 pp. 63-69

——, 'The West Midlands and the Jacobite Rising of 1745', *West Midlands Studies* 1979 pp. 27-31

——, 'Hull and the Jacobite Rising of 1745', *Yorkshire Archaeological Journal* 1980 pp. 75-82

——, *France and the Jacobite Rising of 1745* (1981)

——, 'Newcastle and the Jacobite Rising of 1745', *Journal of Local Studies* Vol 2 No 1 (1982) pp. 95-105

Mahon, Lord, *History of England from the Peace of Utrecht to the Peace of Versailles 1713-1763* 3 vols (1858)

Manners W.E., *Life of John Manners, Marquis of Granby* (1899)

Marchant, J., *A History of the Present Rebellion* (1746)

Mattley, R.D., *Annals of Rochdale* (1899)

Maxwell of Kirkconnell, James, *Narrative of Charles, Prince of Wales's expedition to Scotland in the Year 1745* (1841)

Memoirs of a Royal Chaplain. The Correspondence of Edmund Ryle 1729-1763, ed. J. Pyle (1905)

Midgley, G., *Orator Henley* (1973)

Miller, G.C., *Hoghton Tower* (1948)

'Diary of James Miller', *Journal of the Society for Army Historical Research* 3 (1902)

Mitchell, A.A., 'London and the '45', *History Today* (November 1965)

Moss, F., *Didsbury in the '45* (1891)

Mounsey, G.C., *Carlisle in 1745* (1846)

Mumford, A.A., *The Manchester Grammar School 1515-1915* (1919)

Murray of Broughton, John, *Memorials of John Murray of Broughton*, ed. R.F. Bell (Scottish History Society 27) (1898)

Newton, Lady, *House of Lyme* (1917)

Nicholas, D., *Intercepted Post* (1956)

Order Book of Lord Ogilvy's Regiment (Spalding Club Miscellany, Vol. 1) (1841)

'O'Sullivan's Narrative', in A. & H. Tayler, *1745 and After* (1938)

Palatine Notebook 4 vols (ed. J.P. Earwaker) (1881–84)

Pichot, A., *Histoire de Charles Edouard* (1833)

Pitt. W., *A Topographical History of Staffordshire* (1817)

Potter, G.R., 'A Government Spy in Derbyshire during the '45', *Derbyshire Archaeological Journal* 89 (1970)

Private Correspondence between Lord Chesterfield and the Duke of Newcastle 1744-46 (Camden Society xliv) (1930)

Purcell, P., 'The Jacobite Rising of 1715 and English Catholics', *English Historical Review* 44 (1929)

Quarterly Review (1899)

Ray, J., *History of the Rebellion* (1749)

Remond, A., *John Holker* (1946)

Renaud, F., *The Ancient Parish of Prestbury* (1878)

Revue Retrospective (1885–86)

Richards, R., *Manor of Gawsworth* (1957)

Richmond, Admiral Sir H.W., *The Navy in the War of 1739-1748* 3 vols (1920)

Ritchie, C.I.A., 'The Durham Association Regiment, 1745', *Journal of the Society for Army Historical Research* 24 (1956)

Roberts, G.M., *Selected Trevecka Letters* (1956)

Robson, R.J., *The Oxfordshire Election of 1754* (1949)

Rogers, N., 'Popular disaffection in London during the '45', *London Journal* (1975)

Roper, W.A., *Materials for a history of Lancaster* (Chetham Soc. 61 N.S.) (1907)

Rose, J., *Leigh in the Eighteenth Century 1689-1813* (1882)

Rosebery, Lord & MacLeod, W., *List of Persons concerned in the Present Rebellion* (Scottish History Society 8) (1890)

Rudé, G., *Hanoverian London* (1971)

Sedgwick, R., *History of Parliament. The House of Commons 1715-54* (1970)

Sharpe, R., *London and the Kingdom* 3 vols (1894–95)

Shaw, S., *History of Staffordshire* 2 vols (1798)

Shercliff, W.H., *Wythenshawe* (1971)

Shropshire, Transactions of the Archaeological and Natural History Society of, 'William Cartwright, non-juror, and his chronological history of Shrewsbury' (4 Part 1.4th series) (1914)

Simpson, Llewellyn Eardley, *Derby and the Forty-Five* (1933)

Simpson, R., *Derbyshire* (1826)

Skene, G., 'Account of a Journey to London' (3rd Spalding Club Miscellany, Vol. 2) (1941)

Sleigh, J., *A History of Leek* (1883)

Smollett, T., *A History of England* Vol. xi (1758–60)

Stephens, W.B., *A History of Congleton* (1971)

Stott, B., 'Charles Clement Deacon & William Brettargh', *LCAS* 41 (1924)

——, 'James Dawson & Thomas Syddall', *LCAS* 46 (1929)

Talon, H., *John Byrom: selections from his journals and papers* (1950)

Tayler, A. & H., *Jacobites of Aberdeenshire and Banffshire* (1928)

——, *Jacobite Letters to Lord Pitsligo* (1930)

——, *A Jacobite Exile* (1937)

Tayler, H., *Jacobite Epilogue* (1941)

—— (ed.), *Anonymous History of the Rebellion* (containing 'Elcho's Journal') (1944)

Thompson, J., *Leicester in the Eighteenth Century* (1871)

Tildesley, N.W., 'Richard Wilkes of Willenhall, Staffs, an eighteenth-century country doctor', *Lichfield and S. Staffs. Archaeological and Historical Society* 7 (1965–66)

Tomasson, K., *The Jacobite General* (1958)

Tomlinson, J., *History of Doncaster from the Roman Occupation* (1887)

Transactions of the Gaelic Society of Inverness 21 (1896–97)

'Two Yorkshire Diaries', *Yorkshire Archaeological Society Record Series* 117 (1951)

Verney, M.M., (ed.), *The Verney Letters* 2 vols (1904)

Vernon, E., *The Vernon Papers* (ed. B.M. Ranft) (Navy Records Society) (1958)

Vezzozi, M., *Young Juba* (1748)

Victoria County History of Warwickshire 5 vols (1904–09)

Walpole H., *Collected Letters* (ed. P. Cunningham) 9 vols (1857–59)

——, *Memoirs of the Reign of George II* (1846)

Ward, W.R., *Georgian Oxford* (1958)

Warrend, D., *More Culloden Papers* 5 vols (1923–30)

Wesley, J., *The Letters of John Wesley* (ed. J. Telford) (1931)

Western, J.R., *The English Militia* (1965)

Whitehead, H., 'Brampton in 1745', *Cumberland and Westmorland Association for the Advancement of Literature and Science* 12 (1863)

Whittle, P., *History of the Borough of Preston* (1821)

Whitworth, R., *Field-Marshal Ligonier* (1958)

Whyte, F. & Atteridge, A.H., *A History of the Queen's Bays* (1930)

Williams, B., *The Life of William Pitt* 2 vols (1966)

William Salt Archaeological & Historical Society N.S. Vols 2 (1922) & 6 (1926)

Williamson, R.J.T., *History of the Old County Regiment of Lancashire Militia* (1888)

Yorke, P., *Life and Correspondence of Philip Yorke, Earl of Hardwicke*, 3 vols (1913)

Index

Altrincham 80, 101, 103, 105, 106, 107
Arcy, d', Sir Conyers 40, 53
Ashbourne 74, 80, 113, 116, 118–19, 121, 122, 139–42, 144
Ashton-under-Lyne 102-3, 146, 148, 150
Atholl, James, Whig duke of 18
Atholl, William, Jacobite duke of (Marquis of Tullibardine) 18, 46, 94, 119, 123
  Charles Edward changes orders of 35
  at Carlisle 36–37
    reported killed at Carlisle 37
    at siege of Carlisle 40
    and Lord George Murray's resignation 45
    at Council in Derby 127–29

Balhaldy, Macgregor of 9, 15
Balmerino, Lord (Arthur Elphinstone) 29, 72, 74, 76, 119
  account of 22
  execution of 23
Balmerino's cavalry 172, 175
  at siege of Carlisle 40
Barrymore, Lord 9, 14, 80, 89
  account of 14–15
  letter to from Charles Edward 38
Beaufort, Duke of 9, 15, 77, 80
Berwick 1, 3, 11, 12, 156
Birmingham 99, 144
Bolton 82, 95
Bracken, Henry 72, 73, 74, 76, 158
Bradstreet, Dudley 124, 129, 130, 131, 151, 153
Brampton 35, 37, 43–44, 51, 52, 191, 193
  Council at 39
Bristol 3, 8, 80, 145
Burton 65, 68, 69, 74, 158, 177, 179
Burton, Dr. John 69, 72–73, 76, 148
Bury 70, 95, 146
Buxton 92, 96, 103, 107, 115, 119, 140, 146

Carlisle 3, 4, 6, 7, 8, 11, 12, 31, 75, 83, 100, 104, 108, 112, 126, 128, 145, 156, 167, 171, 174, 175, 177, 179, 190–93, 194
  siege of 34–55
Catholics 2, 7, 36, 45, 46, 74, 82, 137
  in Lancashire 6, 68, 71, 77, 158

  in London 131
  in Preston 76
  in Somerset 145
  in Wales 62
Cattle plague 32
Cheadle (Cheshire) 101, 103, 105
Cheadle (Staffs) 96, 115, 149, 151
Chester 1, 2, 38, 52, 53, 54, 66, 74, 77, 78, 79, 91, 95, 96, 104, 107, 114, 122, 141, 154
Chesterfield, Earl of 7, 54, 74, 75, 83, 104, 144, 160
Cholmondeley, Lord 38, 40, 52, 53, 66, 77, 78, 91, 96
Chorley 82, 153, 155
Clanranald, Ranald MacDonald of 151
  at Council in Derby 126, 128, 129
Clanranald's Regiment 18, 20, 74, 139, 158, 172, 175, 190
Clifton 28, 60, 63, 168, 193
  engagement at, 185–89
Congleton 96, 104, 113, 114, 115, 116, 121
Cope, General Sir John 1, 7, 11, 28, 34, 154, 197
Cotton, Sir John Hynde 9
  account of 14–15
Coventry 48, 66, 71, 81, 96, 122, 131, 141, 149, 157, 171
Culloden, battle of 19, 21, 76
Cumberland (county) 14, 52, 60, 75, 155, 160, 172, 174
Cumberland, Duke of 2, 28, 29, 66, 69, 70, 71, 74, 78, 81, 83, 91, 92, 96, 101, 102, 103, 104, 105, 106, 107, 113, 114, 115, 118, 123, 125, 126, 128, 129, 130, 136, 137, 138, 139, 140, 143–44, 145, 146, 156, 157, 159, 161, 167, 168, 169, 184, 190, 191, 197
  at Stafford and Stone 115, 116, 117, 121, 122
  at Lichfield 124, 141
  commences pursuit 149
  in Macclesfield 151–154, 157
  reaches Wigan 160
  leaves Wigan 170
  recalled to London 171
  and 'French landing' 173, 177

204

210   *The Final Campaign*

Wade, Field-Marshal *(contd.)*
         115, 124, 125, 126, 128, 129, 138,
         139, 141, 142, 148, 154, 156, 157,
         160, 169, 171, 172, 173, 174, 177,
         190, 192, 197
on military committee 1
in Nottingham 1
in Newcastle 1, 6, 11, 13, 40, 46, 61, 63, 64, 75
marches to Hexham 29, 49
his orders from London 36
at Council of War in Newcastle 38
message to Carlisle 41–42
instructions from Duke of Newcastle 47
condition of his army 47, 48, 49, 52
marches to Ovington 48
at Hexham 52
Council of War at Hexham 53
reaches Newcastle 53
second Council of War in Newcastle 67, 70
at Chester-le-Street 78
progress to Wetherby 91, 96–97, 117–18
Council of War at Wetherby 122–23
in Wetherby 131–32
in Doncaster 141, 146–47
march to Wakefield 144
Council of War at Ferrybridge 149
Council of War at Wakefield 152

receives orders from Cumberland 153
reaches Boroughbridge 170
at Ripon 175
arrives in Newcastle 194
Wakefield 66, 102, 144, 146, 149, 152, 154
Wales 2, 7, 12, 52, 54, 61, 65
as possible Jacobite target 8, 62, 64, 66, 70, 72,
         78, 79, 80, 81, 90, 86, 98, 104, 107,
         113, 115, 118, 126, 128, 141, 145, 149
Walley, Thomas 44, 90, 93–95, 97, 105, 149
Walpole, Horace 8, 32, 67, 149, 160
Warrington 53, 66, 74, 76, 77, 79, 82, 89, 90, 95,
         103, 128, 151, 154, 160
Warwickshire 99, 141
Waugh, John, 6, 34, 38; 44
Wentworth, General 1, 49, 141, 149
Wetherby 78, 91, 97, 122, 144
Whitehaven 61–62, 72, 73, 75, 108, 191, 193
Wigan, 80, 82, 89–90, 92, 96, 149–53, 154, 158,
         160, 170, 173
Wirksworth 116

York 19, 54, 61, 66, 76, 97, 102, 118, 147, 148,
         150, 190
Yorkshire 4, 5, 7, 11, 40, 52, 53, 61, 64, 66, 67,
         69, 70, 74, 77, 96, 102, 128, 140, 141,
         147, 152, 170, 171, 174